P9-CKE-787

THE RISE AND RISE OF DAVID GEFFEN

THE RISE AND RISE OF DAVID GEFFEN

STEPHEN SINGULAR

A Birch Lane Press Book
Published by Carol Publishing Group

A Birch Lane Press Book
Published by Carol Publishing Group
Birch Lane Press is a registered trademark of Carol Communications, Inc.

Editorial, sales and distribution, and rights and permissions inquiries should be addressed to Carol Publishing Group, 120 Enterprise Avenue, Secaucus, N.J. 07094

In Canada: Canadian Manda Group, One Atlantic Avenue, Suite 105, Toronto, Ontario, M6K 3E7

Carol Publishing Group books may be purchased in bulk at special discounts for sales promotion, fund-raising, or educational purposes. Special editions can be created to specifications. For details, contact Special Sales Department, Carol Publishing Group, 120 Enterprise Avenue, Secaucus, N.J. 07094.

Manufactured in the United States of America
10 9 8 7 6 5 4 3 2 1

Library of Congress Cataloging-in-Publication Data

Singular, Stephen.
The rise and rise of David Geffen / Stephen Singular.
p. cm.
"A Birch Lane Press book."
Includes index.
ISBN 1-55972-430-7 (hardcover)
1. Geffen, David, 1943– . 2. Motion picture producers and directors—United States—Biography. 3. Executives—United States—Biography. I. Title
PN1998.3.G42S56 1997
791.43'0232'092—dc21
[B] 97-20553
CIP

To B.

"What a journey the man has taken."
Brooklynite Norman Mailer on
Brooklynite Henry Miller in *Genius and Lust*

CONTENTS

PREFACE

Six thousand Los Angelenos had come out to Universal City this evening with the slim expectation of seeing or hearing something special. Most awards ceremonies in the show business community were blandly predictable. Movie stars or film directors usually stood up and thanked their colleagues or families for believing in them and supporting them through the lean years. Acceptance speeches went on too long and revealed too little. Yet tonight's event, taking place at the Universal Amphitheater, was a little different from most such occasions, and this crowd was searching for a deeper kind of hope. One-third of the audience members had tested positive for HIV or were dying of AIDS. Everyone in attendance knew friends or loved ones who'd perished from the illness. All had felt baffled and devastated by the disease. By tonight—November 18, 1992—160,000 Americans had been killed by AIDS, and an estimated one in two hundred Californians was infected with the virus.

The gathering was being sponsored by AIDS Project Los Angeles (APLA), which was presenting its annual Commitment to Life (CTL) Awards. APLA was ten years old and provided housing, food, transportation, legal services, and insurance counseling for thirty-five hundred victims of the illness. The awards were given to those who had raised money for APLA and had shown a "continued commitment to helping people live with AIDS." Past recipients included Bette Midler, Elizabeth Taylor, Betty Ford, Whoopi Goldberg, Madonna, and painter David Hockney. Tickets to the star-driven affair cost $50 to $500, it was open to the public, and this evening would bring in $3.9 million. Bernie Taupin, the lyricist for Elton John, was producing tonight's program, and it had featured performances by Liza Minnelli, Aaron Neville, Lyle Lovett, Eddie

Van Halen, and Johnny Mathis. Shirley MacLaine delivered a speech, Elton John sang "I Feel Pretty," and Warren Beatty presented the awards. This year Barbra Streisand and David Geffen were receiving the honors, and the 1992 ceremony carried an edge of both optimism and outrage.

Two weeks earlier, the nation had elected a young, new Democratic president—Bill Clinton. Most people in the audience felt certain that he would be much more attuned to the gay community and to AIDS causes than his defeated opponent, George Bush, had ever been. Clinton himself had sent a letter of congratulations to tonight's recipients. Yet in the same election, Colorado had passed Amendment Two, which specifically prohibited the creation of legislation based on people's sexual orientation. In short, this meant that the state could not approve a gay rights bill. From coast to coast, this vote had shocked and angered gay communities, as well as many other citizens who were not homosexual. Colorado was generally regarded as a progressive state; if this could happen there, it could happen in other places as well. The vote in Colorado quickly became a call to arms for those supporting gay rights, and Barbra Streisand had emerged as one of the most outspoken critics of Amendment Two and the state that had passed it. She'd demanded a boycott of Colorado by show business personalities from L.A. and New York, many of whom had mountain retreats in the Rockies. And tonight on the stage of the amphitheater, after Warren Beatty had handed her the CTL Award, she'd delivered a broadside against the Centennial State.

Amendment Two, Streisand told the crowd, "voids and prevents adoption of legislation that protects gays and lesbians from discrimination.... There are plenty of us who love the mountains and rivers of that truly beautiful state. But we must now say clearly that the moral climate there is no longer acceptable. And if we are asked, we must refuse to play where they discriminate." Streisand's remarks generated a huge ovation. Then, when she and Johnny Mathis sang "One Hand, One Heart" as a duet, the audience stood and was moved to tears.

While receiving his award, David Geffen took a quieter and more modest approach. For tonight's ceremony, he'd done something almost radical for him: exchanged his constant uniform of blue jeans, T-shirts, and sneakers for a dark suit, dark tie, and dress shoes. He'd also changed his demeanor. The lively, garrulous Geffen looked subdued this evening, a bit overwhelmed by the solemnity of the occasion. He opened his acceptance speech by saying that he'd kept a card for every friend and acquaintance who'd died from AIDS since the early 1980s. He now had a stack of 341 cards—and counting.

He seemed a little hesitant about receiving this honor, unsure of his standing with this audience. He had reason to believe that enemies were sitting out there in front of him, perhaps even some of the same people who'd once called his office and threatened him. Who could have blamed him for being nervous? It was a deeply unsettling thing when your intimate life was turned into a heated political issue. He'd paid a price to stand here before this audience—a terrible price, according to some, but others said that he'd only gotten what he deserved. Even his critics could agree that his recent charitable actions were worthy of the CTL award. In 1992, he'd donated a million dollars to New York City's Gay Men's Health Crisis, the world's largest and oldest AIDS facility. It was the biggest single gift the GMHC had ever received.

Geffen's relationship with the gay community was long-standing, complex, and volatile. Some of the same things could be said about his relationship with his own sexuality. Nearly twenty years earlier, in the mid-1970s, when he'd first emerged as a highly successful recording industry executive, he'd had a passionate and painful fling with the pop diva Cher. After she suddenly dumped him for rocker Gregg Allman, Geffen took up with TV star Marlo Thomas. The affair was soon over, but he did buy her house in Beverly Hills. Back then, Geffen was known as a man who dated and lived with, but did not marry, beautiful, glamorous women.

By the late seventies, his sensual repertoire was expanding. He spent considerable time at Manhattan's Studio 54, as it was racing through its heyday of sex, drugs, and all manner of nocturnal excesses. Geffen was now calling himself "bisexual." As the eighties unfolded, he evolved into an even more successful record executive and a crossover business star, producing films and award-winning Broadway plays, while purchasing extremely valuable L.A. real estate and an art collection valued in the scores of millions. He'd become, by age forty, unique in the history of American entertainment: no other individual had ever touched and helped shape as many parts of our pop culture. By the early 1970s, the Beatles had come and gone. For nearly two decades, Bob Dylan had burned luminously, but by the eighties, he had begun to cool. David Geffen, meanwhile, had continued creating into the nineties in unpredictable and wildly lucrative ways. From the sixties onward, no one had explored America—its music, films, plays, neuroses, drugs, business opportunities, therapies, self-examination, spirituality, and conflicting sexual urges—more than he had.

By the late eighties, most Geffen-watchers (they now made up a cottage industry) were convinced that he was not bisexual, but homosexual. In an earlier and more discreet decade, this issue might have remained a private matter, but the times were neither discreet nor private. A health crisis was taking place in the gay community—men with AIDS were dying by the thousands—and sexuality had become a loud and very political issue. Gay activists in New York and L.A. wanted Geffen to come out of the closet and do it in public. Right now! For the past three years, he'd resisted their pressure and highly personal attacks.

In 1990, he'd sold Geffen Records and become the first self-made billionaire in the history of the entertainment industry. Circumstances had made him rich to a degree that most people couldn't conceive of, but as he'd become more prominent and visible, he'd also become more of a target for derision and scorn. If he gave in to the gay activists and declared himself homosexual, he would open himself up to assaults from the other side—the clamorous, ill-tempered, and growing Christian fundamentalist right, which blamed Hollywood for many of the country's problems. The fundamentalists believed that gay men and women should not just go back into the closet but should also renounce their sexual preference and "choose" to become heterosexual.

Four months before this evening's award ceremony, columnist Patrick Buchanan had stood before the Republican convention in Houston and declared cultural war against those citizens who did not view America as he did. He had many targets to rail against, but a primary one was the gay community, and anyone publicly associated with it was subject to Buchanan's fear and wrath.

If the right wing was against gays in general, Geffen felt that he had even more to fear from the left. In the summer of 1990, Michelangelo Signorile, a gay New York journalist working at *OutWeek* and a pioneer of "outing"—announcing in print that prominent individuals were homosexual—had turned his rage on the record company executive. Signorile believed that Geffen was in denial about his homosexuality and not doing nearly enough to support the AIDS-riddled gay community. He called Geffen "A PIG" and went on to write, "You, David Geffen, are the most horrifying kind of nightmare I've come to study in the grotesque mosaic of the media swirl. The more I hear about you, the bigger my file grows and the more ammunition we have to fire."

In addition to Pat Buchanan and Mike Signorile, Geffen had reasons for concern that were much closer to his L.A. home. "Many people in Hollywood won't admit this," says a show business executive with four decades of experience, "but they resent it when a gay person achieves Geffen's level of success and wealth, regardless of how talented he is. People outside of L.A. wouldn't believe the amount of homophobia in our industry. You hear it in the jokes behind closed doors, and in the hallways when gays aren't listening. There's more fear of homosexuals here than in places like Colorado or Arizona, because there's so much money and jealousy in our community. Many people have seen being gay as a threat to their careers or to the business itself. Your peers in Hollywood are always highly critical of anyone who makes it to the top, and the fact that Geffen is gay makes the criticism doubly nasty. When it comes to sexual behavior, people get ugly."

For a long time, Geffen had not been a particularly handsome man. He was smallish, at five-feet-seven and 150 pounds, and for a couple of decades, perhaps to make himself look taller, he'd grown his curly hair straight up from his scalp, in a kind of Jewish Afro. This hairdo made him look younger but did not flatter his face; it conjured up a prolonged, awkward stage of adolescence. In recent years, as he was approaching fifty, he'd trimmed his hair very short, and something unpredictable had happened. His clear, green, soulful eyes, his sensuous mouth, and his other good features came together in a different way. He looked like an adult now, and an attractive man.

Geffen gazed out at the audience and thanked APLA for honoring him. His reception thus far this evening had been polite but not impassioned. The crowd was lukewarm, waiting, even yearning, for something that hadn't been delivered. He didn't seem inclined to meet their expectations. Unlike many celebrities, Geffen had a curious quality—he did not see himself as being larger than life, and he made a point of not coming across that way in public. He was constantly reminding journalists that he was just another flawed individual "with clay feet." He had no ability to guess the future of the entertainment business, and he had, he sometimes confessed to reporters, things inside of him that would never be healed. He was not smaller than life, either. He was, as he'd once said when referring to Bob Dylan, "lifelike." Many people who'd ascended to Geffen's heights became more and more unreal as they grew more famous. He'd become more real—for better and worse.

He could be vain and arrogant, but just as quickly turn humble and surprisingly vulnerable. He was prickly, quick to anger, and had a sizable ego, which had clashed with many of the stars he'd worked with during the past three decades. He'd publicly compared Mick Jagger's onstage presence to that of a tired stripper. He'd called Crosby, Stills, and Nash "Old Fat Farts" who'd lost their talent. He'd labeled Bob Dylan, in effect, a liar. In Julia Phillips's Hollywood-rocking exposé, *You'll Never Eat Lunch in This Town Again*, Geffen reportedly (although he vehemently denied saying it) described the greatly admired Steven Spielberg as "selfish, self-centered, egomaniacal and, worst of all, greedy."

He'd characterized Clive Davis, the head of Arista Records, as an "arrogant fuck" and had used even more vivid language when talking about the man who'd once run the CBS recording label, Walter Yetnikoff. Geffen took delight in watching mighty figures stumble or fall and was not above sticking the dagger into those who were on the way down. After Madonna published her much-criticized 1992 book *Sex*, Geffen told *Rolling Stone,* "Madonna has a tremendous amount of charisma and talent, but she's no genius. And clearly in the last year we've seen her fuck up considerably." In later years, he would have some deliciously harsh words for Michael Eisner, the CEO of the Walt Disney Company, and for Hollywood's former superagent Michael Ovitz.

Over the years, Geffen had taken his own share of public hits. Two decades earlier, guitarist-singer-songwriter Stephen Stills had quarreled with the record executive and expressed his feelings with a bumper sticker that read WHO IS DAVID GEFFEN AND WHY IS HE SAYING THESE TERRIBLE THINGS ABOUT ME? Another guitarist, Joe Walsh of the Eagles, later performed a variation on this theme. He donned a T-shirt that read WHO IS IRV AZOFF [the manager of the Eagles] AND WHY IS HE SAYING THOSE TERRIBLE THINGS ABOUT DAVID GEFFEN? In the mid-nineties, the obscure musician Mojo Nixon recorded, but never released, a song called "Off With the Head of David Geffen," which claimed that Geffen had killed rock 'n' roll. And in her book, Julia Phillips delivered the ultimate Hollywood statement, when she wrote that Geffen was "an asshole, but he's my asshole."

Some people viewed Geffen as the richest, nastiest kid at the biggest and wealthiest high school in the world. Others found him to be unpretentious and always fresh (back in the seventies, when he met England's Princess Margaret, he wore a T-shirt and jeans for the occasion and greeted her with a loud "Hiya!"). He just didn't seem able to repress himself. In a voice still tinged with Brooklynese, he enjoyed telling listeners how smart he was, how successful he'd been, how much money he'd made, and how many things he owned. He was known throughout Hollywood for handing out unsolicited advice, to men and women, on everything from financial investments to sexual endeavors to collagen implants. He was an incorrigible gossip, especially on the phone.

"David Geffen," went the joke in L.A., "has blisters on his hands from holding the receiver all day long. He's the world's first billionaire yenta."

His sexuality, while a very heated topic among certain people, had never been quite as large an issue with himself. Everyone in Hollywood, he liked to say, knew exactly who he was and had known this for years. He hadn't tried to hide anything from anyone. One of his mottos was "You're as sick as your secrets," so why, he liked to ask, pretend you were what you were not? He'd dated women and he'd dated men, and in a 1991 profile in *Vanity Fair,* he'd openly acknowledged his bisexuality. That was all he'd felt comfortable doing, and all he was going to say on the subject.

If having a billion dollars didn't really change you, it dramatically changed people's perceptions of you. In the public's mind, you were different now, special, and exceedingly powerful. You were a symbol, whether you wanted to be or not. You were a role model to others who were somewhat like you, but not as rich or famous or, in some cases, as healthy. Your life made people envy you, hate you, admire you, and love you—even if they'd never met you face-to-face. You were no longer just a human being but a social phenomenon, whose words and actions were far more visible and important than they'd ever been in the past. Given all that, difficult questions and issues were raised. What was your obligation to the public, and what was your obligation to yourself and your personal truth?

It was fitting that Geffen was making this speech at the Universal Amphitheater at one of Hollywood's original movie studios, because the dilemma he was confronting echoed all the way back to the very first days of the film business. The men who'd founded that business—Adolph Zukor, who'd created Paramount Pictures; William Fox of the Fox Film Corporation; Louis B. Mayer of Metro-Goldwyn-Mayer; Carl Laemmle of Universal; and the Warner brothers, Harry, Sam, Albert, and Jack—all had Eastern European Jewish or Russian Jewish backgrounds. All had come to California early in the twentieth century and made a point of burying their Jewish roots, because of the virulent anti-Semitism of that time.

In the 1930s, these "movie moguls" had been hesitant to make films that negatively portrayed Hitler's Germany, even when it was becoming known that one of the Third Reich's goals was the elimination of Jews everywhere. The moguls did not want to be controversial and regarded their ethnicity as a private matter, something to be kept quiet. Because of this, Hollywood was created around a basic contradiction. Its founding fathers made pictures that were committed to upholding and glorifying the American way of life, even when these men felt excluded from certain parts of it. The entertainment business was built on the conviction that in order to reach and satisfy a mass national audience, things like ethnicity, sexuality, drug use, or strong political beliefs had to be shuffled aside or denied outright. And if ethnicity was tricky, sexuality (and especially homosexuality) was even trickier. Our culture had trouble dealing with the subtleties and complexities of adult reality.

It was a long-standing cliché, of course, that Hollywood was the capital of illusion and phoniness. It was Tinseltown and La-La Land. But this cliché held layers of meaning and nuance that were as rich as those in the Deep South, or those along the Eastern Seaboard, or those in countless small communities of the Midwest. There were significant historical reasons why staying-on-the-surface had been embraced in Los Angeles, and why it had become a way of doing business, if not a way of life. Forty years earlier, Senator Joseph McCarthy had conducted his Communist witch hunt in the heart of Hollywood, going after entertainment figures with left-wing politics, after Jews, and after homosexuals. McCarthy was long since dead, but people he'd harmed were still alive, and his shadow continued to linger over the industry.

In this environment, the truth was often not perceived as a marketable commodity; it was something to be sidestepped, if one wanted things to remain pleasant and the deal to be closed. Superficiality was sometimes necessary. Hypocrisy was just a hidden cost of making a transaction. With all that as a backdrop, for any man or woman to stand up in front of thousands of people and choose to display a measure of personal honesty was something that went well beyond the receiving of an award.

On this November evening, the Commitment to Life audience understood these things, even if they hadn't really thought about them. They lived in L.A., and many of them worked in the entertainment business. They'd hidden their own secrets and buried their own truths, in order to advance a career or just to avoid discomfort.

Geffen paused for a moment in his speech and gazed out at the gathering. Then, in a matter-of-fact tone, he said, "As a gay man, I've come a long way to be here tonight."

The sentence went out through the public address system and reached into the crowd, causing a stir. People were glancing at one another and exchanging nods, as if to confirm that they'd really heard what they thought they'd heard. The remark had been dropped so casually, so nonchalantly, yet it had finally been spoken in a public venue. David Geffen, the richest man in Hollywood and one whose power was decidedly on the rise, had just told everyone present and everyone beyond the amphitheater who was connected to this event through the media that he was indeed a gay man.

With thirteen words, he'd pushed open the closet door with his own hand. He'd crossed a line he'd never been able to cross before. He'd taken the crowd by surprise, and this moment qualified as something more than special. It was in fact unprecedented in the cultural and business history of the United States. No American of Geffen's stature had ever before made such an admission to a mass audience.

Six thousand people spontaneously began to applaud—not loudly at first, but the sound was building.

"And in different places and by different paths," Geffen went on, "we've all come a long way, and yet there is an equally long way to go."

They stood, and the applause grew stronger.

"If I have learned anything," he said, "I have learned this—that we must walk this path together."

The clapping was now thunderous, drowning him out, as if the gathering no longer needed to hear every syllable. Something had been released; people could feel it, and they wanted to whistle and cheer. Geffen himself broke into a smile, clearly pleased with the response. He looked both taken aback and relieved.

Some time later, he would say that making this speech was not a watershed event for him, and that he'd been startled by the significance others had attached to it. To the man on the stage receiving the honor, who was known for his outspokenness, it was just another occasion for him to say what was on his mind. But to those looking up at him, to those who were sick or dying of AIDS, and even to those who'd been his sworn enemies, it was a major revelation—a celebration of personal and public honesty. It was also a shift in the social and political wind.

Geffen's life had always been like that. Since his birth during World War II, what had happened to him had, in a sense, happened to the rest of us. He was almost always at the center of the action, and he was standing there again tonight.

The applause rolled on.

THE RISE AND RISE OF
DAVID GEFFEN

ACT ONE

Money and Sex

CHAPTER 1

The war had recently ended, the Nazi monster had finally been routed, and Brooklyn had a modest feeling of optimism. Money was tight, but there was hope now that one could find a job, buy a car, and eventually move away from the old neighborhood and on to a better existence on Long Island. The great exodus to the suburbs had not yet begun, and for a few more years, at the end of the 1940s and into the 1950s, Brooklyn would occupy a special place in New York City and the American imagination. This Brooklyn had its own newspaper, the *Brooklyn Eagle,* its own dialect—"dem" for "them" and "dose" for "those"—and a deep sense of humor, producing scores of successful comedians, among them Phil Silvers, Jackie Gleason, and Buddy Hackett.

This Brooklyn had a more human face than New York's other boroughs and conveyed more feeling. It was a hardworking, ethnically mixed, solid urban community with good schools, good libraries, and decent neighbors. It had a grittiness that came off the worn-looking, three-story brick buildings, the tar-paper roofs, and the lines of laundry that streamed out of windows and shook in the breeze. It conveyed ethics and values, if not much forgiveness or grace. Ghosts seemed to be standing on every street corner, and this tough, strangely lyrical Brooklyn would move writers to try to capture it in books and movies and plays for generations to come.

In the seventeenth century, the Dutch had settled this part of New York and named much of it, before passing it along to other groups, who then passed it on again. It's been estimated that one out of every nine people in the United States has roots that can be traced back to Brooklyn. Because it had seen so many immigrants come and go, Brooklyn had a sense of poignancy, even of sadness. You could feel that as you watched an old man in a black coat walk slowly along a cracked sidewalk, or glanced into the small shops of the local merchants, who peddled newspapers, buttons, and cigars. People hustled to get out of here, to escape and never come back. Something—some basic struggle to survive and stand out in a harsh, crowded environment—was always changing here, yet always the same. Manhattan, a nickel away on the subway until 1947, conjured up glamour and riches, but the heart of the city had long resided in Brooklyn.

Borough Park lay in the southwestern part of Brooklyn, below Prospect Park and above Bensonhurst and Coney Island. The elevated train that rattled along New Utrecht Avenue divided Borough Park in two. To the east the population was mostly Italian, and to the west it was largely Jewish. Side streets held sycamores and row houses, their front stoops often busy. In the late 1940s, radio was still king, and the sound of Brooklyn Dodger ball games, big-band music, and comedy programs poured out of shops and apartment windows, up from basement doorways.

"In the 'forties and 'fifties, Brooklyn had three things: stickball, the Dodgers, and egg creams," says Joe Sinisi, who grew up in Borough Park and attended junior high school with David Geffen. "The world was fairly simple. Saturdays seemed to last forever, and all games could be played in the street. We had no malls, no Nintendo, and no money, but we had a better time than kids do today. We hung out in the candy store or went to the neighborhood theater. Your world was bounded by three or four blocks. I walked home from school for lunch and ate grilled cheese sandwiches. We listened to Perry Como and the Andrews Sisters. My aunts had Rita Hayworth hairdos and wore the same stockings she did. There were still trolley cars in Brooklyn.

"We'd play a game of basketball in the yard after school, with a little rubber ball. If you didn't play so well, you didn't get chosen. If you were below average on the schoolyard, you were labeled a fag. That was always the brush they tarred you with. That one word determined your place in the hierarchy."

David Geffen was born in Brooklyn on February 21, 1943. He spent his youth in Borough Park, in a row house near where the train ran along New Utrecht Avenue. The Geffen apartment was small, with one bedroom for his parents, Batya and Abraham, and another for his brother, Mitchell, who was four years older than David. Until Mitchell left home for college, David slept on a pullout couch in the living room. He dressed in secondhand clothes that were too big for his short, thin body, never quite growing into many of them. If money was scarce in the Geffen household, it wasn't as scarce as it had been in the Depression, when Batya began taking in sewing to support the family. This activity became a home-based business that turned out undergarments for Borough Park matrons. As the business grew, the small apartment got even smaller. Years later, Geffen would tell *Esquire* magazine that his early living quarters were "always filled with women with big tits."

In time Batya opened her own shop—Chic Corsets by Geffen—and she would eventually buy the building that held her store. While she made clothes, her husband, an unemployed patternmaker, stayed home and thought about things. He read widely in French and Spanish, spoke several other languages fluently, was interested in arcane matters, and devoted most of his hours to private intellectual endeavors. He never aggressively adapted to life in Brooklyn, as his wife had, and seemed content to let her pay the bills. In Hebrew, "Geffen" means "fruit of the vine," and in distant centuries the name had been associated with scholars and thinkers. Abraham may have been carrying on an ancient tradition, but his youngest son would later refer to his father, and not flatteringly, as a dreamer.

Batya Volovskaya and Abraham Geffen had both left their native lands as young adults. She was from Russia but fled that country for Palestine after the Soviet Revolution of 1917. He was from Poland and had saved enough money working as a telegraph operator to travel around the world and visit the Middle East. They met in Palestine, got married, and came to America, settling in Brooklyn. Her family had stayed behind in Russia and for many years Batya did not know what became of her relatives during World War II. Then one day, in 1949, when David was six, his mother received a letter from her sister in the Soviet Union. The young boy did not know about this missive; in fact, he would not know about its contents for almost forty years.

The letter said that everyone in his mother's family, except for the sister doing the writing, had died in the war. They'd lived in the Ukraine, and as the Nazis were marching across the Soviet Union, the Ukrainians had gathered up all the Jews in the area and killed them, by throwing them down wells. Eleven family members, including Batya's mother and father, her grandmother and grandfather, and seven brothers and sisters, had perished in this manner. The one sister had survived, she wrote, only because she hadn't been home on the day the killers arrived at their door.

If young David knew nothing of what was in the letter, he did know that his mother soon suffered a nervous breakdown and had to be taken to an institution. She was gone for several months and the family was taken care of by Abraham's mother. If it was disturbing and painful for David not to have his mother in the apartment, making meals and running the family, it was equally difficult hearing the whispers of kids in the neighborhood, who said that Batya had gone crazy. Then one day, just as suddenly as she'd disappeared, she returned, and their lives resumed as before.

In the 1940s and 1950s, there were really two Brooklyns: the Brooklyn of myth and the Brooklyn of ragged, stinging reality. In the mythological Brooklyn, fathers taught their sons how to throw and catch and hit baseballs, while entertaining them with bittersweet, colorful stories about how one day, the always runner-up Dodgers would rise up and defeat the lordly New York Yankees. Every kid wanted to be Dodger center fielder Duke Snider, and to be cheered as he walked down the street. In the real Brooklyn many fathers knew nothing at all about baseball, and many sons were also ignorant of the sport or disliked it. In the mythological Brooklyn, mothers stayed at home and managed the household, while fathers went off to work and provided for their families. In the real Brooklyn, men and women did whatever was necessary to keep food on the table and clothes on their children's backs. In the mythological Brooklyn, there wasn't any sexual ambiguity. Boys were boys and girls were girls, and the lines of demarcation were very clear. But in the real Brooklyn, down in the alleys and lurking in the darkened apartment hallways, things were always messier.

Men who grew up in the Brooklyn of that time often bring up the subject of sexuality in conversation, as if they can't stop themselves. They talk about it as if it were one of the fundamentals of life in that Brooklyn. In those years, when the Dodgers were repeatedly losing to the Yankees in the World Series, a running joke among New York sports fans went like this:

"What do the Dodgers and certain homosexuals have in common?"

"I don't know."

"They both choke on the big ones."

In the real Brooklyn, any boy who was small and not a good athlete, any boy who could be physically victimized by older, bigger boys, and any boy who was different from the adolescent Brooklyn norm was going to have that difference ground into him on a daily basis.

"Geffen was in my electrical wiring shop class at the Edward B. Shallow Junior High at Sixteenth Avenue and 65th Street in Bensonhurst," says Joe Sinisi. "He was one of those kids that you would shake down for a quarter on the playground, or you'd steal his slice of pizza in the schoolyard. In those days, there were kids who picked on people and kids who got picked on. Everything was based on how many kids above you could beat you up, and how many kids below you you could beat up. That was the food chain. I was in the middle of the pack, and Geffen was lower than I was. He was a target. There was a lot of taunting and harassment. Kids like him were always classified as fags by the tougher boys, some of whom went on to serve time in prison.

"A whole generation of kids from Brooklyn who were picked on went on to great fame and fortune in Hollywood. These kids were driven to achieve, but usually not in traditional Waspish ways or Waspish businesses. You had to hustle your way out of there. Nothing was assured, and you had to have street smarts and savvy or you wouldn't survive. Very early on in our neighborhood, you learned that you did not want to be at the bottom of the hierarchy. That was just not any fun."

Marty Davidson grew up in the Flatbush neighborhood of Brooklyn, which is north and east of Borough Park. After getting his start in show business at a Manhattan talent agency in the 1960s, Davidson moved to Hollywood and became a film director. In 1974, he made *The Lords of Flatbush,* starring Henry Winkler and Sylvester Stallone. The picture was based upon some of his youthful experiences, and one of the smaller, more vulnerable boys depicted in the movie was modeled loosely on David Geffen.

"As a teenager, I was a jock, and that made things a lot easier for me," says Davidson. "If you weren't a jock in Brooklyn in the fifties, your life was shit. If you threw a baseball like a girl, you were called a faggot and you were in trouble. The peer pressure was awful. David's instincts and his sense of humor were the only things that kept him from being thoroughly ostracized. He was not one of the guys, and in *The Lords of Flatbush* you get a good idea of what the world was like if you weren't one of the guys, or if you might be gay. David didn't have an easy life back then. He was on the outside, with a lot of pain and a lot of 'I'll get them later' in his attitude. It was kind of like *The Revenge of the Nerds*. Guys who were nerds in high school do well in show business later on. Guys like Geffen, Jeffrey Katzenberg, and Steven Spielberg. They're driven by something very deep."

"A lot of Jewish kids in our old neighborhood," says Joe Sinisi, "were victimized by Italian kids. Then the Jewish kids grew up, went out to Hollywood, and made movies that portrayed Italians as assholes."

According to one of Geffen's longtime friends, "Through bitter disappointment with his surroundings, David learned an important lesson very early in life. He learned not to seek the approval of other people, because it was never going to be given. He had adversaries at home, at school, and everywhere else. He learned that he didn't need their approval or their permission to survive and to create things for himself. He could do these things on his own by trusting his instincts. That's a very useful thing and may be the key to his success.

"He had a passion for getting things done and then moving on to something new and not getting stuck in the past. Later on, some people looked at him and were annoyed when they realized that he couldn't be controlled as easily as they could be. He was unpredictable, and that kind of behavior makes some people fearful and angry."

CHAPTER 2

In the autumn of 1955, the Dodgers finally defeated the New York Yankees in the World Series and were the champions of baseball. The borough could at last celebrate.

"There were so many people crowding the sidewalks that you could barely walk anywhere," says Dan Rissner, a Brooklyn native and vice president of Neufeld/Rehme Productions at Paramount Pictures in Los Angeles. "The cars from Coney Island were honking their horns and jamming the streets, restaurants gave away free food to everyone, and the day after we won, there was no school."

While local sports fans were relishing their victory, David Geffen was busy reading the nightlife columnists in the New York papers: Walter Winchell, Ed Sullivan, Dorothy Kilgallen, and Earl Wilson. He absorbed everything they wrote, staying abreast of which celebrities were involved in upcoming motion pictures, or Broadway plays and musicals, or heated love affairs. He knew that Debbie Reynolds was dating Glenn Ford, who'd recently been dumped by Judy Garland. He knew which stars had three-picture deals at which studios, and for how much money. Geffen's mother, father, and older brother were mystified by his attraction to such trivial gossip and often made fun of him as a repository of "worthless information." What did the world of Broadway or Hollywood have to do with their mundane existence in Borough Park? Why would anyone bother paying attention to such distant, frivolous things?

In 1955, Geffen was twelve years old. One afternoon, he stopped at a subway newsstand, and his eye landed on a book displayed in front of him: *Hollywood Rajah,* by Bosley Crowther. The youngster bought the book, which chronicled the life of MGM studio head Louis B. Mayer, and quickly read it, enthralled with the story. Over the next forty years, he would be interviewed many times on many subjects, but he would mention only one book as having influenced his life in any meaningful way: *Hollywood Rajah*. Let other kids aspire to be Duke Snider. He wanted to be Louis B. Mayer.

Of all the original movie moguls, Mayer was the most sentimental and the most drawn to blatant acts of patriotism. He was born in Russia in the mid-1880s; since he did not know his real birth date, he later took the Fourth of July as his own. When he was a very small boy, his father, Jacob, brought the Mayer family to St. John, New Brunswick. In Canada, Jacob found work selling scrap metal but could barely make ends meet. Louis eventually went to work for his father, salvaging ships from the harbor in St. John, but the two of them quarreled over business matters and other things.

"There was certainly no love lost between father and son," wrote Neal Gabler in his recent history of the founders of the movie industry, *An Empire of Their Own: How the Jews Invented Hollywood*. "Jacob Meyer was a failure in business and a failure in his family. His refuge, as it was for so many Jewish immigrants of his generation, who felt emasculated by America, was religion."

At nineteen, Louis Mayer fled his family and went to Boston. After briefly moving to Brooklyn, he returned to Massachusetts with the idea of leasing a theater, where he could show the primitive silent movies of the day to the local population. In 1907, he found a burlesque house in Haverhill and signed a six-month lease for $650. The future rajah was on his way. In 1918, eight years after the first movie studio had been created in Hollywood, he moved to Los Angeles, where he aspired not merely to present films but to make them. A year after Mayer arrived in California, Marcus Loew, the New York theater chain owner, purchased Metro Pictures. Then he bought Goldwyn Pictures and merged the two of them. He soon hired Mayer to run Metro-Goldwyn and to produce fifteen feature films a year. In 1926, the studio changed its name to Metro-Goldwyn-Mayer.

Louis B. Mayer steered MGM through its glory days, in the thirties and forties when the studio was considered the epitome of Hollywood class. Its motto was "Ars Gratia Artis"—"Art for Art's Sake"—and Mayer spared no expense in executing both the details and the larger vision of his motion pictures. The grand production of *The Wizard of Oz* was only the most prominent example of how things were done at MGM, and why it became the envy of the industry. Mayer himself was short, highly emotional, bad-tempered, and extraordinarily proud of his studio.

Every Fourth of July he would shut down MGM and use the facility to celebrate the nation's birthday and his own. Bands would play, his employees would gather for the festivities, and Mayer himself, the patriarch, would deliver patriotic speeches. "I worship good women," he liked to say, "honorable men, and saintly mothers." He was corny when that was the thing to be, and he became extremely wealthy.

In the mid-thirties, in the midst of the Depression, Mayer made more money than anyone else in the country—over $1 million a year. He lavishly entertained U.S. senators and governors when they visited Hollywood, and he loved playing the local power broker. He lived in a high style and cast himself in the role of West Coast gentility. The finest symbol of his prosperity was the racehorses he began collecting and breeding. In the mid-forties, he was the nation's second-leading money winner in the sport of kings, and each morning he could be seen at the Griffith Park Riding Academy astride one of his mounts.

One might think that to a twelve-year-old boy living in Brooklyn and sleeping on the sofa in his parents' living room, nothing would seem more remote than the lifestyle and riches of Louis B. Mayer, ensconced in a mansion on the other side of the continent. But young David Geffen didn't see it that way. In *Hollywood Rajah,* he'd encountered something far more exciting than the Dodgers or even the New York gossip columnists. While other boys were out playing stickball in the street or basketball in the schoolyard, he decided that it would be a lot more fun to become a Hollywood rajah.

He already liked going to movies at the nearby Barwood Theater. Now he began attending three or four pictures a weekend, catching double features for a quarter. One evening he didn't come home, and his mother sent the police out to look for him; they couldn't find him anywhere. When he finally showed up at the apartment, he said that he'd been watching *Singin' in the Rain* over and over again, sitting by himself in the darkened theater. On another occasion, when he went with his parents into Manhattan to see the Rockettes at Radio City Music Hall, he left his seat to get some chocolate cigarettes. As he returned, he imagined that the audience was standing and cheering him as he walked down the aisle to take the stage and make his Oscar acceptance speech.

The Wizard of Oz was one of his favorite films. Geffen wasn't captivated so much by Dorothy and her friends or even by the nasty figure of the Great Oz who yelled at the visitors when they came to the Emerald City. He was fascinated by the little man behind the curtain who was pulling the levers and making everything happen. During high school, when people asked Geffen what he wanted to be when he became an adult, he said a dentist. That was pure propaganda: He said it because it was what his mother wanted to hear. His deeper fantasy was to go to Los Angeles, enroll at UCLA, meet some celebrities, and get into the business end of show business. And be rich.

Geffen was a poor student and not very popular with his New Utrecht High classmates. He was small, pesky, restless, energetic, and loud. He was urban, nervous, and jumpy. Very early in life, he'd learned that the only way to get attention in Brooklyn was to get in people's faces and make noise, so he began talking and kept talking when silence might have been more appropriate. Being appropriate was never his highest priority. Getting things out was, regardless of what impact they had on others. In high school, despite his bad grades, he had remarkable confidence in himself and in his intelligence, or at least he acted as if he did.

In later years, people who'd graduated with him from the massive red brick school at 79th Street and New Utrecht Avenue would say that Geffen had "a mouth on him" and was "impossible to ignore." For a young man like himself, school was largely an unnecessary chore. He didn't like most subjects but enjoyed theater classes, an annual music competition called "Sing," and hanging out at Chookie's, the neighborhood snack bar. Studying was tedious and passing a test didn't produce any tangible results. Making money was tangible; with cash in your pocket, you had more choices and more freedom. The most money one could ever make, the teenager imagined, was a thousand dollars a week, and if you earned that amount, you could buy a shiny new Cadillac and drive up and down the streets of Brooklyn, causing people to stare at you and your automobile. Money, he believed, would bring you the kind of respect that he didn't have.

His grade point average at New Utrecht was 66 (65 was needed to pass, and he was known to sign his own report cards, so he wouldn't have to show them to his parents). His formal education wasn't impressive, but during these years he was attending another school, where he was doing much better. This classroom was Chic Corsets by Geffen, on Thirteenth Avenue between 53rd and 54th

Streets. Batya was the only teacher on the premises and her younger son the only pupil.

David came by the shop to eat meals, which his mother prepared in the back while running the business. He dropped in after school and on the weekends. He sat next to Batya as patrons entered, and he watched her interact with them, negotiate prices, work with suppliers, collect money, and do the books. When a customer wanted to bargain, he watched her refuse to take less than she felt her merchandise deserved—and then watched her get the amount she demanded. One day Batya mistakenly quoted a woman a price that was below what the garment in question was worth. Batya agreed to let her have it for this cost, but the woman left to do some comparison shopping at another store. When she returned and wanted to buy the item at the lower cost, Batya was adamant—the answer was no. The woman had been offered a bargain and refused it; she would pay full price now or the sale was off. The woman became upset, but Batya would not back down.

"My mother," Geffen would tell *Forbes* magazine several decades later, "taught me how not to get hustled."

She taught him more than that.

"There's something very significant about the fact that as a youngster David watched his mother do business," says a woman in Los Angeles who's known Geffen for many years. "A father's success can be intimidating. As a child, you watch him and think, 'He's so big and strong. I don't know if I can live up to that.' But when you see your mother asking for money and negotiating, it's different. You think, 'If she can do that, so can I.' She was doing everything else around the apartment—and she was making money. That really affected him.

"Some important things in David's early life were reversed from the norm in Brooklyn. He may have identified more with women than with men. That made him more flexible, more open in some ways. A different role model teaches you a different way of doing things. David's confidence and belief in himself have always been fundamental to his success. I think he got a lot of it by watching his mother."

Batya was shrewd, she was fair, and she consistently made a profit. Everything her youngest son learned about business, he would later say as an adult, he absorbed in those idle hours of sitting in his mother's shop and watching her sell corsets and brassieres. When he was fourteen, Batya insisted that he start ironing his own shirts—so she could stop doing it for him. He resisted but was soon pressing his clothes. She told him that it was time to get a job and have his own money, instead of asking for an allowance. He became a part-time mail clerk and then a busboy in the Catskills. He found that he liked to work, liked having cash in his pocket. He still fantasized about becoming an entertainment executive, but how could he actually go about doing that? What particular skills did he have that would launch him on that career path? What was he really good at? Everyone, some people believed, had one special gift. What was his?

Besides wanting to emulate Louis B. Mayer, Geffen had some other, murkier impulses that pushed him toward show business. When he was eleven, he and a girl his age, who lived in his apartment building, had had a brief, awkward sexual encounter. It was his introduction to a new world, both inside of himself and beyond. The encounter had been fun and secretive and exhilarating, but...he couldn't help wondering if he was exactly like everyone else. He thought that he might be different from other boys in Borough Park, different in ways that were hard to understand or speak about. He had doubts about himself, questions that could not even be whispered.

At New Utrecht High, the older, bigger, rougher boys looked down on kids like him, called them names. It was tough to be labeled a fag, but much tougher if you thought those boys knew something important about you that you couldn't talk about with anyone. Surely there were places where such things could be discussed and dealt with openly. From reading nightlife columns and *Hollywood Rajah,* Geffen sensed that there were locales and businesses more tolerant than the neighborhood he came from. In some industries, there might even be people who were like him. Wasn't show business one of those fields?

Because he was a poor student, and because he was picked on by older boys in the neighborhood, Geffen often doubted that he would amount to anything. With characteristic bluntness, he would one day describe himself in high school as "a complete fuckup." His mother held a different view of her son and saw in him a hidden potential and a power that others would not see for many more years. When he was a boy, Batya sometimes referred to him as "King David," and once, when he came to her and lamented that he was not popular and had no future, she disagreed.

Batya looked down at his small fingers and palms, studying

them intently. "You," she said, "have golden hands. You can be anything you want to be."

He graduated from high school in 1960, the year his father died. The boy and the man had never been close, and in all the media interviews Geffen would give in future years, this relationship would remain opaque. It was his mother who would come across vividly—the hardworking, disciplined, talkative, advice-giving Batya, who was always there running the business and taking care of the family, teaching her son about earning money and expecting him to succeed on his own. Abraham was a shadow, a figure sitting over in the corner with a book in his hand, pondering things other than business, a haunting presence that would reappear before David Geffen, in other forms, throughout his life. As he became more successful, others who evoked Abraham would watch him and judge him—sometimes very harshly—always reminding him that there were other things in life besides money.

If his Brooklyn background were a painting, his mother would be the colors on the canvas and his father would be the negative space. Both would be necessary to create the full artistic effect, just as both parents shaped him and moved him in the direction of his adulthood. His mother's role was more obvious, but not necessarily more important. He may have needed to prove something to Batya—that he could make money, too—but Abraham stirred other needs in his son that were just as deep.

From the moment Geffen began to discover his career, he went in search of older men, of moneyed, powerful father figures who could help him advance in the business. He found them everywhere.

CHAPTER 3

Days after graduating from high school, he got a job driving someone else's car from New York to Los Angeles, where his more straitlaced, conventional brother was a law student at UCLA. David wanted to visit Mitchell and see if L.A. was as spectacular as he'd imagined it to be while sitting in Borough Park theaters, watching movies about beach girls and surfers. Brooklyn and Beverly Hills were more than a continent apart. They were separated by aesthetics, wealth, weather, and a sense of the past: Borough Park embraced the history of Europe and Russia, while in L.A., as the saying went, history was what you'd eaten for breakfast.

Some New Yorkers, of course, view L.A. as glossy and repugnant, but Geffen found the city equal to his expectations. People of both sexes were stunningly attractive, cars were sleek, and gorgeous homes were filled with expensive objets d'art. Lawns were manicured, and money seemed to be flowing in every direction. It was the early sixties and liberation of all kinds was filtering into the Southern California air. The lingering sadness that many Brooklyn natives felt toward their old neighborhoods was not evoked by L.A.

"The poignancy in Brooklyn," says Joe Sinisi, who settled in the Rocky Mountain West, "came from the fact that you could not live as an adult in the place that you'd enjoyed as a child. It had changed too much and no longer belonged to you, but to another group of people from another part of the world. You had to find another home."

In L.A., Geffen met a film producer who cast him in a small role as a high school freshman in *The Explosive Generation*. The picture was not a hit, and Geffen did not envision a future for himself as an actor, but the experience did inspire him to get his nose fixed. It also convinced him that the City of Angels was indeed fabulous and that someday, somehow, he would work there in show business.

After briefly returning to New York, he decided to further his education at the University of Texas, where he had some friends. This effort lasted one semester. Then he enrolled in Brooklyn College, where he lasted another semester. Defeated as a student, he went back to California. His brother, Mitchell, had become engaged to the sister-in-law of music producer Phil Spector. By the early sixties, the young Spector had become a major force in the pop music business, creating the "wall of sound" that accompanied numerous Top Forty hits, including "Be My Baby" by the Ronettes and "Then He Kissed Me" by the Crystals. Two of his backup singers were named Sonny and Cher. Through his brother, Geffen met Spector and began to hang around his recording sessions. He was drawn to the music but more captivated by the fact that someone only a few years older than himself had become an important figure in the recording field.

While visiting L.A., Geffen drove over to a bar on Melrose Avenue. Hesitantly, he entered the Red Raven tavern, not knowing what to expect. He'd been warned by acquaintances not to touch anyone at the bar or he could be arrested, so he kept his hands in his pockets, exchanging glances with the other male patrons. After a short stay, he left cautiously. He'd been told that the police liked to approach men coming out of this gay establishment and hassle them for jaywalking.

Back in New York, Geffen landed a job as an usher for *The Judy Garland Show* on CBS television. He was soon fired. He landed a similar job at the network for *The Red Skelton Show* but was fired again. His superiors found him to be too forceful, too loud, too aggressive—too much. He oozed energy and far more ambition than was needed to seat people in a TV studio. He couldn't seem to stick anywhere, and clearly he hadn't found the thing that causes a young person to say, "*I* can do that and succeed. I know I can."

Mitchell Geffen, who was moving steadily toward adult stability and a career in the legal profession, watched David from across the country, aware that his sibling was floundering. In order to shake him up, Mitchell told David that if he didn't settle down and stay with something, he was going to end up a ne'er-do-well, just like their father. The words stung but didn't solve the immediate problem. Geffen wasn't sure what to do with himself or how to get started in show business. People said you needed more education even to get a low-level job at a talent agency, where many other young men had begun, but he hated school and couldn't face another one.

In 1964, despite his lack of schooling, he decided to apply for a position at the Ashley-Steiner Famous Artists talent agency in midtown Manhattan. It was run by Ira Steiner and Ted Ashley, the nephew of Nat Lefkowitz, who headed the New York office of the renowned William Morris agency. Ashley-Steiner was on the rise and Ashley himself would one day become chairman of Warner Bros. studios. While filling out an application for the lowest position on the Ashley-Steiner ladder, Geffen truthfully acknowledged that he didn't have a college degree. He was then told by management that this admission ended his chances for hire. The young man was already self-conscious about not having any credentials in higher education; this was a further embarrassment. Leaving Ashley-Steiner, he vowed to himself that he would never again experience this particular humiliation.

He went up the street a few blocks and applied for a job in the mailroom of William Morris, the best talent agency in the world. For well over half a century, young men had been going to work in the Morris mailroom and launching themselves in brilliant careers in the agency business and beyond (Ted Ashley himself had started there). For those who were hardworking, patient, and able to suppress some of their own ambitions for the good of the company, William Morris was the epitome of stability, success, and status. Graduates of its training program liked to refer to it as the Harvard of the field.

Naturally, competition was ferocious, and eager young fellows had been known to crawl all over one another—and to throw punches—in the heat of chasing their dreams. To get ahead, you needed to be scrappy, aggressive, smart, committed, stealthy, and not above bending the rules. It was common practice for mailroom trainees to steam open the incoming mail and read it, just so they would know what deals their bosses were involved in. Appearance was important, and young men were expected to be well groomed and conservatively attired. The Morris motto for success was "Dress British and think Yiddish."

While applying for this job, Geffen told his prospective employers that he'd recently graduated from UCLA with a degree in theater arts. They were impressed and he got the job. Soon after starting in the mailroom, he was shocked to learn that another trainee had just been fired for lying on his employment application. The trainee had told the Morris honchos that he was a college graduate, but when they'd contacted his school's registrar and asked for a letter verifying this information, the university wrote back that the young man had earned no sheepskin from their institution. A day later, he was gone from William Morris.

Geffen panicked, then developed a plan. For the next few weeks, he arose very early, went to the Morris office before anyone else, and sorted through every single piece of mail that had just arrived, frantically looking for a letter from the UCLA registrar's office. Finally, it came. He steamed it open and took it to a printer, who was able to reproduce the UCLA letterhead on a blank piece of stationery. On this page, Geffen wrote his own letter, stating that he was indeed a graduate of that esteemed university. He slipped it back into the original UCLA envelope and returned it to the mailroom for delivery to his superiors. No one at William Morris knew what he'd done, and Geffen was on his way. He'd survived his first crisis, through scheming and pluck. He got an apartment in the West Fifties and was earning $55 a week in show business.

For years he didn't speak publicly about this letter-forging episode, and when he finally did, some people criticized him for being dishonest with the Morris agency. He always replied that he'd simply done what was necessary to get ahead in the entertainment industry. In time, these criticisms began to fade, but his feelings of not being well educated—and his peculiar relationship with UCLA—would only deepen.

At twenty-two, he left the mailroom and went to work for the television agent Ben Griefer. A respected veteran of TV's early days, Griefer had handled *The Texaco Star Theater, Sing Along With Mitch,* and *Your Show of Shows*. He'd also negotiated contracts for some of Morris's top TV comedy writers, including Goodman Ace and Neil Simon. As a young man (and even when he got older), Geffen tended to disdain television, but it was a place to learn the business, and Griefer was a good teacher. As his assistant, Geffen got to listen in on phone conversations that his boss was having with clients or the networks, although he wasn't allowed to speak himself.

What Morris agents mostly did was talk on the phone. Their jobs were more diverse than that, of course, but the telephone was central to their work. Geffen knew that he could do this as well as anyone. He could always keep a phone conversation going. He used the receiver not just for business but also for pleasure. He loved gossiping back and forth. The phone was a way of getting close to people, but not too close, and when you tired of interacting with others, you simply said good-bye and hung up. It was neat and clean and quick. It was a form of entertainment. You learned to keep people on the other end of the line interested and amused; you got to use your imagination. Wasn't that exactly what the agents did? If they didn't have a straight answer for a client or a buyer from a network, they just stalled or made something up or used a diversionary tactic. He could do that. He was already as good at it as they were; he just needed a chance to prove himself. He didn't know anything about making music or writing TV scripts, but he was gifted on the phone.

While working for Ben Griefer, Geffen discovered that his boss had accumulated secret headhunting lists of television clients who were under contract with other agencies. These lists gave Griefer an overview of the TV talent base and were used when Morris executives were targeting someone they wanted to lift from a competitor and sign as their own client. The lists mysteriously disappeared one day. When Geffen's boss asked him if he knew where they were, he said yes. He'd taken them to Nat Lefkowitz, the quiet, efficient lawyer-accountant who was in charge of the New York office. Anything this important, Geffen reasoned, needed to be shown to the top brass.

Griefer was deeply offended and wanted Geffen fired for this underhanded tactic, but Lefkowitz felt differently. It had taken some courage to pilfer those lists and bring them to the head man. It had taken some business acumen. Such actions were one way to advance in the cutthroat competition of the lower levels of show business. Maybe this kid from Brooklyn had something that others in the office were lacking. Lefkowitz resolved the dispute by removing Geffen from Griefer's charge and making him a junior agent under Lou Weiss, one of the three powerful TV agents who handled the agency's dealings with the major networks. Geffen learned the rudiments of the TV packaging business, in which an agency brings together the on-screen and off-screen talent for television productions and then sells the package to a network. While doing his job, Geffen made a point of lingering in the hallway outside Lefkowitz's office and running into him as he was coming out. Then he would mention his latest idea for improving the bottom line at William Morris. Lefkowitz was glad he'd kept him.

Geffen was soon talking with another Morris employee on the rise. Jerry Brandt had been making a name for himself over in the music department, not by focusing on established acts from the past but by pushing a relatively new phenomenon called rock 'n' roll. The dark suits who ran William Morris in the mid-sixties knew an enormous amount about film contracts, percentages, TV package deals, residuals, and ancillary rights. They understood legal fine print, marketing, promotion, and finding steady work for their world-famous clientele. But these older men, who were uniformly well groomed, well dressed, and well spoken, had great trouble grasping that a shaggy-haired youth culture was starting to burst up from the soil of American society into the realms of music, politics, and business.

In earlier years, William Morris had made money with pop idols Frank Sinatra and Elvis Presley, but these were special cases that transcended all the entertainment categories. Sinatra was the world's best nightclub singer and couldn't miss. Morris executives learned to tolerate Elvis's slick hair and swaying hips because in 1956 they could book him into the New Frontier in Las Vegas for the astounding sum of $6,000 a week. But such manna did not last, and by the mid-sixties, Elvis's popularity had begun to wane. His twangy, innocent, rockabilly sound had been replaced by something louder, rowdier, raunchier, and even more unpleasant to many adult ears.

If the Morris office was full of executives who would never buy a rock or blues-based album, even sober Nat Lefkowitz felt a twinge of rhythm and excitement when Jerry Brandt came to him in 1965 and said that he could get the Rolling Stones $25,000 a night for a series of concerts across the United States. The Stones may have been skinny, ill kempt, unrespectable, and surrounded by an air of danger, but who cared? The prospect of making 7 percent of that kind of money (the Stones' business manager, Allen Klein, flatly refused to pay the standard 10 percent Morris commission) was more than Lefkowitz could resist. He waived the other 3 percent and signed on.

Jerry Brandt was soon running the burgeoning Morris music department. It had the Supremes, who were topping the charts with "Where Did Our Love Go?" It had the Beach Boys, whose "Help Me, Rhonda" had become a smash. It had Sonny and Cher, who were America's favorite married singing couple. It had Simon and Garfunkel, two kids from Queens who sang sophisticated harmonies, wrote lyrics about intricate personal feelings, and were backed by the accomplished guitar work of Simon himself. Poetry was in the wind and, with the exception of Bob Dylan, no one seemed closer to capturing it than this soft-voiced duo. With acts like these, Jerry Brandt was fast becoming a star at William Morris, riding around Manhattan in limousines and wearing flashy mohair suits. Any ambitious young man in the Morris office would have taken a closer look at Brandt's operation, and Geffen did just that.

The agency, despite its great success, was known for having a hidebound structure, in which junior agents did not easily or quickly replace the older men above them. Often, young men had to wait for their superiors to retire or die before they could move up, and it was a very slow, tedious process. The company was run by individuals who'd spent decades holding power within the agency, and the system was designed for those who could wait—and wait and wait—for their turn.

Geffen was a naturally impatient young man. He'd been impatient in high school, impatient when he tried to attend college, and impatient as a mailroom trainee. He craved action and the chance to show his business talents, but the TV department was already well stocked with executives who were standing in his way. Some of them would be there for many more years. Inside the agenting field, more glamour was attached to film than to television, and Geffen would have liked to work on the motion picture side of William Morris, but that was equally hard to penetrate. For a junior agent sitting in New York, it was even more difficult to get Hollywood to notice you than it was to talk to TV executives in Manhattan.

One day, Geffen mentioned some of his frustrations to Jerry Brandt, who listened and then gave him the best piece of career advice he would ever receive. Start working with people your own age, Brandt said. They're in the music business, and you can represent them because almost no one else is doing that. The turf is new and wide open, yours for the taking.

CHAPTER 4

Geffen began going out at night searching for the kind of talent Brandt was talking about. In the early sixties, the folk scene in Greenwich Village had taken off, featuring performers like Bob Dylan, Fred Neil, Judy Collins, Dave Van Ronk, and Tom Paxton. Undiscovered talent, such as Joni Mitchell or the Lovin' Spoonful, was still passing through the Bitter End, Gerde's Folk City, and other small clubs, where patrons sometimes passed the hat to keep the musicians going. Out of all this activity, one man had emerged as the most astute manager of talent on the emerging scene: Albert Grossman.

The gray-haired, pot-bellied, chain-smoking Grossman handled Odetta, Big Bill Broonzy, and Peter, Paul, and Mary, but he'd carried himself to another level when he'd signed Bob Dylan. He'd seen the superstar potential in Dylan and helped him reach it. Yet Grossman was more than a businessman; he knew folk and rock music and cared passionately about these art forms. He would go on to manage such seminal groups as the Paul Butterfield Blues Band and the Band, as well as Richie Havens and Janis Joplin. Like Jerry Brandt at the William Morris office, Grossman had created visibility for himself and was a role model for any young person who wanted to become a part of the music business. Geffen was well aware of Grossman and in the future would be compared to him—usually unfavorably.

Geffen's first musical signing was Biff Rose, a small-voiced, eccentric performer, but then he represented two acts with more legs. Jesse Colin Young and his group, the Youngbloods, would have several hits, while the Association had two huge singles in the mid-sixties: "Windy" and "Along Comes Mary." Geffen was beginning to get noticed in the Morris office. When older agents heard about a group that was passing through New York, or were struck by something they'd heard on the radio, they went to him and drew upon his expertise. Was this band any good? Did they sell? Should the Morris office be working with them? In a place where hipness was never the order of the day, he was becoming a recognized authority on the new music. He was also building a reputation as a serious phone user, a reputation that over time would expand into legend.

"I was on the phone with him the night of the New York City blackout in 1965," says Jack Winter, a Morris client and comedy writer for *The Jackie Gleason Show, The Dick Van Dyke Show,* and Johnny Carson. "David and I were talking when we both realized that the lights had gone out around us, but the phones were still working. He was in his office and I was at home. Then we realized they'd gone out all over the city. He waited a few moments to see if they would come back on, but when they didn't, he just kept talking. It was a lot more important for him to make the point he was making than to worry about something like a blackout."

Despite his growing clout inside the Morris office, not everyone was enthusiastic about the direction Geffen's career was taking. Unlike Albert Grossman, he wasn't an integral part of the folk or rock scene. He wasn't a fervid fan of new music, and he didn't know an A minor chord from a tuning fork. Some people believed that he was just clutching at the latest thing. The rock music business was very young, and still widely regarded as little more than a scruffy and disreputable fad.

"I knew David back in the mid-sixties when we were both starting out in the business," says film director and Brooklyn native Marty Davidson. "He was at William Morris and I was at the Ashley agency, just a few blocks away. We'd meet once in a while for lunch, and since we were both in TV packaging, we would compare notes. I was making $65 a week and he was earning about the same thing. We could barely pay the rent, but we had expense accounts for the first time in our lives, so we could go out at night and eat in restaurants, go to clubs and concerts and parties. We both liked the nightlife.

"One day we were having lunch, and I told him that my ambition was to get into motion pictures. He said that he'd been offered a position in the music department at William Morris. I said, 'David, don't be stupid. That's a dead end. Take my word for it. It's a big mistake to go in that direction.'"

Davidson laughs at the memory. "I guess he did all right. David's ego was enormous, but he used it in such a way that he was lovable. He was aggressive, he had balls, and he knew how to mix things up when it was necessary. Nothing ever stopped him from making phone calls or pursuing talent."

▪ ▪ ▪

Laura Nyro was born in 1947, and her father was a piano tuner in the Bronx. Early on she began playing the instrument and composing music. One day, her father went to the office of Artie Mogull, an associate of Albert Grossman's, in order to tune Mogull's piano. The tuner told Mogull that his daughter wrote songs and he ought to give her a listen. Mogull had heard so many lines like this before that he never wanted to hear one again. But the tuner was so insistent that Mogull agreed to audition the girl the next day. The eighteen-year-old Nyro walked into his office, sat down at the piano, struck the keys, and began singing her future hit "Stoney End." Mogull immediately became her manager.

She soon had a contract with Verve/Forecast, and in 1966 she debuted with the album *More Than a New Discovery*. Her music was a fascinating amalgam. She combined the soulful and gospel elements of black music with the angst of a white urban teenager, and she appeared on the scene when many young white people were trying to identify with and understand the experience of black Americans. This phenomenon took several forms. Some white kids were drawn to the blues, as performed by black artists like Muddy Waters and B. B. King. Others were drawn to the funk of James Brown or the almost-religious sounds of Aretha Franklin. With her bluesy phrasings and sophisticated lyrics, Nyro offered listeners a kind of white soul music.

She was, most people believed, a far better songwriter than performer. With her long dark hair, dark eyes, and black clothes, she looked morbid. She sat on stage at a piano and drove her music into the audience. She wore lavender lipstick, and some of her dresses had plaster-of-paris fruits sewn onto them. A cult following adored her, but she was not for the masses.

"In person," says one of her fans from the sixties, "she wasn't very good, because she was obviously neurotic and had no sense of what people could endure. She was an artist who needed someone else to interpret her music."

In 1967, she appeared at the Monterey Pop Festival, in front of a juiced-up crowd that had come to see Janis Joplin and her electrified hard rock band, Big Brother and the Holding Company. When Nyro sat down and plunged into her songs about the intricacies of love, the audience booed and jeered, nearly heckling her from the stage. It was a grotesque failure, and some critics felt that it signaled the end of her career.

After her Monterey disaster, Geffen heard about Nyro from Bones Howe, the producer for the Association and the Fifth Dimension. Geffen listened to a tape of her material and was moved by two songs in particular: "Wedding Bell Blues" and "He's a Runner." He instinctively felt that anyone who could create as strong a reaction as she had at Monterey had something going for her. Geffen visited her in her Eighth Avenue apartment, where she lived in splendid squalor with numerous cats. She was, he could instantly tell, a born nerd, and he'd already developed a lifelong dedication to those he categorized in this way. Something happened between the two of them, and for the first time ever, Geffen became passionate not just about making a deal, but about an artist and her music. He had a talent for connecting with female performers—and in this case, the feeling was something like love.

Elliot Roberts, a William Morris trainee who would become Geffen's partner in the music managing business, had seen this trait in the man before. Roberts had once played a Buffy Sainte-Marie album for Geffen in his apartment, and as Geffen listened to the protest lyric, "My country 'tis of thy people you're dying," he began to weep. Roberts never forgot this spontaneous show of emotion. Geffen was mistrustful of the world and most of the people he met, yet he had a sentimental, vulnerable spot that music, and mostly the songs of women, could penetrate.

After connecting with Laura Nyro, he began telling friends that he was thinking of marrying her.

"I met David in the mid to late sixties," says Larry Marks, a pianist and music producer in L.A., who now runs a talent agency for composers. "He'd just signed Laura Nyro and was starting out as a manager in the music business. He completely believed in her, and was a totally driven human being on her behalf. Back then I lived in Beverly Hills, and he popped into my house one day and had a recording by her. It was her first album, I think. We played it, and he began raving about how she would be a star soon. He went on and on. Not everyone in the room was as much of a believer in Laura Nyro as he was.

"The thing about David was that he was never distracted by anything other than business. While other people had wives or families to think about, he had nothing else to do but push his own personal agenda. From the moment he began in music, his work was his life. He would literally move in with someone he wanted to sign or move them into his home. He was very, very seductive when he wanted to turn on the charm—and smart as a whip. When he made up his mind about something, it was impossible to modify it. There's a lot to be said for that kind of maniacal drive. One of the quickest ways to succeed is to make a decision, any decision, and then stick by it. David did this with Laura Nyro and he never wavered. He yelled at the wind, and eventually it changed direction. Then he looked like an economic god."

From the beginning, Geffen sensed that Nyro's music could be leveraged into something more than capturing a small, fervent group of admirers. He knew that she wrote first-rate pop music, but he felt that she needed big-name performers to record her material. After her debacle at Monterey, Artie Mogull was looking to unload her—but at a decent price, since he'd negotiated her recording contract with Verve and owned her music publishing rights. When Geffen called Mogull and said that he wanted to manage her, Mogull agreed to let Geffen become her agent but held on to everything else. Geffen talked Nyro into hiring a lawyer to void her contract with Mogull, and a court ruled that because she'd signed her papers with the man when she was a minor, they were invalid. Mogull, however, still owned the rights to her old songs.

Geffen became her manager and set up a new publishing company, Tuna Fish Music (named after Nyro's favorite food). Tuna Fish would own her future compositions, with 50 percent of its proceeds going to the singer and the other half to Geffen. Then he took her to Clive Davis, the head of Columbia Records, the most prestigious label in the business, and got Davis, in the wake of Monterey, to give her a second chance. Davis was impressed enough to sign her to a recording contract. Geffen peddled one of Nyro's songs, "Stoned Soul Picnic," to the Fifth Dimension, who had a hit with it. Then he began lining up other headlining performers to record more of her material. His long-range goal was to sell Nyro's publishing rights to CBS, but first he had to get Artie Mogull out of the way. When he offered Mogull $470,000 for the rights to Nyro's past songs, this struck Mogull as a colossal sum for a performer who had recently been unmercifully booed. He took the deal.

Nyro's debut album for Clive Davis and Columbia Records was *Eli and the 13th Confession*. The album climbed into the top two hundred, but more important, it exposed her music to other artists, who now began covering (recording) her songs. The Fifth Dimension had another big hit with "Sweet Blindness" and Three Dog Night took "Eli's Coming" to number ten on the pop charts. From Nyro's first album, Blood, Sweat, and Tears recorded "And When I Die," while Barbra Streisand covered "Stoney End" and "Flimflam Man."

One evening in 1968, after Geffen had moved in with Nyro, they were standing on the balcony of her Central Park South apartment looking out over the city. In a spontaneous outburst of poetry, she said, "New York is a tender berry." Due to her Bronx accent, the words came out sounding like "tendaberry." Legend has it that she then went inside, sat down at the piano, and wrote three songs that would appear on her next album. *New York Tendaberry* was released in 1969 and became her bestselling record. It contained "Time and Love," another song that Streisand would cover.

In 1968, Geffen left William Morris and went to work for what had been the Ashley-Steiner Famous Artists agency. Six years earlier, Ashley-Steiner had purchased Famous Artists, an L.A. agency whose biggest client was John Wayne. Less structured and less stodgy than William Morris, Ashley Famous, as it was now called, was a business on the rise, with a client list that included Vanessa Redgrave, Sean Connery, Burt Lancaster, and Ingrid Bergman. Ashley Famous had been aided by the federal government's 1962 decision to enforce its antitrust laws and order MCA—the vast Music Corporation of America—to divest itself of the agenting business, since it was now getting into movie production. Ashley Famous had hired some of MCA's top film talent and picked up Tennessee Williams and Arthur Miller. Yet the agency's strongest division was TV packaging, and on that front it competed vigorously with William Morris. Its music department was weaker, and Geffen was hired to change that. His Ashley Famous tenure was short-lived but reverberated through the rest of his career.

In 1967, Steve Ross, a former funeral parlor director who had become the aggressive young head of the Kinney parking lot chain, began buying other businesses—rather mundane ones at first. He acquired Hudson Painting and Decorating, Star Circle Wall Systems, Inc., Panavision, Inc., Circle Floor Co., Inc., and the Wachtel Plumbing Company. Tall, handsome, and dynamic, Ross had ambitions that went far beyond overseeing parking lots and plumbing stores. He envisioned an empire and was drawn toward the glamour associated with the entertainment business. When he first expressed a desire to buy Ashley Famous, Ted Ashley wasn't interested in selling his firm to an outsider but agreed to meet with Ross as a favor to someone else. The next day the deal was done.

In November of 1967, Kinney National paid $13 million for Ashley Famous, by now the second largest talent agency in the country. Then Ross looked toward California and something much bigger: the Warner Bros.–Seven Arts studio in Hollywood. Warner had a highly profitable music division led by a young executive named Mo Ostin and featuring artists like Bill Cosby, Peter, Paul and Mary, Dean Martin, and Nancy Sinatra. In 1967, Warner Music had purchased Atlantic Records, the successful label headed by Ahmet Ertegun. Warner leaped into the rock business by signing a ragged group of musicians out of San Francisco named the Grateful Dead.

After only a few months at the Ashley office, Geffen went to his superiors and asked to be released from his contract. He told them that he didn't want to be an agent anymore but to manage the careers of Laura Nyro and other musicians. The Ashley brass valued Geffen—he knew more about up-and-coming musical talent than anyone else in the office—and were not pleased. People were regularly bringing him tapes of new groups, and he was becoming well known throughout the rock world. He'd met Robbie Robertson of the Band, he'd invited Jimi Hendrix and Buddy Miles over to his apartment, and he was with an aspiring young songwriter named Joni Mitchell in early April of 1968, when Martin Luther King was murdered. Ted Ashley and his top lieutenants didn't really appreciate the new music, but they knew that brashness, street smarts, a fast tongue, and nerve were not liabilities in the realm of rock but assets. They didn't want Geffen to go.

In the talent agency business, which runs on proprietary information, the only thing worse than losing a good hire is having him or her take some of your clients or secrets to a competitor. When Geffen asked to be released from Ashley Famous, his boss took this request to Ashley himself, who then took it to Steve Ross. The situation was more delicate than it normally would have been. Ross had already set in motion the steps to buy Warner–Seven Arts. When this deal closed, Ross would have to divest Ashley Famous, because under antitrust laws his company could not be in both the agency and the movie production businesses.

With all this unfolding, Ted Ashley was in the process of

negotiating with Marvin Josephson, the owner of the Marvin Josephson Associates talent agency. Ashley wanted Josephson to buy Ashley Famous and all its assets. Geffen was one of those assets, and Ashley strongly desired to keep him in the office, at least until these negotiations were finished. But Geffen was adamant about leaving. The impasse was resolved when he promised the Ashley leadership that if he were allowed to depart, he would never again reenter the agency business. He would stay in the music management field and not go to work for one of their rivals. Under these conditions, he left Ashley Famous and took Laura Nyro with him. Several months later, he accepted a job at Creative Management Associates, run by the highly successful agent Freddie Fields. In the eyes of the Ashley office, he'd broken a very significant vow.

His hiring at CMA unleashed anger toward him that would resonate across the rest of his career. A small, close-knit community makes up the business side of entertainment. It runs on trust and on long-term relationships. It has its own rules and unwritten code. Young men tend to advance in the field by keeping their word and doing the bidding of older men. Those who violate this code can set off feuds that last indefinitely. Nearly thirty years after Geffen left Ashley Famous, there were still people in the business who'd never forgotten, or forgiven, his departure.

"Ted was very affectionate toward David," says someone who worked in the Ashley office in the 1960s, "and he was really sorry when Geffen double-crossed us and left. You want me to tell you who David Geffen really is? How can I best describe him? He's a little putz who shits on people. He's Sammy Glick, that's who. He was always Sammy Glick."

Insults don't cut much deeper than that: Sammy Glick, the ultimate hustler, is the creation of novelist and screenwriter (*On the Waterfront*) Budd Schulberg, whose father was in charge of production at the Paramount studio in the 1920s and 1930s. Originally published in 1937 in *Liberty* magazine, *What Makes Sammy Run?* appeared as a novel in 1941. According to Neal Gabler in *An Empire of Their Own,* this book is "an account of an ambitious first-generation American Jew named Sammy Glick who claws his way to the top of the Hollywood heap by forsaking everything decent.... Glick, ferret-faced and nervous, is an irrepressible schemer and user, a bolt of ambition who climbs his way from errand boy at a newspaper to columnist to screenwriter to producer without missing a beat." Gabler writes that the book's narrator, Al Manheim, believes that "what really made Sammy run was his war against his father, his Judaism, his environment, his poverty, his world."

Yet Geffen, despite the ire he'd generated by joining CMA, was not hurt by what had happened at Ashley Famous, but helped. He'd encountered Steve Ross, the man who would play the most significant role in his business future. Geffen would develop the same kind of relationship with Ross that he'd already established as a pattern with very successful older men. Nat Lefkowitz had allowed him to stay at William Morris when others wanted him gone. Ted Ashley was not happy with Geffen's leaving his agency but would work with him again. And Steve Ross would be his greatest supporter. They all sensed Geffen's passion for making deals, his incredible feel for what was about to come around the corner in popular entertainment, and his essential hunger. They understood him, because they were hungry too.

Lefkowitz was a Brooklyn native who'd started at William Morris in 1927 and laboriously worked his way to the top. His nephew, the slightly built, diminutive Ted Ashley, had grown up in a tiny Brooklyn apartment, sleeping on a cot and watching his father eke out a living as a tailor. At age sixteen, he'd started in the Morris mailroom, and within half a decade, he'd become an agent. Unlike Lefkowitz, Ashley didn't want to stay at the Morris office and turn into another lifer. He left there at twenty-three—enraging his uncle Nat—and began managing comedians, including Henny Youngman. Steve Ross came from the Flatbush section of Brooklyn and had grown up in a tough Irish, Jewish, and African-American neighborhood, where he quickly learned about being called names and fighting. He also learned about business. As a boy, he sold cigarettes to his father, a heavy smoker, for a nickel more per carton than the youngster had paid for them.

When Lefkowitz or Ashley or Ross looked at Geffen, they saw not merely a son but a piece of himself. Each man had felt the searing ambition that can come from growing up without money, and all were determined to achieve a level of wealth and respectability that would gloss over, if not obliterate, their pasts. Geffen knew exactly how to treat them.

One afternoon years ago, Marty Davidson was at the Beverly Hills Hotel, relaxing by the pool with producer Steve Tisch (*Forrest Gump*) and his extremely successful father, Robert Tisch, who'd made millions in real estate.

"Bob Tisch was very, very rich, and this was before David had made his really big money," Davidson says. "I saw him sitting at the far end of the pool with Warren Beatty and Michelle Phillips. Warren and Michelle were necking at a cabana, and David was just looking around, as if he were a little uncomfortable. Warren kept kissing her, and finally David spotted us and jumped up and came over to our table. I think he was glad to get away from them.

"He sat down and immediately began talking to Steve's father. He just charmed the hell out of this man for the next thirty minutes. It was an incredible performance. Then he asked Bob Tisch if he would adopt him, so that he could be his son. He said, 'If you'd adopt me, I could really become something.' David is an incredible charmer, and he always knew where the money was. He knew how to deal with the men with the money, and he let them know that he enjoyed other people's success. He loved associating with people who were what he wanted to be.

"I don't think he ever got over being this kid from Brooklyn. I'm sure that it's amazing to him now that he became David Geffen."

CHAPTER 5

In 1968, Geffen met yet another father figure: Ahmet Ertegun, the head of Atlantic Records. Born in 1924, Ertegun was the son of the Turkish ambassador to the United States. At age twelve, he came to Washington, D.C., and in 1947, he started Atlantic Records with money given him by a Turkish dentist. A passionate jazz and blues collector, he once owned twenty-five thousand albums. He had a perfectly shaped balding head and wore a trimmed goatee, expensive blue blazers, and highly polished shoes. He could speak French or he could speak jive—while moving comfortably through the monied realms of New York or Paris, or the impoverished world of undiscovered black musicians. Ertegun had a hip, raspy voice and an abiding sense of humor. While courting a young Romanian woman named Mica, he stashed a five-piece band in her closet and instructed them to come out playing "Puttin' on the Ritz." The couple were soon married.

Despite his Turkish heritage, Ertegun was deeply connected to black American music. In the 1950s, he and two partners—his brother, Nesuhi, and Jerry Wexler (the man who coined the phrase "rhythm and blues")— recorded Joe Turner, Clyde McPhatter and the Drifters, Ruth Brown, and Ray Charles. On the jazz side, Nesuhi Ertegun signed John Coltrane, Ornette Coleman, and Charles Mingus. Much of Atlantic's music seeped across racial lines and was embraced by white audiences. In the sixties, this trend became even more prominent when Atlantic, along with Stax and Volt, distributed recordings by Otis Redding, Solomon Burke, Sam & Dave, Wilson Pickett, and Aretha Franklin. As much as anyone, Ertegun and Wexler helped bring together black and white culture through music. In the early seventies, the Rolling Stones signed with Atlantic, not because Ertegun could offer them the most money but because Mick Jagger wanted to be on the label that first recorded some of his musical parents.

Ertegun had something more than taste and style, something subtle and unusual in his profession. As rock music executives get older, they continue to deal with new artists in their twenties or thirties. It's always tempting for aging music execs to try to hang on and be hipper than they are, by chasing young women or drinking excessively or taking drugs. For two decades, Ertegun had managed to stay on top of several musical worlds without the need for any of these things. In a business that celebrates adolescent feelings and behavior, he came across as a mature adult. It was a far rarer accomplishment than one might have guessed, and people seemed drawn to him for reasons they could not quite explain. In later years, Geffen would say that Ahmet Ertegun, more than anyone else, was his role model in the music business.

One of the seminal bands of the 1960s was the short-lived Buffalo Springfield, whom Ertegun recorded for Atlantic Records. Their 1969 *Retrospective* album became a rock classic, and in the liner notes, he wrote, "Of all the groups to have emerged in America in the middle sixties, Buffalo Springfield will be remembered as one of the most creative and exciting. The very power of the individual writing and performing talents of the members was also the reason for the breakup of the original group. It was comprised of Steve Stills, Neil Young, Richie Furay, Dewey Martin, and Bruce Palmer, later replaced by Jim Messina. More will be heard from all of them."

Ertegun was prophetic. Richie Furay and Jim Messina formed Poco, a successful country-rock band of the early seventies, and then Messina became even more popular after teaming up with Kenny Loggins. Neil Young, one of the genuine wild horses of the rock world, would still be creating new music in the 1990s. Stephen Stills, the singer and acoustic blues guitarist with perhaps the finest talent in Buffalo Springfield, would go on to have a good solo career (in the late sixties, Stills had nearly been derailed as a musician when he'd tried out for the Monkees, the made-for-TV band that became a big hit; fortunately, his teeth weren't good enough for television, and Mike Nesmith got the gig).

Elliot Roberts had worked with Geffen at William Morris before becoming the manager for David Crosby, lately of the Byrds. In 1968, Crosby wanted to join with Stephen Stills and Graham Nash, the ex-Hollie, to start a new band. The three musicians also wanted to record, but all were under contract to different labels. Roberts asked Geffen to help him get their releases from these companies, and Geffen began doing just that, with the intention of taking the new group to Clive Davis at CBS. Freeing up Crosby and Nash was easy, but Stills was another matter.

"David first contacted my partner, Jerry Wexler, about getting Stephen Stills released from Atlantic," says Ahmet Ertegun. "David wanted Jerry to let Stephen out of his contract, and when he made this suggestion, Jerry threw him out of his office. Physically. I called David up and invited him to come back and talk to me. He did that, and I found him to be very charming. He had a keen perception of what was happening, and he was no bullshit. His observations on the music business were to the point and we both had enthusiasm for young artists who were not exactly in the mainstream. David was very good at getting people to make deals that were favorable to him. But then he would deliver on his promises and make them happy.

"I told him that I couldn't give him a release for Stephen, but that I would be interested in recording this new group myself. When he saw that his idea wouldn't work out, he agreed to mine. From the start, my wife, Mica, and I could both see that he was going to be very big. He doesn't give up, and he's a killer in business. He can smell disaster coming and get out of its way. He's great with numbers and knows exactly where they are going. He also had a feel for new artists, and he could lead them into good situations.

"The only thing that would have surprised me is if he hadn't become a huge success. He's smarter than anyone else in our field, and he will not let anything, including friendship, interfere with business."

Laura Nyro learned that the hard way. In 1969, Geffen sold Tuna Fish Music to CBS for $4.5 million. The songwriter received half of the proceeds, and Geffen got the other half, becoming a multimillionaire at twenty-six. Nyro hadn't fully understood the fine print of her arrangement with Geffen and was upset with his taking 50 percent of the sale. It was the beginning of the end of their relationship.

Marty Davidson, who'd once advised Geffen against going into the music business, was shocked by his friend's sudden wealth.

"The difference between me and David," he says, "was that when I made my first deal at Ashley Famous, I got a $150 raise. I thought I was going to the top, and whenever I thought about David scrambling to be a music manager, I asked myself, 'Where is he going?' On his first deal, he got more than two million dollars. Oh, well."

In 1969, while Crosby, Stills, and Nash (soon to be joined by Neil Young) were recording their debut album for Atlantic, Geffen and Elliot Roberts were trying to get them concert dates. As it turned out, their first live performance came that August, at Woodstock, before several hundred thousand people, where Stills gazed out at the multitudes and confessed that the band was "scared shitless." Some earlier concert dates had had to wait.

In June of 1969, Denver rock promoter Barry Fey was putting together a three-day music festival, with Janis Joplin as the headliner. Rock festivals were still in their infancy, and Fey himself was just beginning in the business. It was a time of chaotic creativity.

"David called up and said, 'Here's Crosby, Stills, and Nash, the act that will make your festival,'" says Fey, whom *Billboard* magazine voted the best rock promoter in America for 1978, 1979, and 1980. "This was going to be their first performance ever. He told me that their album was coming out in May of '69, so I offered him

$10,000 for the act. Today, that wouldn't pay for the lights. He accepted it, but their album didn't come out in May and it wasn't out in early June, either. I got worried and called David. 'I can't do this,' I said. 'I can't pay ten thousand dollars for a band with no album. I'll have to cancel them.' You've got to understand that I'd hocked everything I owned and mortgaged my car to put on this festival. I was totally stretched.

"David got real upset with me, and things got heated on the phone. He said, 'You can't do this to me, Barry. You can't do this to Stephen. He's really looking forward to playing Denver.' I said, 'Then let him come out and play for nothing.' He said, 'You know I can't do that.' After a while, he calmed down and said, 'Look, Barry, this isn't going to work out, but we'll do business together in the future.' They didn't play here, but David was right. We did plenty of business later on, and he was first class all the way. Whenever I called him, he talked to me personally on the phone and never passed me along to someone else. He never avoided conflicts. He understood musicians a lot better than most people in our business do. He could speak to them on their level, and he cared about them. Who deserved success more than he did?"

In the fall of 1969, the much-awaited *Crosby, Stills & Nash* LP was finally released. It had a rustic-looking, sepia-colored jacket, showing the three young men sitting on a worn-out couch; Stills held a Martin guitar. Inside the jacket, the trio were dressed in Eskimo parkas. The air surrounding them looked tangibly cold, and their long brown hair reflected the sun as it rose behind their heads. No photograph from the sixties captures more of the youthful energy, self-involvement, and hopefulness of that time. In a day when the release of albums was a major event on college campuses and at musical scenes across the country, this recording caused a visible rush of excitement. Everyone had to hear it. Everyone had to learn the lyrics and harmonies. Lasting friendships were formed over these songs.

For brief periods during the fifties and sixties, certain records represented something more than songs pressed into wax. They signified a breaking down of racial barriers or a protest against warfare or a general rebellion against all that was oppressive, harmful, stupid, and limiting in the human experience. A palpable sensation of freedom accompanied these albums, and a "counterculture" grew up around this music. The first Crosby, Stills, and Nash album was one such LP, and Geffen had helped create it. He even had the psychic scars to prove it—after being busted for trying to sneak a satchel of dope through an airport for David Crosby. (Geffen's brother, Mitchell, handled the legal issues, and the case never came to trial.)

For five years, he'd been slowly building a reputation inside the music business. Now it had solidified. From 1969 on, Geffen would not only have more and more success but would show an astonishing capacity to be at the epicenter of the action. When Ahmet Ertegun held a fancy gathering in Manhattan, Geffen was there. When the beautiful people in fashion or cinema came together to entertain one another, he received an invitation. When celebrity photographer Annie Leibovitz asked him to take off his clothes in front of the Beverly Hills Hotel, so she could shoot a picture of him with nothing but a leaf over his genitals, he daringly complied with her wishes. He'd crossed the threshold of celebrity and was gradually becoming famous himself.

Yet respect did not come with his fame and riches. There was something about Geffen that annoyed people, just as it had when he was in high school and then later on, when he bolted the Ashley Famous agency for his next opportunity. He was still, in the eyes of his critics, too transparently ambitious for his own good.

"In the late 1960s," says George W. S. Trow, who has written extensively about contemporary American culture, "some musicians and other people genuinely believed in something beyond entertainment and making money. They held a white-hot energy that could not be contained. They had a deep commitment to something, which they couldn't quite define, yet it was real. Back then, they understood the difference between money and meaning. Today, of course, it's all just a business.

"David Geffen was the link to the marketplace for some very talented people in the counterculture. He deserves credit for that, but you could never really believe in him as a countercultural figure who stood for anything other than succeeding in business. You just sensed in him the same upwardly mobile drift that you sense in so many other Americans. From 1969 to 1971, some people really did represent something more. John Lennon is an example. Or Jerry Garcia. Or Ahmet Ertegun, perhaps back in the fifties. But

David...we're always disappointed when people rise to Geffen's level and then behave the same way rich people have always behaved in the past."

Even Geffen's mother had trouble believing how successful her younger son had become. When he invited Batya to a Crosby, Stills, and Nash concert, she was taken aback by his status in the rock world. While watching the group perform, she turned to Geffen and asked him what he did for these musicians.

"I'm their manager," he said proudly. "I'm responsible for their careers."

Batya gazed at him, incredulous.

"*You?*" she exclaimed.

CHAPTER 6

Geffen's stay at the Creative Management Associates agency was as brief as his stint at Ashley Famous. He worked there long enough, however, to meet Sandy Gallin, a young agent who'd gained recognition a few years earlier by booking the Beatles for their legendary 1964 appearance on *The Ed Sullivan Show.* In the 1970s, Gallin would become a talent manager and go on to represent some of the biggest names in show business, including Dolly Parton, Roseanne Barr, and Neil Diamond. He would also develop a close friendship with Geffen and become one of his key allies in a future power play. While at CMA, Geffen realized that he didn't want to continue being an agent and didn't much like working for others. At heart, he was an entrepreneur, who loved making deals and championing his own artists.

Late in 1969, Geffen went to Ahmet Ertegun and offered him some other bands to record, besides Crosby, Stills, and Nash. Ertegun begged off and came up with a better suggestion. Now that Geffen had sold Tuna Fish Music to CBS and had some working capital, why didn't he start his own record label and run it himself?

Ertegun had great faith in Geffen's business acumen and could provide him with the necessary advice about renting studio time, making albums, and marketing and promoting new products. Why not record the people he was pushing so hard, instead of trying to get others to do that for him?

Geffen had recently moved to L.A. and begun looking for office space. In 1970, he found an old French château on Sunset Boulevard and grabbed it as the headquarters for his new label: Asylum Records. He chose the name for two reasons. One was because both the music business and the inner workings of his small company struck him as insane. Second, he wanted Asylum to be a refuge for talent not welcome elsewhere. He assumed that his first big signing at Asylum would be Laura Nyro, but she was still smarting from the Tuna Fish deal. She spurned Asylum and stayed with Columbia Records. Geffen was embarrassed and hurt by her actions—and not merely because he'd lost a fine artist.

He'd lived with Laura Nyro and allowed himself to get close to her, to trust her, and he'd worked very hard on her behalf. He'd touted her when others didn't want to listen to her music and had taken her to the top of the business—to Clive Davis himself. Geffen didn't trust anyone easily, but on this occasion he'd made himself vulnerable. After she rejected Asylum, the two of them could not bring themselves to discuss her decision, and they never spoke again. She made a few more recordings before retiring to a fishing village in Massachusetts. In time, she returned to performing, until her death from cancer in 1997.

Following his split with Nyro, Geffen tried to keep his professional endeavors and his personal emotions clearly separate. He would never get quite that close to a performer again. At the same time, his career was always about more than business. He looked to certain artists and to older men to provide things that he couldn't get elsewhere or had never received from his father. And if he felt anything like betrayal or dishonesty in these people, he would lash out with no mercy. The credo that he'd learned on Brooklyn playgrounds—you don't take an insult without giving a harsher one back—was the backbone of his life. Enormous success would not change this.

While he ran Asylum from West Hollywood, Elliot Roberts, his partner in the management company of Geffen-Roberts, Inc., oversaw the booking and touring end of their music business. Geffen did not go on the road with bands but stayed in the office and constantly worked the phones. As his own boss, he could give free rein to his own rock-'n'-roll style of getting things done. He made instant decisions about almost everything, implicitly trusting in the electrical impulses that traveled up from his viscera and hit the traffic signal in his brain that said yes or no. Once he'd made up his mind, little could alter it. Yet he was open to advice from his employees. He wanted their input and didn't care if they raised their voices; to be good in the music business, he believed, you had to feel very strongly about getting your artists in front of the public.

He was almost always willing to listen—at least for several seconds. Geffen expected his staff to be as fast and entrepreneurial as he was, and he generously rewarded those who were. Once he'd heard a piece of information, he didn't need to hear it again. Repetition was dangerous. The music field was ragged, unpredictable, and ever changing, and the best working environment was one where people could openly vent their feelings.

"I think it's important," says a woman in L.A. who's known him for many years, "that he grew up watching a small business operate, because he understood that almost everyone, on some level, wants to run his or her own business. They want to be given responsibility for making choices and decisions. If you don't give people that, it will lay the groundwork for rebellion later on. At Asylum, he didn't demand that people conform to his way, but find their own ways. That's how a company can grow and stay ahead of the trends.

"He removed some of the fear from the working environment by encouraging people to let their thoughts out. You can waste a lot of time in business worrying about what the people above you are thinking. If you get this stuff out, you're way ahead. David didn't plan any of this or strategize it; he just followed his instincts and went forward. Get the input, decide, and move on. It's a very fluid style. He has an innate ability to say what he feels, right when he's feeling it, and then let others respond to it. Most people don't have that instant access to their words and emotions. Words are what people are mostly afraid of, but he learned at a very early age that he could say what he felt and get away with it. So he just kept talking."

For years he worked without a desk, because he had no use for one. A couch, a worn Eames chair, and a phone sufficed. He also disdained paper. Memos were generally unnecessary, and he was certain that he could retain any pertinent information in his mind.

Paper just cluttered up the office. His ability to compute numbers in his head astounded many people. While they were still debating whether or not to do a deal, he'd already made that decision, run the figures through his brain, and calculated how many units of a product had to be sold to break even or turn a profit. One of his early colleagues at Asylum said that while he himself worked in the music field, Geffen was involved in finance.

He didn't buy art for his offices, or other expensive furnishings. After his company began producing gold records, he didn't hang them on the walls. Gold records were about the past and the past was finished. Geffen didn't enjoy long staff meetings or in-depth analysis of market potentials. He didn't mind being wrong about a product, but what he truly disliked was not being the one responsible for making the crucial decisions. Mistakes were inevitable; all that really mattered was not letting them control your future choices. When there was good news to deliver to an artist, he sometimes let an employee make the call. When there was bad news, he made the call himself. He wasn't the first one at work every morning but was still there when the others had all gone home—and still gripping the phone. The most difficult thing wasn't finding another deal but turning off his mind. After leaving the office, he rode around L.A. in the darkness, with the night wind blowing in through the windows, listening to demo tapes that budding musicians had sent to his label.

To young artists, he pitched Asylum Records as an intimate company where they would be free to make exactly the music they wanted to, without interference from any executives. He was committed to producing a relatively small number of albums each year, only twenty or so, and because he was highly selective, he could heavily promote and market Asylum's material. Geffen was striving for a kind of closeness in his business—a family atmosphere—and he achieved it. Along the way, he also handed out streams of personal advice to his staff and his musicians, whether they wanted it or not. People listened to him, not so much because they liked what he was saying but because there was something about him that was sad and lonely.

While he stayed in L.A., Elliot Roberts traveled with the bands represented by Geffen-Roberts. The two men developed something of a good cop–bad cop routine, in order to better the interests of their clients.

"Geffen I could always deal with, but Elliot Roberts...," says music promoter Barry Fey, who was not the sort of man to be intimidated by the wildcat nature of the rock business. Once, when the six-foot-seven, three-hundred-pound road manager for Cheap Trick told Fey that his band would not go on until Fey provided better food for them backstage, the promoter jumped him with both fists. "Elliot was always meaner than David. David would sit in L.A. and talk to me nicely on the phone, but Elliot was hands-on and would come out on the road with the bands and torture you. Nothing was ever enough for him. Ever."

In 1967, Roberts had heard a twenty-three-year-old woman performing in Greenwich Village coffeehouses for $15 a night. Joni Mitchell was from Alberta, Canada, and had studied art in Calgary before moving to New York City. Roberts was so taken with her music that he soon quit his job at William Morris to become her manager. When the singer was approached by executives from Warner/Reprise to make an album, Roberts needed help in putting together a record deal. He turned to Geffen, his mentor in the music business, to help negotiate her contract. Geffen took Mitchell to Clive Davis, who listened to her sing and dismissed her with the pronouncement that folk music was out. Geffen never forgave the remark, and eventually signed Mitchell to Asylum.

Like Laura Nyro, Mitchell had initially gained a reputation as a songwriter. Tom Rush covered "The Circle Game," then Judy Collins had a Top Ten hit with "Both Sides Now." Mitchell did not attend the 1969 Woodstock festival but was so moved by the massive gathering that she wrote a song about it—while sitting in Geffen's New York apartment (they would later live together, as roommates, in L.A.). "Woodstock" appeared on the 1970 release, *Ladies of the Canyon,* her first popular album, which was followed by *Blue* and *For the Roses*. In later decades, hugely successful artists—Prince, Sting, Melissa Etheridge, Shawn Colvin, and others—would pay homage to Joni Mitchell.

No one her age wrote melodies as complex or elusive as Mitchell's, and no one had a more intriguing voice. She could sing folk, rock, country, or jazz. Her lyrics poked delicately at the mysteries of passion, yet she could also be bawdy: "I'm a pretty good cook, sittin' on my groceries. . . ." Her writing captured the fragility that people everywhere were finding in their romantic attachments, as if something had been set loose that could not be contained. Love was maddening, nothing seemed to last, and every new intimacy felt exhilarating but treacherous. She was of the first generation of women with the freedom to explore just how slippery liberation could be.

"Her songwriting is significant," says one of her longtime female fans, "because it's an education, a whole learning experience given to you by a very intelligent and creative woman. When love affairs don't work out in her songs, she talks about her own vulnerability, her own flaws. She sees herself as others see her. She's not conventionally beautiful, and she writes very honestly about that. She wonders why a man has left her and if it's because of her looks or some other perceived shortcoming. That's how women feel and think. She talks openly about jealousy between women and the subtle nuances that occur in relationships. She gives you the joy of love, but also the bitterness and the irony."

Geffen strongly believed in her gifts, and she repaid him well. On her first Asylum album, *Court and Spark,* she wrote a song for him entitled "Free Man in Paris," which originated after the two of them had traveled to France together. During their sojourn, Mitchell had noticed that Geffen only seemed relaxed and "free" in Paris, when he was a continent away from the music business and its "dreamers and telephone screamers." He would return to Paris tomorrow, the chorus states, "but for the work I've taken on / stoking the starmaker machinery behind the popular song."

There was more to "Free Man in Paris" than the story of a music executive getting away from the office for a few days. Many of those who worked with Geffen felt that he was a genuinely unhappy individual, who paid too much attention to others' personal affairs because he had no private life of his own. He was permanently disgruntled, people said, and would never find anything resembling inner peace or true intimacy. He didn't, he sometimes confessed to friends and colleagues, see himself as normal. When others left the Asylum office to go home at night, he was alone with his telephone, trying to structure or restructure another deal. Some people had wives or lovers or children or even pets to think about. Others lost themselves in alcohol or drugs. Geffen would occasionally smoke a joint, but mostly he did numbers and looked for talent.

▪ ▪ ▪

In the mid-sixties, Linda Ronstadt had made three albums with the Stone Poneys, and in the early seventies, she released several solo efforts on Capitol. After Geffen signed her for Asylum, she worked with renowned producer Peter Asher and brought out *Don't Cry Now,* in 1973. It became one of that year's top fifty albums and the first big hit for Geffen as a label boss. The LP had been produced by another Geffen signee, J. D. Souther, who'd made *John David Souther* for Asylum in 1972. Geffen loved to bring artists together, as he'd done with Crosby, Stills, and Nash, and see what new music could be generated. At his suggestion, Souther teamed up with Chris Hillman, formerly of the Byrds, and with Richie Furay to form the Souther-Hillman-Furay Band. Their first album sold more than half a million copies.

After leaving work in the evenings, Geffen often went to the Troubadour in West Hollywood, the proving ground for many new acts in L.A. It was a magnet for anyone interested in hearing undiscovered musicians or in seeing established stars in the audience, like James Taylor or Kris Kristofferson. One night at the Troubadour, Geffen was standing in line to go to the bathroom when he began talking with a rusty-voiced hipster. The fellow was articulate and had a set of pipes that conjured up darkness, whiskey, cigarettes, and complicated women. He said he wrote songs and performed them himself. Geffen wanted to hear his sound.

Tom Waits was already a local cult figure, but with his first Asylum album, *Closing Time,* and then with *The Heart of Saturday Night* and *Nighthawks at the Diner,* he became a national success. Waits was the kind of artist who anchors and improves a record company: His signing told the world that the person running the label was willing to take a chance on offbeat talent and let it find its own following. Geffen had wanted to create a musician-friendly environment, and in Asylum's first years everyone agreed he'd achieved that. A number of performers at the label toured with one another and played on each other's albums. It was a freewheeling family atmosphere, and the early music that came out of Asylum would later be referred to as "good feeling."

By the summer of 1972, Asylum was becoming well known in the music business, and the *Los Angeles Times* did its first article on Geffen and his young company. The paper's rock critic, Robert Hilburn, wrote the story. His lead sentence would become an underlying theme of Geffen's entire career, as it was chronicled in the media. Depending on one's point of view, Hilburn said, Geffen was either "the smartest or the luckiest" man in the record industry. In the photograph accompanying the article, Geffen had big hair in the mode of Bob Dylan and looked eerily like a cross between Dylan and Paul Simon.

Geffen came across as a very focused executive with an extremely clear plan. His job was to protect his artists "from all the people who want to rip them off.... I know what I want. I can't be pushed around.... You can't go through life worrying about what people are going to think about you. That's one of the roles of being a manager.

"My best friends are the people I work with and represent.... You can't take a month's vacation. You've got to be there when the artist needs you. They need talk, love, assurance. It takes an insane, even demoniacal devotion to be a good manager. It's an obsessive thing. Elliot and I are both obsessed with our clients."

CHAPTER 7

Another aspiring singer-songwriter living in L.A. had grown up around music and wanted to be a performer himself. His father had been a jazz pianist in Europe and played with the great gypsy guitarist Django Reinhardt. The young man was looking for a label that would take a chance on an unknown, and when he heard about Asylum he mailed his tape and a glossy photograph of himself to the company. A busy Asylum employee tossed these items into the trash. A secretary noticed the picture in the wastebasket and thought the guy was cute. She retrieved the tape and slipped it into a deck. The song "A Child in These Hills" moved her so much that she insisted Geffen listen to it. He was also impressed and went looking for Jackson Browne at his home, in the Echo Park neighborhood.

Geffen found the young man and talked to him about making

an album for Asylum. Browne was ecstatic and told him about another group of guys who lived upstairs. They had a band named the Longbranch Penny Whistle, Browne said, and they were good. Geffen went up and met the group, which already had some outstanding credentials. They'd played behind James Taylor, Linda Ronstadt, and the country-rock group Poco. Geffen liked the musicians and their sound so much that he bought their recording contract from Amos Records for $5,000. He then fronted them the money to live on while they wrote more songs and polished their act, telling them to make a dentist appointment to get their teeth cleaned. He liked everything about them but their name, so he told them to come up with a new one. Then he sent them to Aspen, Colorado, to rehearse at a local bar, the Galley, until they were ready to make their first album for Asylum. It was called *The Eagles* and had three smash songs: "Peaceful Easy Feeling," "Take It Easy," and "Witchy Woman."

Don Henley, the Eagles' drummer, and Glenn Frey, their guitarist, were both singers and the stars of the band. They'd begun by trying to capture some of the countrified sound of Gram Parsons and the Flying Burrito Brothers, but when they began recording for Geffen, their simple melodies and excellent harmonies were all their own. Their first album made the charts and their next one, *Desperado,* was even more successful. Their third disc, *On the Border,* contained two number one songs, "Best of My Love" and "One of These Nights." Guitarmaster Joe Walsh now joined the Eagles, and they became Geffen's first supergroup. In the mid-seventies, many people considered them the best band in America, and their *Hotel California* album, released in 1976, sold a stupendous eleven million copies.

Jackson Browne never became as big as the Eagles, but he was one of Asylum's signature artists. Geffen allowed him to mature slowly, and nearly two years passed before he released his first album, named for himself, which contained the Top Ten single "Doctor My Eyes." His later albums, *For Everyman, Late for the Sky,* and *The Pretender,* the last produced by a young music critic named Jon Landau, established him as one of the more important songwriters of the seventies. Browne was forever grateful to Geffen for giving him a chance and mentioned him on each of his Asylum LPs. He also wrote a song for Geffen, which evoked the label boss's favorite movie as a boy. It was called "The Wizard of L.A."

■ ■ ■

In the late sixties, Steve Ross and his corporation, now called Warner Communications, Inc. (WCI), had begun buying record companies. He'd purchased Atlantic from Ahmet Ertegun. He'd acquired the Reprise label, previously owned by Frank Sinatra and now run by the singer's former accountant, Mo Ostin. And he'd bought Elektra from Jac Holzman. The three companies together were called WEA and comprised one of the strongest recording businesses in the field, second only to CBS. WEA's hit list included the Doors, Aretha Franklin, the Rolling Stones, Carly Simon, James Taylor, and Jethro Tull. By 1972, it had become obvious to the music industry that Geffen's antennae for upcoming commercial trends was impeccable and that Asylum was going to be a great success.

Geffen's former boss, Ted Ashley, was running the Warner Bros. film studio for Steve Ross, and Ross himself had been closely following Geffen's career. Despite the flap that the young man had created by quitting Ashley Famous, Ross liked Geffen and was a man who appreciated executive talent.

"Steve Ross," says independent Hollywood producer and long-time Warner exec Jerry Leider, "always nourished the biggest asset that our company had, which was the people who went down the elevator every night. There may have been better or worse negotiators, there may have been better or worse managers, and there may have been people who were better with numbers. But Steve knew that his major asset had to be looked after, and it was not the studio library or the filmmaking hardware. It was the people riding in those elevators."

Ross decided to buy Asylum. When he asked Geffen how much he wanted for his label, the younger man gave him the biggest figure he could think of: $7 million. Ross accepted the offer, and WCI acquired Asylum for $2 million in cash and $5 million more in stock. When the deal closed, the WCI stock was trading at $45 a share. Six months later, it had fallen to $8, and it looked as if Geffen had made a bad bargain. He went to Ross distraught and laid out his feelings; he hadn't realized that his $5 million was going to be worth about a sixth of that half a year later.

Ross then did something extraordinary. Like Geffen's early Hollywood hero, Louis B. Mayer, Ross saw his employees and his ever-widening circle of show business contacts as part of his extended family. He loved playing the patriarch to them: paying them very well, helping them out when they needed it, and lavishing expensive gifts upon them. If all of this ultimately redounded to his advantage, that was simply a smart way of doing business. He'd done this as a funeral parlor director and as a parking lot executive, and he was doing it now as the leader of WCI. In return for his generosity, he wanted respect and complete loyalty.

He promised Geffen that over the next five years, he would pay him one-fifth of the difference (per year) between $45 a share and where the stock was at the end of the half decade. In other words, Geffen would make money if the stock rose above $45 but could not lose money if it fell. It was a very generous offer, and not the last such thing Ross would do for the younger man who'd also grown up in Brooklyn. Some people thought it was too kind and felt that Geffen had a peculiar hold over Ross that no one else did.

One person Geffen didn't have a hold over was Irving Azoff. An Illinois native, Azoff was shorter than Geffen by several inches and even more ruthless when it came to representing talent. Inside the music business, his nickname was the "Poison Dwarf." Rock bands loved him because he understood the rigors of the road and had a reputation for trashing motel rooms that was equal to theirs. Geffen had originally hired Azoff to work for the Geffen-Roberts management firm, but when Azoff saw his chance to be more than an employee, he grasped it.

As Asylum had become more successful and as the Geffen-Roberts management company had also expanded, some bands didn't want to be represented on the concert circuit by the same person—Geffen—who was recording them. The Eagles, for one, felt this was an inherent conflict of interest. Azoff persuaded the band to leave Geffen-Roberts and go with him. It really didn't take much persuasion. While the Eagles were grateful to Geffen for helping them get started, they were angry when he sold the label to WCI and reaped all the profits himself. He was fond of telling his acts, "We are not partners," but some people didn't really understand that concept until Geffen received $7 million from Steve Ross and they got nothing. The sale to WCI was the beginning of the end of the family atmosphere at Asylum.

As he'd done with Laura Nyro, Geffen retained the publishing rights to the songs the Eagles had written. In 1977, the group went to court to get back those rights, suing Geffen for $10 million in damages, plus the return of their copyrights. They won an out-of-court settlement.

Azoff went on to form Front Line Management, which would become the most successful firm in the music business, representing Jimmy Buffett, Chicago, Steely Dan, and Boz Scaggs. In the 1980s, Azoff and Geffen would carry on a running spat in the media, hurling insults at one another with something like glee.

When WCI purchased Asylum, Jac Holzman was running Elektra, but in 1973, he stepped aside. Ahmet Ertegun went to Ross and suggested that Geffen take over the label. Ross agreed, and Elektra/Asylum/Nonesuch was the result of the merger. Geffen soon dropped twenty-five of Elektra's thirty-five artists, fired the art director, and got rid of the production and promotion staffs. He lured the Band away from Capitol and began romancing Bob Dylan, in the hope that he would leave Columbia. Geffen promised all his artists that he would raise their royalty rates to 15 percent—about twice the industry average.

His first year running the triple label, sales were an impressive $18 million and Elektra/Asylum/Nonesuch produced several gold records, including Joni Mitchell's *Court and Spark* and Carly Simon's *Hotcakes*. In February of 1974, *Time* magazine called Geffen "the new financial superstar of the $2 billion pop music industry." His reputation was soaring. "One of the best things I ever did," says Ahmet Ertegun, "was to bring David into the fold at WCI. He turned Elektra/Asylum/Nonesuch into a major record company." For the past several years Ertegun had been watching Geffen, convinced that he was going to be not merely another success story but something much more.

"In the early seventies," Ertegun says, "David and I and my wife, Mica, went to London together. I took him to an art gallery, and while we were there I told the man running the gallery that David was going to be very wealthy one day and would become a great art collector. I suggested that he sell David something by a painter he knew and give him a deal now, because some day he would be a tremendous customer. The man did just that and sold him a small Picasso for [about] $35,000. David couldn't believe that he owned a real Picasso.

"He was very proud of the painting, but he was also very worried that it would get stolen from his home in the Hollywood Hills. I told him to insure it for $75,000, which he did. The painting did get stolen, and he was extremely depressed about it. But then he became very happy when he was paid $75,000 for it by the insurance company. He'd spent $35,000 and gotten back $75,000, so he'd made money on the deal. Then someone found the painting, and the insurance company asked for its money back, but he didn't want to do that. So he kept the money and let the company have the painting. They sold it for $140,000, and that really upset David because he felt that he'd lost money on the deal."

Ertegun chuckles, remembering. "That's how he got started collecting art."

CHAPTER 8

One morning Geffen was lying in bed at the Inn at the Park Hotel in London, smoking a joint and pondering his future. Marijuana was like that; it could make you think. Ever since high school, his goal had been to make money, because he'd believed that cash was the route to happiness. Now, less than a decade into the music business, he had $12 million and more success than he'd ever imagined having. He could drive Cadillacs in ten different colors up and down the boulevards of Brooklyn, honking his horn and causing people to stare, but what would that prove? He was living in L.A., where he'd always wanted to live, and doing what he wanted to do, but his emotional climate remained turbulent. Happiness, it seemed, was far more elusive than money.

Geffen went into psychoanalysis five days a week, determined to confront his inner questions and perhaps the biggest one of all: his sexual ambiguity. Although he'd had encounters with men, he didn't think of himself as gay. He was just...perplexed, hurt, confused by the past. The time had come, as he once put it, "to deal with the little David inside" of him. He was ready to make a commitment to heterosexuality and to start dating women seriously.

On a summer evening in 1973, Geffen went to the Troubadour with Janet Margolin, a woman he was seeing, and with Ahmet Ertegun. Bette Midler was performing and there were several celebrities in the audience, including Sonny and Cher Bono. Years earlier, Geffen had met this duo when they were backup singers for Phil Spector, and he'd watched them become one of the most successful pop acts of the sixties. "I Got You Babe" was their first megahit, reaching number one in the United States and the United Kingdom, followed by Bob Dylan's "All I Really Want to Do" and "The Beat Goes On." The couple were married in 1964, made two forgettable movies (*Good Times* and *Chastity*), and eventually had their own TV show. By the early seventies, they were coming apart both as an act and as marriage partners.

As Geffen studied Cher at the Troubadour, he promptly fell in love, for the first time in his life. She was long, lean, dark, and black-haired, wore provocative outfits, and had made a career out of appearing exotic. She played upon the vamp theme, and to the young man sitting in the crowd with Janet Margolin, she was irresistible. On this evening, Geffen didn't know that she and Sonny were separated; all he knew was that she made him feel something he'd never quite felt before. The switch on his natural distancing mechanism suddenly flipped to off. Of course, she was only a fantasy. Not only was she married, she was a pop star and an unattainable siren.

For years, the Troubadour had been a musical showcase, the place where agents and record company executives went looking for their next score. In 1973, Geffen and several prominent rock businessmen decided that L.A. could use another night spot, something that would challenge the supremacy of the Troubadour and its owner, Doug Weston. Most of the clubs on Sunset Strip, like the Whisky-a-Go-Go and the Ash Grove, were rock-'n'-roll funky. Geffen and his partners wanted to create a step up in class, an intimate venue where listeners could enjoy the music in a more stylish setting. Woodstock, and rolling in the mud during concerts, had become passé.

The Largo Burlesque emporium stood at 9009 Sunset Boulevard, just across the street from Asylum. Geffen and the president of Ode Records, Lou Adler (who'd produced hits by the Mamas and Papas, Johnny Rivers, and Carole King), now took over this address and began refurbishing it for their new club: the Roxy. It was named for the old Roxy Theater in New York, one of the grandest entertainment palaces of the vaudeville era. Other partners soon joined in the venture, including Chuck Landis, who'd run Largo Burlesque, Elliot Roberts, and Bill Graham, who worked out of San Francisco and was the most revered concert promoter in the nation. The Roxy would be a great leap forward in rock venues. The dressing rooms were carpeted, unheard of in certain grungier night spots. The rooms also had showers, a novelty for a generation of musicians that was slowly embracing the virtues of hygiene.

On Thursday evening, September 20, 1973, Neil Young opened the Roxy to a standing-room-only crowd of five hundred people. The club's debut had originally been scheduled for the previous May but had been delayed for several months, causing the buzz about it to intensify throughout L.A. By early September, the Roxy's impending opening had become a major event in the city's nightlife. Geffen had had to turn away so many people seeking tickets to Young's performance that he would later say he'd made more enemies on this occasion than in all his previous years in show business.

The Roxy's doors opened at seven-thirty, but long before, a crowd had lined up along the Strip. Bill Graham, a hardened veteran of the concert scene, looked out at the gathering and kept muttering to himself, "Amazing, amazing, amazing. . . ." Graham, who was known as a demanding perfectionist, was astonished at the job Geffen and, more particularly, Lou Adler, had done in bringing the Roxy together. Throughout the past week, Adler had been at the club until the smallest hours of each morning, overseeing the installation of light fixtures from the 1940s and other finishing touches. Details were important, and even the matchbook covers had a forties theme. The bar upstairs, "On the Rox," featured a mural of Jimi Hendrix, Paul McCartney, Diana Ross, Joni Mitchell, Bob Dylan, Janis Joplin, Stevie Wonder, Mick Jagger, and other gods of rock.

Nils Lofgren was supposed to open for Neil Young, but he was too sick to go on. Cheech and Chong took the stage and did their famous routine about driving on dope, followed by Graham Nash singing several numbers. Neil Young then emerged in a white suit, white shoes, and dark shades, his brown hair flowing. With all the energy and edge he was known for, Young performed songs from his new *Tonight's the Night* album. The audience, which contained some notables, loved him. Carole King had shown up to watch the show, as had Dickie Betts, a guitarist for the Allman Brothers. The biggest celebrity in the crowd, Elton John, was seated in the center of the room. On one occasion, he became annoyed when an aggressive waiter tried to keep adoring fans away from him; after admonishing the young man, John allowed himself to be fawned over at close range.

At eleven-thirty, the first crowd of five hundred was swept out the door and replaced by five hundred more people. The Roxy had officially been christened and would take its place as one of the premier nightclubs on Sunset Strip. In coming months, audiences would hear acts as diverse as Poco, Richie Havens, B. B. King, Miles Davis, the Temptations, and Argentinian saxman Gato Barbieri.

One night at the Roxy, when Geffen, Bob Dylan, and Robbie Robertson were sitting together in the audience, Lou Adler approached them and whispered something to Geffen: Cher was in the club and had noticed him and Dylan. Would he mind if she joined them? Geffen did not hesitate with his answer. She came over and sat down with the men, and before long, Geffen suggested that they have dinner some evening. Within a week, he and Cher were living together in his house, two blocks from where Sonny was living in the Bonos' house—with another woman. Because Sonny and Cher still had a successful TV show, the couple remained business partners, but they'd begun the nasty process of ending their nine-year union.

In becoming Cher's lover, Geffen crossed a significant threshold of visibility and notoriety. For years, he'd had his picture taken with people more famous than he was, and it could be said that he was one of the most unfamous famous people in the country. Any middling-serious rock music fan walking into the Roxy that evening would have known the faces of Bob Dylan and Robbie Robertson, but you had to be quite close to the music business to recognize the third man at the table. Geffen was still a background figure, who liked publicizing his record company but had never expressed much interest in personal publicity. Like many good businessmen, he felt that he could accomplish more by making decisions from the wings. As long as he got invited to the right parties—which he did—what difference did it make if his name appeared in the gossip columns?

No man could have fallen into Cher's arms and maintained his cover. She was not merely a nationally heralded pop singer and part of one of America's best-known marriage teams—she was a cultural icon. Her image provoked people, stirred them in ways that could not be denied. She dressed outlandishly, and her figure set off feelings about sex, ethnicity, and emerging female boldness. She was a very loud reminder that both Queen Victoria and the prudent America of the 1950s really *were* dead. Now that she was breaking up with Sonny, her personal life was tabloid material and, unlike many celebrities, she enjoyed being outspoken, outrageous, and shocking. One of her first public appearances with Geffen was at the Grammy Awards, where he showed up in a tux and she wore all white, with her midriff exposed and a butterfly in her cleavage. More than a decade later, when she was well into her forties, she would be singing on MTV clad in a black G-string.

If you were a thirty-year-old male and had serious questions about your sexual identity, you might easily have turned to Cher. If she couldn't resolve your sexual ambivalence, who could?

She convinced Geffen to trade in his old Mercedes for a Rolls-Royce Corniche with wire wheels. She talked him into slicking up his image with some better clothes, after looking at his wardrobe and disdainfully pronouncing him "Mr. Beige." He'd never paid much attention to haberdashery before, but suddenly he was buying new shirts, shoes, and trousers, while also pricing diamonds and pearls for his lover at Tiffany's. Then he began vigorously promoting Cher for movie offers, TV specials, a solo album, and an upcoming tour.

When Sonny Bono came to the realization that his sex-symbol wife had left him for a skinny, unshaven, curly-headed, scruffy-looking record executive, he was very disgruntled. He was bitter toward Geffen, and his feelings would not change much during the next twenty years. In his 1991 autobiography, *And the Beat Goes On*, Bono described Geffen as "a little wimpy guy, and I never thought he had the stuff that allowed him to accomplish all that he has in life." Geffen, Bono added, was "a brilliant, calculating, extremely shrewd man who would do whatever he had to do, no matter the cost—moneywise or human—to achieve his goal. Geffen was exactly the kind of man Cher was attracted to—a powerful guy who took charge of her life and made things happen. To me, he was a ruthless cutthroat."

In January of 1974, when Cher told Sonny that she wanted out of the *Sonny and Cher* TV show, Sonny blamed Geffen for causing the career split between the duo. In mid-February of that year, Cher filed for divorce, asking Sonny for $32,000 a month in alimony. CBS then dropped *Sonny and Cher* and replaced it with *The Cher Comedy Hour,* a further insult to her ex-singing partner. Sonny retaliated by going out and getting his own show with ABC (hers succeeded and his bombed). Then he sued Cher for $14 million, claiming that she spent $600 a month on her fingernails and $6,000 a month on clothes. Then he sued Geffen for $13 million for butting into Sonny's contractual arrangement with his wife.

Cher fought back by letting Geffen handle the phone negotiations with Sonny over Sonny's rights to visit the Bonos' young daughter, Chastity. Geffen was unmatched at phone combat, and his skills with a receiver only made Sonny more livid and nastier. Things got so bad that Geffen began chain-smoking and Cher gained five pounds. In the end, Geffen negotiated for Cher a magnificent divorce deal: she got $25,000 a month, plus the house, plus custody of Chastity, plus direct control of her share of the income still being generated by their duo projects. Sonny got angrier.

All this marital mudslinging landed Geffen's picture in the *National Star, Rona's Barrett's Gossip, Movie Screen, Movieland and TV Time,* the *National Enquirer,* and other literary outlets. He'd entered tabloid heaven. Batya Geffen, who had finally, at her son's behest, given up her bra-and-corset business in Brooklyn and moved across the country to the home Geffen had purchased for her in Beverly Hills, began calling David and asking him why he'd landed in this mess with another man's wife.

For more than a year the court battles raged, while Geffen and Cher were ensconced in their Los Angeles home. Geffen would later say that this was the most exciting period of his life: being with a woman he adored, feeling genuine love for her, running Asylum Records as it achieved its greatest success, widening his circle of friends to include Bob Dylan, Jack Nicholson, and Warren Beatty—and getting richer by the day. There were moments when he worried that Cher might not be the most faithful companion—he suspected that she was sleeping with the bass player for the Average White Band—but still, this was the most important relationship he'd ever had.

Toward the end of 1974, *Esquire* magazine assigned a snappy, young, talented reporter named Julie Baumgold to do a story on Hollywood's hottest couple: David Geffen and Cher. He had been written about in prestigious magazines before, including *Time* and *Newsweek*, scribes had been interviewing him for years, but no one had really captured him in action. The *Esquire* piece would be his coming-out party, the introduction of this powerful, behind-the-scenes entertainment player to a national audience. No one had ever made quite such an entrance before, although some people had come close.

Back in the 1950s, Lillian Ross had earned an enduring reputation as a magazine profiler by spending some time with Ernest Hemingway as he was unwinding with his pals in Manhattan after finishing another novel. In the *New Yorker*, Ross nakedly portrayed Hemingway as full of arrogance and bluster and some other things. While the reading public greatly enjoyed seeing someone stick needles into the world-famous author's public persona, Hemingway himself would never quite forgive the young woman for revealing him so bluntly on paper. He felt betrayed, which is, of course, what many people feel after they've been interviewed and written about. This kind of betrayal is exceptionally painful for those who have trouble trusting people—like David Geffen. By comparison, Hemingway was lucky.

It wasn't just that Baumgold showed the music exec hopping along Fifth Avenue on one foot because his new boots hurt his toes. Or wrote that his socks were in bad taste. Or that the salespeople in Tiffany's tried to ignore him, because he looked like a schlemiel. Or that he crassly enjoyed walking through a Tower Records store in L.A. and pointing at the best-selling albums on display while chanting, "That's mine...that's mine...that's mine." Or that she quoted a friend of Geffen's saying that when he "focuses his whole attention on you, it's like being licked by a cat. For a while, it feels good, but then you realize the tongue is ragged and scratchy."

The very ghost of Sammy Glick was rising from the pages of *Esquire*. Baumgold's style perfectly encoded the manic energy, gaucheness, and drive to succeed that Geffen embodied in the mid-seventies. He was all over the place, couldn't slow down, and she was unmerciful in her observations.

Baumgold caught Geffen eating a hot dog at Pink's famous L.A. wiener stand, then getting sick to his stomach and running off to the bathroom. She described Cher and Geffen's art collection as being of the "draped-shepherds-relaxing-against-columns school" and said their sense of interior design created the effect of "clobbering gloom." She reported on Cher sticking her tongue deep inside Geffen's mouth during a kiss, and quoted the singer asking her lover to "feel my ass....hard as a rock." Baumgold showed the couple mock-arguing about which one had the larger bank account: Cher claimed $900,000, while Geffen had only $780,000. The two of them, the story concluded, would marry as soon as Cher's divorce was final.

CHAPTER 9

In February of 1975, the article ran as the cover story in *Esquire*. Cher was featured on the front of the magazine, looking beautiful and slightly malicious. In green letters near her face were the words "Who's man enough for this woman?" Inside, the story was titled, "The Winning of Cher and Some Other Major Achievements of David Geffen." Just before the magazine hit the newsstands, Geffen and Cher had gone to the Troubadour to watch Gregg Allman perform. By the mid-seventies, the rough-edged, blond-haired organist-singer for the Allman Brothers had developed a solo act with a band of his own. While Allman was working his way through his last set, a note was delivered to Cher at her table. She read it, smiled, folded up the sliver of paper, and slipped it into her pocket. Geffen watched her, not thinking much about this: Notes from admirers were always arriving for Cher; people always wanted to meet her. That was part of the kick of going out with her at night.

She excused herself and went to the restroom, not returning until considerably longer than it takes to powder one's nose. The set ended, and as she and Geffen were exiting the club, Allman walked by and told Cher that he would see her later. Outside, when Geffen asked her what he'd meant, she displayed the kind of cutting honesty that would later characterize some of the roles she played as a film actress. What it had meant, she told Geffen, was that she was interested in Gregg Allman.

When Geffen had suspected Cher of sleeping with the bass player in the Average White Band, he'd opted for forgiveness and understanding. It was a fling and it would pass, although he later compared receiving this piece of news to having a can opener scraped over his brain. But when he now learned that Cher was attracted to Gregg Allman, his powers of rationalization failed him. This hurt. It hurt more than anything he'd ever experienced. It was, in fact, so painful that he immediately decided that he had no choice. He had to walk away from the relationship as soon as possible, even after Cher asked him to stay, while she went off and explored her own desires with others.

The breakup of Geffen and Cher, and her instant romance with Gregg Allman, which was wildly celebrated in the tabloids, coincided with the publication of the *Esquire* cover story. This article would have been difficult for Geffen under any circumstances, but the circumstances were now excruciating. He clearly had not "won" Cher but had just lost her to another man, a rock star who was the opposite of Geffen himself. Southern, macho, whiskey-drinking, bad-ass Gregg Allman had come along and in less than an hour taken away the woman whom *Esquire* said Geffen was going to marry. It was tough enough to lose the first person he'd allowed himself to feel this deeply for; it was worse to lose her in such a wrenching manner; it was worse still to have this happen in public. The steamy Cher–Gregg Allman affair and their short-lived marriage were exquisite gossip column fodder for months to come.

What could be more humiliating than having your personal life collapse just as a national magazine was touting your "major achievements"? For any man, this would have been debilitating. For one with significant questions about sexual identity, it was something more than that.

Geffen felt crazed, nauseous, sick all over. He saw his therapist every day and called him on the weekend. He couldn't eat and lost forty pounds, dipping down to near one hundred. He moved into Warren Beatty's house, seeking refuge there. Beatty was very supportive, but Geffen could not find solace. Cher's solo TV show was preparing to air, and she'd become the darling of the popular press. Each time he glanced at a magazine, Cher seemed to be staring back at him with that alluring, dangerous smile. When Geffen could endure no more, he packed up and flew to Brazil, hiding out and waiting there for his broken feelings to heal. For once in his life, the mistrustful, hardened street kid from Brooklyn had opened up, made himself emotionally vulnerable, and committed himself to a relationship with a future. Then his heart had been smashed.

He flew back to L.A., checked into a bungalow at the Beverly Hills Hotel, and tried to resume working and conducting a normal life. His pain was only deepened when he saw Cher on her television program or read her statement in *Time* magazine that when she left Sonny Bono for David Geffen, she'd merely "traded one short ugly man for another."

The *Esquire* story was important in more ways than its bad timing and its effect on Geffen's emotional stability. It set the tone for much of the writing that would be done about him in national magazines in the future. Reporters in general would see him as a pushy, overrated, "lucky" businessman, who did not quite deserve all his riches or his reputation for turning everything he touched into cash. He would be portrayed as an almost comic figure, a near-nebbish who'd somehow made it big, a Woody Allen type who wasn't redeemed by Allen's sense of humor. What other major American executive had ever been seen hopping down Fifth Avenue in his stocking feet?

If Geffen had died from heartache or permanently disappeared from our popular culture in the mid-seventies, this might be how he would be remembered. But he was far more resilient than that. He'd learned many things in Brooklyn, and one of them was that when someone steals your pizza on the playground or calls you a fag, you just don't quit.

In the early seventies, Geffen had set about trying to lure Bob Dylan away from Columbia and over to his own label. Eventually, he did this, in the same way he'd done it with others: using relentless wooing and seduction, on men and women alike, and convincing them that he was their friend and could help. Geffen had met Dylan through Robbie Robertson, the estimable songwriter-guitarist for the Band, and soon began establishing a friendship with him. That was no mean accomplishment, as Dylan was a notorious recluse. For stretches at a time, Geffen called him every day, talking to Dylan about his career, which was not where it had been a decade earlier. Geffen praised him, pouring out his admiration. He offered suggestions, and confidence-building advice. He worked their common ground.

Both men were small, thirty-something, Jewish, and brilliant, with deeply scrambled feelings about their pasts. Both had humble origins and reservoirs of unexamined anger. Each had a muddy relationship with his father. One was the very symbol of a gifted, enigmatic artist, the other the archetype of a driven businessman. One was a pursuer, the other the pursued. They were two halves of a whole (not unlike Geffen's own parents). Geffen often went up to Malibu, where Dylan had a home, and made a point of running into him there, just as he'd once "accidentally" run into Nat Lefkowitz in the halls of William Morris. He wanted to stay in touch, to be of service. He inquired about buying a house next to Dylan's, so he could be closer still. Eventually, he bought the property and moved in. For many people, Bob Dylan was like a magnet.

The Irish poet William Butler Yeats wrote that rhetoric comes from the argument an individual has with his society, while poetry comes from the argument he has with himself. In the early sixties, Dylan had made poetry out of both things. No one since Henry Miller had seen through the American façade with such scathing precision, or been able so seemingly effortlessly to translate into words (and, in Dylan's case, music) what he felt. He wrote some of his best songs in a couple of hours. He had an acidic sensibility, and something more. No other young songwriter was capable of penning a lyric with such evocative power as "The ghost of electricity howls in the bones of her face" (in "Visions of Johanna" on the 1966 album *Blonde on Blonde*). It is a line with the visceral impact of the Edvard Munch painting it recalls.

Dylan had a ferociously hungry gift and did his finest work in his mid-twenties, inadvertently creating the impression to millions of young fans that it would always be this easy. In the 1960s, he wasn't simply revered but worshiped. Geffen himself would say that he once viewed Bob Dylan as God.

By the early seventies, the musical landscape had fragmented, and was going in half a dozen directions at once. Some people had embraced country or bluegrass, some still liked hard rock, and others favored the softer rock that Asylum represented. Dylan's voice had once reflected the shared feelings of a generation of young Americans. His songs created a sense of unity and purpose, but that moment had passed. The challenge was different now. It was more subtle and more difficult. What his still-adoring public seemed to want from the man were the clues that would help them step over the threshold of adolescence and into the adult world.

It was an ironic development. Thanks largely to Bob Dylan, the sixties generation now realized that war was bad, poverty was ugly, racism was insidious, and injustice often prevailed. But after coming to this awareness, how do you proceed to grow up and find something to believe in? How do you live with the knowledge of what is wrong and still discover some peace, happiness, and grace within? How do you deal with the violence inside yourself? And what if you, finally, are part of the problem, instead of the solution? It was childish, absurd, and unfair, of course, to expect anyone to answer such questions, but Dylan's aura was large enough to unleash these kinds of demands.

He came to Asylum in 1974, when his career was past its white-hot prime, but he remained the biggest—or at least the most serious—name in the rock music business. He made two albums for Geffen and on the first, *Planet Waves*, he was backed by the Band. It contains one superior ballad about his son, called "Forever Young," and some other good, if not very memorable, material. His second album, *Before the Flood*, also recorded with The Band, was a live two-disc set featuring songs that he'd brought out earlier. He toured successfully for Geffen's management company and did well at Asylum by almost any standards, except the ones he set for himself back in the sixties.

Another literary figure, F. Scott Fitzgerald, once said that there are no second acts in the lives of Americans—his way of declaring that it's tough to grow older and continue to develop as a human being. In example after example in the entertainment business, Fitzgerald's words can be applied with accuracy. They are not exactly true for Bob Dylan, who's kept on writing songs, including some notable ones, since the mid-seventies. But he would never regain that instantaneous ability to feel and to capture in music what was taking place inside of himself and an entire generation of listeners.

In later years, Dylan often gave the impression of a man whose consciousness had outstripped his ability to express himself. He'd perceived and felt more than he was comfortable feeling. He couldn't find a framework for what he was experiencing. In these circumstances, one can either give up, go mad, retreat further within, or develop a sense of humor. Dylan went further within, often talking cryptic mumbo-jumbo in public. It was as if he could be anything in the world except the one thing—vulnerable—that might have opened another door. In time, he was superseded by more ironic songwriters, like Elvis Costello, David Byrne, Joe Jackson, Warren Zevon, and Lyle Lovett, all of whom were able to make fun of their own painful problems.

After recording two albums for Asylum, Dylan returned to CBS. Columbia was a far larger company than Geffen's label, with more money and other resources. Some people believed that Dylan's reunion with CBS was a direct rejection of Geffen, but others knew that Dylan was restless and always changing something; it was unlikely that he would have stayed at the smaller company for the duration of his career. In later years, when Geffen spoke about Dylan to reporters, there was a wistful quality to his words, as if he were both saddened and disappointed by what had happened between the two men. And he more than hinted that Dylan had not kept his word about their working together in the future.

"I couldn't believe it," Geffen told *Esquire* magazine in 1982, "that Bob Dylan would lie."

The record executive had met "God" face to face, and it had been an unsettling experience. Bob Dylan was not all that different from anyone else. He was an uncertain individual, about to enter middle age and still trying to confront the most basic questions: How do you love yourself when you're filled with entangled, hurtful emotions? And if you don't love yourself, how can you possibly love others?

Some people think Geffen was profoundly affected by his encounter with the songwriter.

"Dylan flirted with David and then stiffed him and went back to Columbia," says George Trow, who observed Geffen throughout the seventies, in preparation for a profile of Ahmet Ertegun that he would publish in the *New Yorker* in 1978. "When Dylan left Asylum and went for the bigger money at Columbia, I think this was a transforming moment for Geffen. He saw that even with Bob Dylan it was still all about money, and since David knew how to make more money than anyone else, he looked at this and said, 'Fuck it, that's what I'm going to do.' So that's what he did."

Says a friend of Geffen's from the late seventies, "I was at a party once with David and Paul Simon. The two of them were talking about money and Simon said, 'When you have a million dollars, you think about getting five million.' Geffen nodded in agreement. 'When you have five million,' Simon said, 'you think about getting ten million.' Geffen nodded again. 'When you have twenty million,' Simon said, 'you think about fifty million, and when you have fifty million, you think about a hundred and when you have a hundred—'

"Geffen interrupted him and said, 'No, Paul. That's enough for anybody. Nobody thinks about getting more than a hundred million dollars.'"

CHAPTER 10

The really big money, many people believed, was in the movie business. Wasn't that where Louis B. Mayer had made his fortune and wasn't that the most prestigious arena in the entire world of entertainment? Everyone deferred to film stars. Everyone wanted to produce, direct, write, or appear in motion pictures. Hollywood was where the rich went to get richer. And hadn't Geffen reached the zenith of the music industry by recording Bob Dylan? What other challenges did that venue have to offer? The Eagles were the bestselling band in the country; Joni Mitchell, Linda Ronstadt, and Jackson Browne had all become successful; running Asylum was now routine. Geffen was tired of talking about music deals on the phone all day long and wanted to expand his knowledge and business experience. Wasn't that what some of his peers were doing?

Back in the sixties, when Geffen had accumulated vacation time at the Morris office in New York, he didn't fly down to the Caribbean and lie on the beach. He didn't even drive out to Long Island and gaze at the Atlantic. He went to Los Angeles and visited the Morris office in Beverly Hills. The agency's top executive, Abe Lastfogel, worked there, so Geffen traveled west to be nearer the center of power. He sat in on meetings in L.A., offered suggestions, and, according to some accounts, steamed open the West Coast mail. That was his idea of fun and relaxation.

During one of these trips to Southern California, he met an aspiring young Morris employee named Barry Diller, who was working under Phil Weltman, one of the most respected veterans in the agency's chain of command. Weltman had a military bearing, was demanding as hell, and was beloved by most of his charges. He was hard but fair in the treatment of his men and trained several future business stars in Hollywood. At one point, three Weltman protégés—Joe Wizan at Fox, Barry Diller at Paramount, and Bob Shapiro at Warner Bros.—were all running studios.

Geffen was drawn to Diller, a UCLA dropout and the son of a high-rolling California real estate developer. When Geffen learned that Diller had attended Beverly Hills High with Marlo Thomas, the daughter of comedian Danny Thomas, he was star struck. The young men had things in common and enjoyed talking about their ambitions and career dreams. Both of them saw the Morris office as a stepping stone to something bigger. Geffen was veering toward the music field, while Diller was moving in the direction of the film business. In 1969, he started the ABC *Movie of the Week*, and by the mid-seventies, he would be running Paramount Pictures. "Killer Diller," as he was called because of his toughness and managerial acumen, was a studio head at thirty-two.

In 1975, when Geffen looked at his friend, he saw another world to conquer. He'd become one of the hottest young entrepreneurs in the music industry, but there was nothing quite as sexy in the business end of show business as saying that you were responsible for a smash film that had made scads of money and been nominated for several Academy Awards. Of course, many pictures lost money and cost executives their jobs. Despite the odds, people kept diving into this fray.

In the early seventies, the film industry had gone through a bad slump. The era of dominance by the old movie moguls and their "studio system" was essentially dead and had not been replaced by anything as stable or profitable. The business needed an infusion of managerial talent at the top. Steve Ross had been very prescient in hiring Ted Ashley to run Warner Bros., and by 1972 the studio had turned out a series of relatively low-budget ($2 to $3 million) hits: *Dirty Harry, Klute, A Clockwork Orange, Summer of '42,* and *Deliverance,* along with several others.

Geffen was keenly aware of what was taking place at the studio and increasingly restless to make a change. Since selling Asylum to WCI in 1972, he'd become part of its corporate fold, making millions for the Elektra/Asylum/Nonesuch labels. He was in high favor with Steve Ross, and when the WCI brass learned that Geffen was looking at his options, the idea of his working for Ashley at the studio arose. Surely he could bring the same golden touch to motion pictures that he'd brought to music.

In 1975, he left Asylum to become vice chairman of Warner Bros. Pictures. While holding this title, he was involved with three reasonably successful films—*Greased Lightning,* starring Richard Pryor, *Oh God!* featuring George Burns, and *The Late Show,* starring Art Carney and Lily Tomlin—but it wasn't his movies that made the greatest impact on the organization. It was his behavior, which was not exactly in the mold of corporate correctness. He didn't look corporate, with his scruffy chin and tall hair, his blue jeans and tennis shoes. But in Hollywood in the mid-seventies—a time of questionable fashion statements all around—his attire wouldn't have gotten him into trouble. The real problem was that he was not attuned to making group decisions, he had almost no use for weekly meetings, he wasn't particularly interested in reading scripts, and he failed to carbon-copy his memos (he intensely disliked paper, after all). Conflict was inevitable.

As one of Hollywood's first successful vigilante-kicks-and-kills-the-bad-guys pictures, *Billy Jack* had recently been a big hit. Ted Ashley was now considering a sequel and requested that his top managers take a serious look at the original movie and give him their considered recommendations, before Warner committed millions to a follow-up film.

"Geffen was passionate about getting this sequel made," says a Warner executive from that era. "He couldn't stop talking about it. One afternoon, he was in a meeting with Ted, going on and on about how much better the second *Billy Jack* would be than the first one, although it would cost more money. He kept promoting it and promoting it, and finally Ted said, 'Tell me, David, what did you think of the first *Billy Jack*?' 'I never saw it,' Geffen said, 'but I heard it was a real piece of shit.'"

Former Warner exec Larry Marks says, "Warner Brothers was a big company, and Ted was chairman. He liked long meetings and keeping his employees up to date on our corporate life. He ran things so that Steve Ross would not be caught off guard in a situation and not have good information. We had ninety-minute staff meetings on Mondays, Wednesdays, and Fridays, from nine A.M. sharp to ten-thirty sharp. And we had a marketing meeting once a week for ninety minutes. So we had four formal meetings a week, plus the informal ones. You were expected to be there and to be prepared.

"Ted brought David into Warner Brothers, and at first they were very close. But there were arguments and creative differences between the men over who was in charge of the show. David was used to running his own business and he's a very creative, very intuitive guy. Ted's a very analytical guy and a great administrator. He liked to put people in a room and ask them a lot of questions and get the right answers. David likes to make immediate decisions, once something has sparked his interest. He doesn't like to stop and take the time to convince anyone else that he's right. He likes to decide and then drive things to fruition.

"Ted was organizationally oriented. He wanted information from his people after they'd done all their research. He once asked us to watch a film that another studio was involved with. It had a lawsuit attached to it. Ted wanted us to tell him if we should pick the film up. Did it have a box office life? Could we buy it in exchange for dropping the lawsuit? David knew the people who'd made the film and thought it was a waste of time to view it. So he didn't bother. There was a very heated tiff."

Geffen lasted a year at Warner, before he and Ashley called it quits one evening at an est seminar (they reportedly parted with a hug). After leaving the job, Geffen remained under contract to Warner Bros. for several more years. Ross offered him another position, at corporate headquarters in New York, but the general consensus was that he was simply not made for this kind of duty. Geffen himself later acknowledged that he didn't have the personality to be a corporate leader.

"Today," he told *Vanity Fair* years later, "if you said to me, 'Hey, would you run a movie studio?' I would kill myself. I can't think of a more horrible job."

At Warner Bros., he'd discovered something important about the movie world: it was very different from the faster, looser way things were done in rock music. His footing had always been steady in the record business, and he knew how to use the unvarnished truth in that arena. That had worked well at Asylum, but the motion picture industry, he'd discovered, was filled with tentativeness and fear. Too much money was at stake for too much outspokenness or risk-taking to be encouraged. Too many layers of humanity had to be penetrated or persuaded before you could get anything done. Geffen saw and felt the fear in the business, and his response was to back away from it, at least for now.

While he was leaving the film industry, some other young men in Hollywood were just getting started in it. One of them in particular, a twenty-eight-year-old named Michael Ovitz, was also aware of the fear that lurked in the underbelly of the business, but his approach to it would be very different from Geffen's. Early in 1975, Ovitz and four partners had been summarily fired from the Beverly Hills William Morris headquarters after their superiors learned that these five TV packaging agents were thinking of leaving and opening their own office. Ovitz soon became the leader of their new business, Creative Artists Agency, and began telling people that within a decade he would have the most powerful talent agency in the field. Some people thought he was mad.

Like Geffen, Ovitz had perceived that beneath the Hollywood façade were great insecurity and trepidation, an almost tangible feeling of fragility. But unlike Geffen, Ovitz would use that insecurity and fear to do something that had never been done in Hollywood before. Geffen and Ovitz were opposites—fire and ice. Their paths were bound to cross in the future. And when they did they would not become friends.

CHAPTER 11

In 1976, Geffen began urinating blood. When the bleeding didn't stop, he checked into L.A.'s renowned Cedars-Sinai Medical Center, where he underwent a series of examinations. After his doctor had studied the test results, he told the patient that he had cancer of the bladder. In the not-too-distant future, Geffen might lose this body part—he might even die. He was thirty-three years old, had never confronted a serious disease before, and had lived a relatively carefree life. Now he'd been invaded by the most frightening, mysterious, and doom-laden word in our national vocabulary: "cancer." The sound alone was enough to make the throat catch. "Cancer" seemed like something worse than a terrible malady—almost like a form of punishment.

There were people in Hollywood who were happy that Geffen—the nouveau riche boy wonder of the music biz and the loud-mouthed promoter of his own causes—had lost Cher to another man. There were people who were pleased that he and Warner Bros. had had a sudden parting of the ways; he couldn't succeed at everything, could he? There were people who were less than glum that he'd contracted an illness, perhaps a serious one. And there were people who laughed when they heard that he was moving in the direction of self-help therapies. L.A. being what it is, and Geffen himself being a grating presence, there were snipers all over town ready to pronounce him dead in the entertainment business. Like some of his recording artists, he'd peaked young and could devote the rest of his life to spending his money.

There were also people who believed that he was not ill but had either made the cancer story up in a play for sympathy or concocted it to mask the fact that he was really in the hospital because he was having a nervous breakdown. "I'd still like to see the X-rays from that cancer diagnosis," says one of his former friends.

For years, the facts surrounding all this were vague, and it wasn't until the early eighties that Geffen would even use the word "cancer" when talking about this episode. In time, he filled in more of the medical details, and the reality that gradually emerged was that he'd had both physical and psychological problems. He'd also had a bad scare, which had a clear effect on the man.

Geffen had never had a reputation for vulnerability but after Hollywood superagent Sue Mengers and Elliot Roberts visited him in the hospital during this time, they said that he was visibly frightened and could not stop crying. Others found him to be quiet, subdued, introspective in a way he hadn't been before. After leaving the hospital, he sat for hours on the beach, just watching the waves, pondering what to do with himself. He gave the telephone a rest. He thought about who he was and what he was running away from. Changes, he decided, were in order.

Following his breakup with Cher, Geffen had gone on a blind date with another celebrity, actress Marlo Thomas. They'd had a heated affair and briefly lived together, but the romance was short-lived. None of his involvements with women—Janet Margolin, Cher, or Marlo Thomas—seemed to be going anywhere. The end of his relationship with Cher in particular had shaken Geffen; with her, he'd not only uncovered a level of pain that was deeper than anything he'd experienced before, it wouldn't go away. He'd undergone intense therapy, and that had been helpful, but he was looking for something more.

In recent months, he'd moved into his beach house on the Pacific Coast Highway in Malibu, a twenty-three-hundred-square-foot residence that bordered the ocean. It had four bedrooms, four bathrooms, and a pool. Fronted by a stucco fence and evergreens, the house was handsome and erect, evoking a small southern estate more than a California bungalow. In later years, he would buy other, much larger homes, but this would remain where he lived—alone. The house suited his lack of ceremony and casual lifestyle and was within hearing distance of the great Pacific roar. Driving home on the PCH in his silver Porsche, with the breeze in his face and salt water tingling the nostrils, was as close as he could get to making a fast escape from L.A. Wending along the very edge of the American continent carried a rush of freedom and just a hint of flying. That kind of liberation was what he was searching for.

A year before he and Cher fell apart, Peter Guber, a friend of his who would one day run Columbia Pictures with Jon Peters, had told Geffen about a phenomenon that was sweeping through Southern

California and the rest of the nation. It was called est, for Erhard Seminar Training.

The initial est program involved spending two weekends in a hotel conference room with a group of total strangers and the trainers of the sessions. You were not allowed to leave the room, even to go to the bathroom, until the trainers gave you permission. You were not allowed to use your last name, because everyone was supposed to shed his or her previous identity at the door. Inside these walls, all were regarded as equals. You were not allowed to take aspirin or any other pills during the sessions, not allowed to drink or take drugs between the two weekends of the program. You were encouraged to stand up and talk about your most intimate difficulties in front of people you'd never seen before.

When Guber first suggested to Geffen that he take est training, Geffen dismissed the idea as quacky. But a year later, he was ready to give it a try. (He once confessed that after the debacle with Cher, he would have joined the Catholic Church if that would have lessened his suffering; his friend and former business colleague, Bob Dylan, who was going through his own identity crisis at roughly this same time, did publicly embrace Christianity.)

Est was controversial and had as many detractors as supporters. Some saw it as a radical new way to approach human growth. Others viewed it as crypto-fascism.

"The est concept," says Bob Richards, a business executive who went through the program in L.A. at the same time as Geffen, "was designed to break down ingrained habits and defenses using a very hard, military sort of regimen. The trainers wanted you to bust through the stories you normally tell yourself, in order to get down to your real feelings—your more authentic self—and to share that with others. They wanted you to expose in public the very things you most wanted to protect and keep unknown. It was like shock treatment, and you were receiving it in front of a group. The trainers kept saying, 'This is it, this is it,' which means that everything is right now, and there is nothing else. It's their way of trying to get you out of the past and into the present moment.

"What you learned in est was that everyone else in the room was as neurotic as you were, so you weren't the odd man out. That part of the training was good. You also learned that once you'd exposed your inner self to others, they were either compassionate toward you or didn't give a damn about what you'd revealed. Either way, you saw that you could survive doing something like this, and that was also good. The training was supposed to give you a greater sense of freedom and power. From that perspective, it was fairly effective."

A woman in L.A. who took the training says it was "like being locked up in a mental hospital. People were curled up on the floor around you. Some had their eyes closed and were visualizing things. Some were moaning, and others were crying. Some were laughing hysterically. It was very surreal, and you could not get away from the group. It was like brainwashing—or instant enlightenment: Do this for two weekends and you won't have to work on yourself again. At the end of it, they expect you to have a revelation. The trainers walk around and say, 'Did you get *it*? Did you get *it*?' I never understood what '*it*' was. They also push you very hard to recruit a new batch of people for another seminar. I now think that est was really all about marketing the next round."

Geffen himself was always quite charitable toward est and two other programs, Lifespring and Marianne Williamson's Course in Miracles, which he would take in later years. He spoke publicly about these adventures and was grateful for what he'd received from them. In est, he often said, he'd learned that he was not a victim of circumstances, he was responsible for what had happened to him in the past, and there was no one to blame for what he was feeling.

One afternoon, he'd been sitting in his est group, thinking about himself and his own self-importance. Here he was, a multimillionaire in his mid-thirties, who'd already been a major player in the record business. He'd befriended Joni Mitchell, Bob Dylan, and many other celebrities. He'd gone to parties with Warren Beatty and Jack Nicholson. He was wealthy, famous enough, and invited where everyone else wanted to go. Looking around the hotel room, he knew that he was easily the most accomplished and celebrated person in the group. Thinking these things, he felt self-conscious and decided not to share them with the others.

Moments later, a young woman sitting next to Geffen stood up and began telling the group how important she was. She worked as a waitress at the Copper Penny cafe near Encino and saw herself as unique and quite significant. She hadn't planned to tell everyone in the room how special she was, but then she had changed her mind. As Geffen listened to the woman, her speech made a great impression on him. With some chagrin, he realized that all the others in the room, regardless of what job they held or how much money they had or who their friends were, felt pretty much the same way he did. They all wanted to see themselves as special, as having value and being worthy of love. He never forgot the waitress's words.

"Many people," Geffen once told an interviewer for *Playboy* magazine, "view all that stuff [the self-help therapies] as flaky. People who are cynical about those kinds of things are cynical in general. Well, they get to have their cynicism. I aspire to be better. It's hard to judge the value of things you have not tried yourself. I might try something and decide it's a waste of time. But more often, I think I get something valuable out of these experiences....

"You die unhealed. If you work on yourself your whole life you will still die unhealed, but you'll have a better life if you continue to work on it. If you can heal some of the damage that comes from life, I think that's good."

According to a longtime Geffen observer in Hollywood, "There are many different levels to David's involvement in programs like est. He not only went into these things because he wanted to deal with his own pain, but he's also a true explorer and experimenter in our popular culture: with music, sex, films, drugs, and ideas. He wanted to know what went on inside these programs—and inside himself—and he had the willingness, curiosity, and passion to find out. A lot of other businessmen would not have done that. A lot of them would have balked at exposing themselves in such a public manner.

"At the same time, I think he had another agenda. I always imagined him sitting in these seminars doing marketing research, asking himself, 'What kind of albums do these people listen to? What kind of movies do they want to see? What will they buy next?' If you were not in touch with these sorts of questions and intensive processes of self-discovery, then you were out of touch with your consumers. Your target audience was sitting right there with you, pouring out their souls. And he was listening and absorbing everything they said and did. The more street smart you are, and David is very street smart, the more you're going to take away from any situation.

"On still another level, I think he wanted to understand the psychological principles that are taught in these seminars. If everyone in your business is neurotic, then how do you work with neurotic people in a productive way? How do you keep your artists happy and get them to create what you want? How do you talk to them about their pain or depression? Or their doubts and fears? He wasn't learning about just his neuroses, but everyone else's. These are very important things to know how to do in show business.

"Finally, I think he wanted to know more about himself and how he really operates. David's a seeker and a very unusual creature. He doesn't study things over a period of time and then form an opinion or plan. He just takes it all in very quickly and acts. Stimuli goes straight into his pores and then he turns it around as new entertainment products for consumers in the marketplace. That's his gift. He's never been a remote, calculating strategist but a master dancer with the moment. He's consistently invested in his gut instinct of what the future will buy and sell, and he's usually been right.

"It's as if he's able to tap into the consciousness of large groups of people and know what many of them will want to experience next. But he's never created too far into the future, so he's never too far ahead of the pack. That can get you into trouble as a businessman. He has the ability to create just at that point where reality will gravitate to next. He puts the bait right in front of people's noses, and they take it. If you can do this without even having to stop and think about it, that's truly remarkable. It might cause you to go into all kinds of seminars in order to find out more about where your gift comes from and how it works."

Being told he had cancer shifted something within Geffen. He decided that acting like a straight man and dating women—or women alone—was not the answer.

"It was a mind-boggling realization that came at the same time I was diagnosed as having a tumor," he later told *Playboy*. "I was in the hospital waiting to find out whether it had spread, whether I was going to be mutilated or whether I would die. It all sank in then. I realized there is no time to waste in life. You have to live your life one day at a time. But I had been living a lie. Trust me, when someone tells you that you have cancer, it changes your life in a profound way....

"I thought, I'm going to live my life and see who I really am and what I really like, because I don't know. I had been trying to be something else, but from that point on I had to be who I was. Cancer made it imperative not to waste any more time."

Since he believed that he might be dying, he considered making a will, but when he sat down with his lawyer, he realized he didn't own much of anything. He'd been too busy working all those years to spend the money he was generating. That was going to change as well.

CHAPTER 12

He bought a seven-room apartment in Manhattan, overlooking Central Park, then hired Charles Gwathmey, an esteemed interior decorator, to redo it to his specifications. The apartment had green marble floors and high ceilings: Geffen ordered them lowered so that he would appear taller. He hung on the bedroom walls pictures of himself with John Lennon and Yoko Ono, with Jackson Browne, and with Cher. He bought another seven-room house, this time in Beverly Hills, and paid cash. He bought a 14,908-square-foot lot in L.A. and again paid cash.

Back in the 1960s, while working at William Morris, he used to spend part of his lunch hour strolling through the nearby Museum of Modern Art, learning about contemporary painters and sculptors. He loved staring at beautiful things and longed for the aesthetic pleasures that had been missing from Borough Park. Since traveling to London in the early seventies with Ahmet and Mica Ertegun and being introduced to the world of art galleries and collecting, he'd developed a fascination with owning objets d'art. He began buying Tiffany lamps and glass. He purchased every David Hockney print in existence. In his New York apartment, he hung paintings by Magritte, Fernand Leger, and Edward Hopper. In L.A., he had a Jasper Johns and a Frankenthaler.

He got rid of the clothes Cher had bought for him and replaced them with others. He purchased some of the same garments for his Manhattan closets that were hanging at his California address: two of everything, sometimes two in every available color. He went to Barbados five times in one year. He bought expensive furnishings for all of his homes and then decided to have some fun. Because he believed that his health was deteriorating and he couldn't assume anything about his future, he wanted, as he later put it, "to get laid as much as possible." Fortunately for Geffen, the zeitgeist was moving in exactly the same direction he was. In the late seventies, everybody wanted to get laid as much as possible.

If the sixties had seen some bodacious sexual behavior, it was frequently tied to vaguely altruistic impulses. People were making love to ban the bomb. They were making love to end the fighting in Vietnam or to abolish racism. They were making love as a personal insult to Richard Nixon. They were "making love," as the slogan had it, "not war." In the seventies, it was sex for the hell of it—sex all over the place and in every configuration. At any time of day or night, you could find couples in the bushes of Manhattan's Central Park, and the bathhouses were jammed. You could walk past the boathouses in Riverside Park and find people groping one another at random.

Sex parties were rampant, but they carried a hollow, uncomfortable air. People were having public sex because it had become the thing to do, even among strangers, and if they did it often enough, it might eventually take on some meaning. Prostitution and pornography were flourishing. People took drugs in order to have sex and had sex in order to get drugs. There was a great deal of talk about bisexuality, and when someone stepped forward and announced that he or she was bisexual, a common response, at least in America's biggest cities, was "Isn't everybody?"

In this atmosphere, it was inevitable that someone would create Studio 54, *the* nightclub in New York for a couple of years at the end of the decade. Located on West 54th Street between Eighth and Ninth avenues, it had once been the CBS-TV studio where *What's My Line?* was shot. Now it had a fifty-four-hundred-square-foot dance floor, five thousand blinking lights, bare-chested bartenders, and coed bathrooms. It had faux art-deco trappings and twelve large poles that came down from the ceiling and ascended back up, in rhythm. It stocked Quaaludes; lighting effects showed a man in the moon snorting cocaine from a spoon; a huge replica of an amyl nitrate popper doused the dancers with confetti.

Head-splitting disco, with its pounding, insistent beat, permeated Studio 54, causing everyone to stampede. Young women were flexing their sensual muscles, and young men lay belly down on the dance floor while other young men gyrated just above them. In the club's basement was the "playground," featuring Astroturf, a pinball machine, and children's toys. Down there, in the most private part of the operation, nothing had to be feigned or simulated.

Studio 54 was known as much for turning away wannabe hipsters as for letting more famous people in. Drag queens, fashionable women in evening clothes, hookers, muscular young men, kids from New Jersey, and wide-eyed out-of-towners all tried to crash the party. Night after night they gathered outside, under the black-and-silver marquee, sealed off from the front door by red velvet ropes and huge bouncers, begging to be let in. While they groveled, the paparazzi swarmed around them, like gnats with flashbulbs. Limousines came and went, dropping off their fawned-over passengers, and virtually everyone with a name took a turn at the club: Cher, Truman Capote, Mick Jagger, Liza Minnelli, et cetera. At the gates of Studio 54, America may well have crossed a line—where fame became more important than any other human attribute—that has never been recrossed.

Steve Rubell, the club's owner, stood by the entrance and played God, separating the celebrity wheat from the hoi-polloi chaff. As Steven Gaines and Sharon Churcher wrote in their Calvin Klein biography, *Obsession,* it was now Rubell, of all people, and not Lady Astor or one of the Vanderbilts or Whitneys or Rockefellers or Jacqueline Bouvier Kennedy Onassis who became "the social arbiter of all New York." This was quite an achievement for a postal worker's son who grew up in a three-room apartment in Canarsie, Brooklyn.

Rubell had started in the restaurant business, then moved into gay bars and small discos. In 1977, he opened Studio 54 and New York simply could not stay away. There are many snapshots from the late seventies that could stand for that particular time in American social history, but none is quite as provocative as that of Steve Rubell sitting on his bed and masturbating over $80,000 in cash spread out on his mattress—that night's take at the door.

Calvin Klein never had any trouble getting into Studio 54. Whenever the fashion designer arrived at the entrance, which was often, Rubell practically prostrated himself in front of the man. Also welcome at the club were Klein's friends, among them David Geffen, Barry Diller, and Sandy Gallin, whom Geffen had met during his brief stay at Creative Management Associates, back in the late sixties. These four individuals were wealthy, extremely well connected, and often celebrated in the media. In some circles, they would become known as the Velvet Mafia, a term that all of them despised.

None of the men had made any public declarations about his sexuality, and each was intensely interested in keeping his private life private. It was common knowledge at Studio 54, as well as around Manhattan and L.A., that these men were sexually flexible, but this information had to be kept safely inside the walls of the entertainment and fashion businesses. If mainstream America were to learn about such things, went this line of reasoning, feelings would be hurt, careers would be damaged, money would be lost, and the special position they held in relation to that mainstream would be altered—if not shattered. Square America was there to be entertained and exploited for gain, but its citizens had to be kept in the dark and treated like children. Otherwise, the game might end and privileges could be lost.

For many years, going back into show business history, this particular agreement among the people in the know had been rigorously kept. It was indeed one of the few sacred cows left in American journalism. Savagely criticizing the president of the United States in public was now fair game on every talk show in the country, but this other subject was taboo. Reporters would talk among themselves but not write about certain kinds of sexual behavior; even gossip columnists would not betray this trust. You simply didn't put in the paper or on television screens or in movies the reality that men went to bed with men and women with women. The adult truth of the matter had always been protected and would remain so for a while longer—but not forever.

When he wasn't partying at Studio 54, Geffen taught a music business course at Yale, under the aegis of a Hoyt Fellowship, and later taught a similar class at UCLA. Lecturing students amused him for a while, and he seemed healthy enough to perform these duties. (strangely enough, as the months passed, he didn't seem to be getting any sicker).

It was at UCLA that his straitlaced brother, Mitchell, had gone to law school. It was UCLA that Geffen himself, while a teenager in Brooklyn, had fantasized about attending. It was UCLA that he'd traveled west to see right after leaving New Utrecht High, and it was UCLA that he'd told the lords of William Morris he'd graduated from when he lied about his educational background. To Geffen, UCLA was the Holy Grail, representing tanned, blond-haired, rich kids with college degrees and a background of solidity and security that he'd never known.

Now he had a teaching gig at UCLA. Then, in 1980, his friend Governor Jerry Brown appointed him to the California Board of Regents, making him an overseer of the institution whose letter he'd once forged. In the future, he would do something even more dramatic in relation to the university. Geffen had an attitude toward the place, and it showed.

"He would come into the classroom dressed in tennis shoes, blue jeans, and a T-shirt," says one of his former students at the UCLA graduate business school. "Very casual. Nonchalant. He liked to tell the story about his secretary discovering Jackson Browne's picture in the trash can at Asylum and how he turned him into a star. He was very funny and fey, in a dishy sort of way. You would ask him a question, and he'd give you the body language that says, 'I don't know,' but you knew damn well that beneath that pose he knew the answer and he had the numbers to back it up. You knew he was ruthless as hell in business but tried to cover it up with a theatrical style.

"I don't think he fooled anyone in that class. He had the killer instinct. That's why he was teaching us."

CHAPTER 13

Money and sex and excellent paintings were easy to come by, compared to respect. In 1978, George Trow's superb profile of Ahmet Ertegun was published in the *New Yorker.* With more sophistication, Trow continued the tradition of Geffen-chronicling that had been established by Julie Baumgold in 1975 in *Esquire.*

Over a period of seven years, Trow had observed Ertegun, and on several occasions Geffen had been present and doing business with the head of Atlantic Records. Trow portrayed Ertegun as a smart, elegant figure of style and grace, who sometimes spoke in almost poetic phrases. He was enigmatic and a little prickly but essentially irresistible. Geffen, by contrast, came across as grasping. Ertegun himself is quoted as saying that the younger man had an "eager greed."

"With a certain humor," Trow wrote of Geffen, "with a certain honesty, with an exuberant pleasure (but with no grace), he had shaken off the obscure world in which managers and record hustlers —however rich—scruffle unnoticed."

In the most resonant passage in this long profile, Geffen, acting as the manager for Crosby, Stills, and Nash, asked Ertegun to advance the group $50,000 to cover their studio costs for an upcoming album (the year was 1971). Ertegun balked at the amount. Geffen kept doing what he did best—demanding more for his artists and himself. Trow wrote:

"Ahmet was annoyed by this request, but he treated it with a jaunty humor. 'We'll give you ten thousand dollars,' Ahmet told Geffen, 'and you can go to Santa Monica Boulevard and watch a couple of movies, or whatever you do all day.'

'You should give me the fifty thousand dollars,' Geffen said.

'Why?' Ahmet asked. 'No one else gets it.'

'Because it's sound business practice, and besides, I want it.'

'No.'

'Why don't you concede for once? Why not make a gesture of goodwill, taking into account the entire relationship? Why not give the fifty thousand dollars?'

"Finally, Ahmet agreed to advance thirty-five thousand. 'I'm not giving you fifty thousand dollars, because I need the money to run my company,' Ahmet said.

'If you're in that kind of trouble, I'm selling my stock,' Geffen said.

'You're very chintzy,' Ahmet said.

'*You* are chintzy, not me,' Geffen said.

Ahmet ceased to be jaunty. 'You know, a soldier is sometimes too good a soldier,' Ahmet said. 'Whatever happens, I'm your friend and I love you, but don't squeeze the juice out of every situation.'"

▪ ▪ ▪

By the late seventies, Geffen was confronted with a deepening dilemma. His health appeared to be quite good. If he wasn't going to die or deteriorate, what was he going to do with himself? He was bored with Studio 54, he was essentially unemployed, and he was growing increasingly restless. His public reputation was fading, and some people regarded him as a has-been.

"There was a brief vogue for David Geffen," Trow had written near the end of his *New Yorker* story. "David Geffen was seen with Cher. David Geffen went shopping with Cher. David Geffen shared a cover article in *Esquire* with Cher.... David Geffen struck out on a new career. He left the record business and went to work for Warner Brothers–Seven Arts, Ltd.... Later on, David Geffen broke up with Cher and Cher began to go out with Gregg Allman, and Ted Ashley came back to work at Warner Brothers–Seven Arts and couldn't get along with David Geffen and so David Geffen left."

The clear implication was that he'd failed at Warner Bros. and his moment had passed. There was other evidence to support this notion.

"I was with David once in the late seventies," says a New York friend. "We ate lunch and came back to my apartment. He asked if he could use my phone to check for messages. I said sure, so he sat down and took out a little pad and pen. He wrote on it, from top to bottom, the numbers one through three in anticipation of his first three messages. Then he dialed his message service. They told him that no one had called, so he quietly put away his pad and pen. His phone had stopped ringing, and he looked rather shaken. For David that was rare.

"Even in those years, when he wasn't working and was worrying about his future, he had this underlying layer of superconfidence. Maybe it's because he'd escaped Brooklyn and his mother and father. Maybe it's because he felt he was beating back cancer. Maybe it was always just there. David was occasionally in error, but he was never in doubt. Even in retirement, he had all this energy pouring out of him. All this ballsiness. When you watched him closely, you could tell that he was the kind of guy who liked to break people in negotiations. He really understood what power is. He loved exercising it and had a great sense of where the other guy would buckle and run. He never had any difficulty in asking for what he wanted. I couldn't imagine him sitting around and doing nothing much longer."

At the end of the swinging seventies and the heyday of Studio 54, Geffen once summed up his sexual philosophy to this same friend. It was no great achievement, he confessed, to become aroused by beautiful people of either gender.

"One time," the friend says, "David and I were talking about things, and he told me that he loved women, really loved them, but he just couldn't give up guys on the side. He had to have that other thing going to keep himself satisfied. I always assumed that he was bisexual."

Nearly four years after receiving his cancer scare, Geffen visited a doctor in Manhattan who put him through another round of tests. The physician carefully examined the patient and said that there was no tumor growing inside of him and that he was a perfectly healthy man. Someone had misinterpreted the original medical data; there never was anything seriously wrong with him.

When Geffen's ex-lover Marlo Thomas learned about the new diagnosis, she wanted Geffen to sue his first doctor. When his mother—all four feet eleven inches of her—heard about the second opinion, she wanted to go after the L.A. physician with a baseball bat. In private, Geffen complained about the "asshole who'd taken away four years of my life," but in public he had a more subdued and vaguer response, which was in keeping with the entire cancer issue.

He expressed relief and said that he never wanted to hear the word "cancer" again. He'd been able to take some time off from his early hectic years, he'd grown a bit mellower and wiser, he'd confronted some aspects of his sexuality, and he was now rested and anxious to reenter the marketplace. His experience with Southern California therapies had taught him that he was not only responsible for everything that happened to him but that everything had a purpose. Maybe this illness, whatever its real source, had surfaced because he'd needed a break from his former self.

Now that he was going to live, he needed a new plan. He'd already been through several career options and father figures, but none was a fit. He didn't want to be Nat Lefkowitz, because he didn't want to be a talent agent or run an agency himself. He didn't want to be Ted Ashley, because he didn't want to be in charge of a movie studio. He didn't want to be Steve Ross, because he couldn't adapt to a corporate structure and the behavior it demanded. Much more significantly, Geffen would never be Ahmet Ertegun. This wasn't simply a matter of style or grace but of something more basic.

Ertegun's reputation in the music business had been established in the 1940s and 1950s, because his tastes had led him toward the most significant aspect of American social life: race and racism. His instincts had taken him into the heart of our historical legacy regarding skin color, and he had played an important role in the introduction of black music to white audiences. He had a personal passion for black sounds and rhythms, which carried him into realms that had nothing to do with making a buck. All this gave him an aura of seriousness, and he received respect that others in the business could not command. At a ripe moment in the country's racial history, he had taken the initiative to do something that needed to be done. As a result, he became more than just another successful record company executive.

Unlike Ertegun, Geffen held no such position in the music business or the psyche of the American entertainment industry. He'd backed some important artists—all of them white—but his work did not expand outward in the same way that Ertegun's did. It built no multicultural bridges, nor did it mine the richness and diversity of American life. Geffen had never produced albums, as his mentor had done; nor had he written songs, as Ertegun had done under the pseudonym "Nugetre," which is his name spelled backward; nor had Geffen gone into the Deep South and traipsed around small towns and dingy bars looking for undiscovered talent. If Geffen's recording resumé was not as distinguished as Ertegun's, almost no one else's was, either. He was a tough act to follow.

"Ahmet," George Trow wrote, "at some moments, has *presided over* American cool."

Geffen, a profoundly competitive man, had only presided over Elektra/Asylum/Nonesuch within Warner Communications, Inc. If he were ever to make a greater mark on the entertainment industry, he would have to move into new and different arenas. In a sense, this came naturally to him. He already moved in many directions at once—psychologically, financially, sexually, and spiritually. But first of all, he had to get back into the business. He had to start making calls—and getting some calls in return. A silent phone, or an underemployed message service, was the equivalent of professional death.

Geffen was aware of Trow's article about Ertegun, and the

phrase that had stung him and stuck in his mind was "a brief vogue for David Geffen." Those words had hurt and perhaps even stirred some doubts. He knew that some people perceived him as nothing more than, as he would put it years later, "a flash in the pan." He was still being dismissed by his critics as a music executive's version of a one-hit wonder. Hadn't that always been true?

His parents and brother had made fun of him for reading the gossip columnists about the stars in Hollywood, but now he socialized with those stars. Journalists had spent years underestimating his resourcefulness and grit, even after he'd become a multimillionaire at twenty-six and the vice chairman of Warner Bros. at thirty-two. Now people were saying he was finished—but he would show all of them that he was more than a passing vogue... if he could just figure out what he wanted to do with the next act of his life.

ACT TWO

Big Business

CHAPTER 14

Geffen and two friends—Lorne Michaels, who produced *Saturday Night Live* for NBC-TV, and Paul Simon—took a trip to Barbados, with the intention of helping Geffen discover his future. During their excursion, Simon told him a very simple thing: Start with what you already know and work outward from there, because you can never predict where it will take you. That made sense to Geffen, and when he thought about it, he realized that the one thing he clearly knew was the music business. After returning to the States, he contacted Steve Ross and Mo Ostin, the chairman of Warner Records, which included the Asylum, Elektra, Atlantic, Nonesuch, and Warner labels. WCI was cash rich from its recent sales of the current national fad, the Atari video game, and looking for new investments or acquisitions. The two men were happy to hear from Geffen, who told them that he wanted to start a new record company.

Outside the WCI fold, there were many Geffen doubters, but inside the corporation, the faithful were still in charge. Steve Ross, just as he'd done back in 1972 when purchasing Asylum, now made the younger man an extraordinary offer. Geffen would put up the labor and find the talent for his new label. In return, WCI would provide all the start-up financing—$25 million—would pay the recording costs for albums, and would market, promote, and distribute Geffen's products under the Warner umbrella. WCI and Geffen would jointly own the label and evenly split the profits.

If an album failed to sell, Warner took the loss. If it succeeded, both partners made money. Either way, Geffen could not lose a dime and had total freedom to run his company. For no dollars down, he was back in business and associated with one of the largest and best entertainment corporations in the country. He had access not only to its system of record distribution but to its filmmaking capabilities, which he also wanted to explore. This agreement was set in place in 1980, with the stipulation that after five years Ross and Geffen would renegotiate the deal, based upon how the label was doing. Much later, Geffen would contend that Ross had promised him, right from the start, that he would eventually buy Geffen's half of the company.

Once again, there were critics throughout the entertainment world who felt that shrewd and calculating Steve Ross had been taken by his former employee. For some reason, Ross did things for Geffen that he wouldn't do for anyone else. By 1980, Geffen had been out of the record business for five years, and musical tastes had changed dramatically. The Eagles were still popular, but Joni Mitchell and Jackson Browne were starting to wane. Geffen had no connection to disco, the huge fad that was just dying, and no attachment to two other movements that had come into fashion: punk rock and a new art form emerging in the black community, called rap. It seemed that Geffen's era—that of the white folk-rock singer-songwriters—had passed, and music trends seemed to have left him far behind.

Given all that, his deal with Ross was a supreme vote of confidence for Geffen, who could hardly have asked for anything more. It didn't take long for him to come up with a name for his new label: Geffen Records. He set up shop in his old Asylum digs on Sunset Boulevard and began working the phones from sunrise till midnight. His party days had faded. He arose at six A.M., read three papers (the *Los Angeles Times,* the *New York Times,* and the *Wall Street Journal*), and ate a breakfast of bran cereal and herb tea. He bought another home in L.A.—Marlo Thomas's former residence in Benedict Canyon—and he now lived there, as well as at his beach house. In Benedict Canyon, he worked out at his in-house gymnasium, lifting weights and performing aerobic exercises in front of mirrors. He began scrupulously taking pictures of his physique, in order to chart its progress from scrawny to buff.

At Geffen Records, he again ran a no-frills operation, shunning a desk and other unnecessary furniture. He took a small, undecorated office for himself, so that none of his employees could complain about their own cramped conditions. The premises had no executive parking spaces and no autographed pictures of famous musicians on the walls. But he paid his people well and encouraged loud input from his staff. His credo was that you should never punish an employee for telling an uncomfortable truth, because in business the truth was always the most important thing. Geffen Records would have no titles, except for two: Geffen himself was the CEO, and Ed Rosenblatt, a music business veteran, became the president. The rest were all equals striving to impress the boss, and not just as employees but as entrepreneurs.

"Eddie has a pretty big ego," says an early Geffen Records employee, "but there was room in the office for both him and David. That says a lot about how Geffen ran his business. He gave people the freedom to fail—or succeed."

Reentering the music field in 1980, Geffen faced some serious challenges. The previous year had been one of the worst ever. Industry sales slipped 11 percent compared to 1978, the first drop in these numbers since World War II. The larger record companies were paying up to $10 million annually just to get their songs on the radio (this practice was once called "payola" but had now been upgraded to "independent promotion fees"), yet even this tactic wasn't inspiring the public to buy their products. CBS Records, long the most prestigious label in the field, would soon fire three hundred people and shut down nine of its nineteen national sales branches.

Doomsayers were predicting that the business could not bounce back or find a new group of superstars to push it forward. AOR—album-oriented rock, played and promoted on radio—was what had made the record business so successful, but AOR had fallen in the ratings. In addition, the corporate musical landscape had changed since the early seventies; competition was nastier than before. Under Mo Ostin, Warner Records was making inroads into the dominant position held by CBS, but "Big Red," as the venerable label was called, was fighting back.

Thirty years earlier, CBS Records had risen to prominence by signing some of the country's most original musical talent. The legendary John Hammond, an early CBS employee, was credited with discovering jazz greats Billie Holiday, Teddy Wilson, Count Basie, and Charlie Christian. He would later sign Bob Dylan, Aretha Franklin, Bruce Springsteen, and Stevie Ray Vaughan. In the mid-fifties, Goddard Lieberson, who had a taste for show tunes and the more sophisticated sounds of music, began running the label. Inside CBS, Lieberson was much admired (he playfully signed his memos "God"), but in the sixties, he gave way to a Brooklyn native and Harvard Law School graduate named Clive Davis. During his tenure, Davis brought some major acts to CBS— Blood, Sweat, and Tears, Janis Joplin, Santana, Chicago, Billy Joel, and Pink Floyd—but then he fell into difficulties over allegedly misappropriating funds and was soon gone.

Davis was replaced by a forty-two-year-old Brooklyn native named Walter Yetnikoff, whose parents were Russian Jews and whose father had been a house painter. The music business had long been filled with free spirits, wildcatters, and con men; Yetnikoff now joined this tradition of rogues. He was fond of liquor, Yiddish, and gentile women (it was said that his sex drive had caused him to create and sustain a "shiksa farm"). He was also fond of an irreverence that was becoming increasingly unfashionable. As the seventies gave way to the eighties and as social issues and public sensibilities became more delicate, he didn't tone himself down but grew louder and more politically incorrect.

After attending Columbia Law School, Yetnikoff had landed a job as an attorney at CBS, with no intention of entering the record business. He was tone deaf and not musically inclined. One afternoon he was invited to a party with some record executives, and the gathering wowed him. It wasn't because of the sophisticated patter or the food or drink or even the music, but because of the young women at the fete. They were attractive and friendly, and maybe, Yetnikoff concluded, there was something worth pursuing here.

In 1975, he began running the largest and most successful record company in the world. He was a new breed, who cast himself in the mold of a rock star. He wore his shirt buttons undone, revealing a hairy chest, looked like a street fighter, and loved being called "the king of the grooves." He chain-smoked Shermans and was a screamer who broke glasses and plates during tantrums. When speaking with an artist on the phone, he liked to say, "From God's mouth to your ear." His favorite epithet was "cocksucker." In his office, he kept a faux six-foot screwdriver and a sign that read THE MENSCH WITH SPILKAS ("man with the jitters"), which was a perfect description of virtually everyone who succeeded in the record business, except Ahmet Ertegun. Yetnikoff was outspoken about his Jewish heritage and once drove an Arab sheik out of a London hotel room by repeatedly blasting CBS artist Johnny Winter's latest recording through the man's wall.

In the sixties, three big record companies had struggled for supremacy in America: CBS, RCA, and Capitol. By the mid-seventies, RCA and Capitol had fallen back, and the current field—with yearly sales over $6 billion—had only two major players: CBS and Warner. The latter, led by Mo Ostin, had signed the late Jimi Hendrix, Van Morrison, and James Taylor. In 1976, Yetnikoff plucked James Taylor away from Warner, by offering him $1 million an album plus a $2.5 million advance (and by sitting with Taylor until four A.M., when he finally, exhausted and in tears, signed the deal). In 1977, as payback, Warner nabbed Paul Simon, whose Simon and Garfunkel album *Bridge Over Troubled Water* had sold eight million copies for CBS. Yetnikoff increased the CBS market share by introducing new artists like Elvis Costello and the Clash. Warner countered with the Talking Heads and Prince. The companies fought bitterly over the rights to Billy Joel and Rod Stewart. It was, in pugilistic terms, an unrelenting heavyweight championship bout.

Yetnikoff once orchestrated a rabblerousing CBS convention, designed to inspire his employees vis-à-vis their archrival. He printed up FUCK THE BUNNY signs, a reference to Warner's most notable corporate symbol, Bugs Bunny. During his keynote address, Yetnikoff declared war on Warner Records and handed out GI combat boots to his assembled troops. In the halls of Big Red, people often reminded one another that Walter absolutely hated Mo Ostin.

Onto this field of battle, at age thirty-seven, walked David Geffen. He'd not only been out of touch with the music scene for several years but was entering a crowded, depressed industry. No one, with the exception of the top Warner execs, was really happy to see him back in business on Sunset Boulevard. Walter Yetnikoff didn't need any more competitors. Geffen and Clive Davis, now over at Arista Records, were old professional enemies. And even Joe Smith, who was running Elektra for WCI, would eventually get annoyed when Geffen tried to lift the lead singer of the Cars, Ric Ocasek, from Smith's label and record him as a solo act. Just down the road from Geffen's office, another man had become extremely successful in the recording business. Neil Bogart ran Casablanca—the Studio 54 of record labels. In its brief prime in the late seventies, Bogart had young women walking through the office taking daily drug orders for its executives. A few years later, the boss was dead.

And finally there was Irving Azoff, who'd always enjoyed watching Geffen suffer. The former Geffen-Roberts employee had started his own very prominent management firm, Front Line, but now wanted to run a major label. In 1983, he got his wish, taking over MCA Records in Hollywood. MCA, the vast Music Corporation of America, was known throughout the entertainment industry as "the Octopus," because it had a tentacle in nearly every part of the business. Most of those tentacles generated large amounts of revenue, but MCA Records did not. When Azoff took over the label, it was so flat that wags in L.A. referred to it as the Musical Cemetery of America.

Azoff, a.k.a. the Poison Dwarf, was a lot like Geffen, only more so. He used the phone as much as Geffen, or more, and he threw louder fits. He had added to his legend as a maniac by lighting a menu on fire in a chi-chi L.A. eatery because the service struck him as laggard. On another occasion, he had a messenger deliver a live, gift-wrapped boa constrictor to the Beverly Hills home of Michael Lippman, a music manager in Azoff's disfavor, during Lippman's fortieth birthday party. The enclosed card read, "Happy Birthday, Michael. Now you have two of them!" The "two of them" was a reference to Lippman's now enraged and terrified wife.

Azoff appeared demonic but was good at the music business (or he was good at the business because he *was* demonic). After assuming control at MCA Records, he got rid of approximately 80 percent of the label's acts and began turning the company around. In 1986, he sold Front Line to MCA and pocketed $15.7 million.

Geffen now looked at Azoff as a lot of people had once looked at Geffen. "What he is," Geffen said of Azoff in Fredric Dannen's 1990 music business exposé, *Hit Men,* "is devilish. And that's interesting on some level, but not nearly as interesting as intelligence, or charm, or wit, or real, true ability. Irving is involved in some drama of self-importance. And he thinks that in order to be powerful or important, you have to fuck with people. Or frighten them, or be awful to them, which I find unacceptable behavior."

CHAPTER 15

Soon after opening his new record company, Geffen got a call from Donna Summer, lately the queen of disco and a megaselling artist for Casablanca Records. She'd won two Grammy Awards and earned her disco title in 1975, with a seventeen-minute LP rendition of "Love to Love You, Baby," complete with erotic sound effects. That was five years ago, and now she was so disgruntled with Casablanca that she was suing the label for $10 million. Would Geffen, she asked him over the phone, be interested in signing her to a recording contract? He thought this was a crank call but said yes anyway, and she became one of his first artists. Although Summer would never again be the star she'd once been, and although some people felt that Geffen badly overpaid for her services, giving her $1.5 million for her first album, his company needed a name on its roster, and she sufficed. Her first album for the label, *The Wanderer,* had a single by the same name that rose to number three on the charts.

After signing Summer, Geffen went to a party in L.A. and ran into one of pop music's longest-running superstars. Born in Middlesex, England, in 1947, Reginald Kenneth Dwight began his career as a pianist for Long John Baldry in the Bluesology band. Baldry's sound was a bit harder than Dwight wanted, and in time he began a letter-writing correspondence with another young Englishman from Lincolnshire, named Bernie Taupin. The two of them penned songs back and forth through the mail, Taupin handling the lyrics and his newfound partner composing the melodies to these tunes, sometimes in less than half an hour. By the time they met in person, they'd created future hit material together. In 1970, Elton John, as the pianist-composer was now called, had his first big single in the States with "Your Song." His next album, *Tumbleweed Connection,* pushed him into the pantheon of fame, and for a decade he'd remained atop the small, shaky pinnacle of the contemporary music field.

If his personal life, entwined with martinis and cocaine, had long been tumultuous, the scale of his professional success was almost immeasurable. As the sixties generation grew older, John and

Taupin's "soft rock" had a way of reconnecting listeners to their own youthful, romantic emotions. In the 1970s, John had seven consecutive number one albums in the United States, and it was said that 2 percent of all records sold were his. "Rock's Liberace," as John was called because of his flamboyant onstage costumes, regularly sold out Madison Square Garden and many other venues. His worldwide following had purchased sixty million of his LPs and made him spectacularly wealthy.

The record business works like this: It costs between $300,000 and $400,000 to record an album—or, starting in the early eighties, a compact disc—and get it onto the shelves. At $7 to $8 wholesale per disc, you have to sell fifty thousand of them to break even. If a disc sells a million copies, at $7 per unit, the performer gets approximately $1 million and the remaining pretax revenue—$6 million—goes to the label. (Royalty payments are complicated, and the industry is filled with stories of light-fingered executives cheating artists out of these payments, or giving them long, shiny Cadillacs in exchange for tens of thousands of dollars owed in back royalties.) Based upon this arithmetic, it's easy to see why the recording business holds allure—but only if you can sign the stars. Geffen was many things to many people, but everyone agreed that he was a signer. Elton John was soon in his stable.

Then he got a call from Yoko Ono. She and John Lennon were living at the Dakota apartment complex in New York, and for the past half decade Lennon had been in seclusion, exploring his inner realms and raising their son, Sean. Early in 1980, Lennon decided, as he once put it, "that the housewife would like to have a career." When Yoko learned that Geffen was back in the music business, she remembered his enormous success at Asylum, rang him up, and asked if he would be interested in recording the ex-Beatle—and herself—on a new album. Geffen didn't grope for an answer.

Some people are exceptionally good at what they do, some are exceptionally fortunate in their timing, and some are both things simultaneously. No amount of analysis can explain away the mystery of how all these elements intersect in one human life at precisely the right moment.

Geffen set to work on the Lennon-Ono *Double Fantasy* album, which contained seven songs by him and seven by her. On this LP, Lennon was able to transform some of his obsession with his own youth into a wondrous father's anthem for his young son, "Beautiful

Boy." The album's other break-out hit, "Just Like Starting Over," reached the Top Ten. Under any circumstances, the autumn 1980 release of this disc would have been an event in the music world: People were always talking about a Beatles reunion, or about which direction the most relentlessly inquisitive, introspective, and exploratory member of the group, John Lennon, would move in next. Lennon was the only Beatle who clearly transcended the band and its fame. His honesty, self-absorption, ever-shifting identity, and constant search for ultimate answers were emblematic of the entire Baby Boomer generation. He devoted all his time to what others could only do as an avocation, and in the end, he seemed to be edging closer to some kind of peace.

On December 8, 1980, right after *Double Fantasy* came out, he was shot to death on the steps of the Dakota by a young man named Mark David Chapman, who would later be diagnosed as schizophrenic. In the bizarre logic of megafame, many people described the killer as a great Lennon "fan." On the day of the shooting, Geffen was in New York and immediately went to Roosevelt Hospital, where doctors were unable to keep Lennon alive. One of the most famous photographs generated by this murder depicts a grief-stricken Yoko Ono emerging from the hospital after her husband's death. On her arm is David Geffen.

There are omens and there are omens. None is entirely trustworthy, but some of them command attention. If the clumped-together deaths of Janis Joplin, Jimi Hendrix, and Jim Morrison near the turn of the previous decade signaled the end of the sixties, Lennon's execution may have foreshadowed the 1980s. He was slain about a month after Ronald Reagan was elected president of the United States and George Bush, a former director of the Central Intelligence Agency, became vice president. For many Americans, the eighties would be a hugely prosperous time, a time of unfettered business expansion, a money time. But it would also be a time of death.

Murder, as the nation had learned in the past and would relearn again and again in the future, could be sensational for business. *Double Fantasy* went multiplatinum, selling three million copies (a "gold" LP sells five hundred thousand units, while "platinum" breaks the million mark). It won the Grammy for 1980's Album of the Year. Geffen Records had been given a huge boost by the coinciding of the album's appearance and the assassination of one of the greatest cultural heroes from the 1960s. The new company and its leader once again had instant visibility and credibility. Like many other people, Geffen himself, who'd recently been released from a possible death sentence from cancer, was deeply shaken by Lennon's demise. Years later, he would say that this shooting had taught him something very important: there is no such thing as the future. It simply did not exist, as something one could count on. There was only now—so there wasn't a moment to waste.

He went back to work with a vengeance, finding and corraling talent for his label. Ever since the success of Crosby, Stills, and Nash, Geffen had been drawn to bands comprised of the best parts of famous ex-bands. He now signed Asia, a "supergroup" from the United Kingdom. Drummer Carl Palmer had once played in Emerson, Lake, and Palmer, while guitarist Steve Howe and keyboardist Geoff Downes had been members of Yes. Bassist John Wetton was a veteran of King Crimson, Roxy Music, and Uriah Heep. Geffen would never find another Crosby, Stills, and Nash, but Asia's first album spent nine weeks at the top of the charts, was the year's best-selling disc, and delivered two Top Twenty singles: "Heat of the Moment" and "Only Time Will Tell." In late 1983, the group played a live MTV gig that was broadcast to twenty million people in the United States and Japan.

Geffen signed the ever-experimental Neil Young, his old cohort, who would soon record *Trans,* an extremely personal LP about his small son's battle with cerebral palsy. The lyrics were hard to decipher, and the album was not an easy sell. *Trans* began a tumultuous relationship over creative differences between Geffen and Young, and it would end badly. Geffen traveled to Europe, where he used his renowned powers of persuasion to lure away from Polygram the young singer Peter Gabriel, who'd already fronted the successful British rock group Genesis. Gabriel's first Geffen disc, *Security,* contained the hit "Shock the Monkey," and he developed into an MTV star, making some of the best videos for this new rock venue. A good songwriter and an adequate singer, he was more imaginative, both visually and lyrically, than most of his competitors. He would be writing challenging music for years to come. Geffen signed another longtime friend, Joni Mitchell, who made a strong comeback album for his label, *Wild Things Run Fast,* in 1982.

He signed a group from Portland, Oregon, called Quarterflash, formerly known as Seafood Mama. Their first hit, "Harden My Heart," went to number three in the United States and number one in France, Italy, Australia, and Japan. Geffen signed the novel duo Was (Not Was), comprised of two men who called themselves Don and David Was. Their debut Geffen album, *Born to Laugh at Tornadoes,* featured as unlikely a trio of guest artists as one could find anywhere: Ozzy Osbourne, Mitch Ryder, and Mel Tormé. Geffen signed the bands Lone Justice and Style Council. As solo acts, he signed the former Eagle Don Henley, the very promising young songwriter John Hiatt, and the soon-to-be-famous lead singer of Van Halen, Sammy Hagar.

Most of Geffen's acts were either short-lived successes, like Was (Not Was) and Quarterflash, or much larger names who were no longer at the height of their popularity. Bringing them into his company was a significant achievement, but none of the real stars—Donna Summer or Elton John or Neil Young—would do their most memorable work for Geffen Records. John's first disc for the label, *The Fox,* was called "a disaster" by one critic, and Summer's initial release, *The Wanderer,* was characterized as a "major disappointment." These artists helped launch the company, but it would have to find its legs elsewhere. On the other hand, Geffen was back in business—and not just the music business.

CHAPTER 16

In the late seventies, Geffen had met Michael Bennett, the creator of the hugely successful Broadway musical *A Chorus Line*. Bennett decided to produce another musical, *Dreamgirls,* but it ran into fiscal difficulties and needed extra backing to reach the stage. Bennett contacted Bernard Jacobs, the president of New York's Shubert Organization, the largest landlord on Broadway and the owner of theaters in L.A. and two dozen other cities. Shubert had been responsible for such hits as *Amadeus* and *Children of a Lesser God.*

Then Bennett rang up Geffen to ask if he would like to provide financial help for his new musical and, in effect, get into the business of theatrical production.

Geffen was always looking for a new challenge and willing to place his money where his faith was, and he believed in Michael Bennett. For his part, Bennett knew that Geffen was a risk-taker and a superb entrepreneur who not only worked well alone, but was also a good partner. When Geffen got paid, the entertainment scuttlebutt had it, he made sure that his partners got paid at the same time; that naturally made people want to do joint ventures with him. He pledged an estimated several hundred thousand dollars to keep *Dreamgirls* moving forward. Geffen also set about working another angle on the project.

In the 1950s, Goddard Lieberson had made his reputation at CBS Records by bringing out the original cast recordings of some of the most successful musicals in Broadway history. In 1956, after the celebrated composers Alan Lerner and Frederick Loewe came by his office and played him the score of *My Fair Lady,* Lieberson decided to put the songs on an LP. CBS shelled out $360,000, and *My Fair Lady* ran on Broadway for six years. The album became the largest-selling one of its kind to date and made CBS millions. In 1968, the cast album of *Hair* was another hit; and in the seventies, *Jesus Christ Superstar* sold seven million copies worldwide. The 1977 recording of *Evita,* with music by Andrew Lloyd Webber and lyrics by Tim Rice, was the best-selling LP in the United Kingdom that year.

After investing in *Dreamgirls,* Geffen wanted to release an album in conjunction with the opening of the play. This would, he believed, not only make the Broadway production more popular but might even help get the music business, which was slumping, out of the doldrums. The Geffen Records art department created the logo and poster for *Dreamgirls* (the musical), and Geffen himself signed one of the show's stars, Jennifer Holliday, to a recording contract. The show opened in December of 1981 and ran for four years, while the *Dreamgirls* album became the bestselling cast LP in America since *Hair.* Geffen not only received a huge return on his *Dreamgirls* investment but reignited a trend, as CBS, Arista, RCA, and Atlantic began bidding on the rights to make cast albums from other musicals.

Geffen was soon working with the Shubert Organization on several other theatrical productions. By the end of 1982, in fact, he was being called a "mini–Broadway conglomerate." He owned 20 percent of *Master Harold...and the Boys,* a play about a white teenager's relationship with his family's black servants, which ran on Broadway from May of 1982 until February of 1983. He owned 50 percent of *Little Shop of Horrors,* an off-Broadway musical about a man-eating plant, which ran from July of 1982 until November of 1987 and evolved into a Geffen Records album and a feature film. He owned 20 percent of *Good,* a drama that was set in World War II and dealt with a college professor's drift into Nazism; it ran for three months in late 1982. But most profitably of all, he owned 33 percent of *Cats,* the Andrew Lloyd Webber musical that opened in October of 1982, won seven Tony awards, had the biggest advance ticket sales ever on Broadway, and is still running. The *Cats* album, on Geffen Records, was also a smash.

To his credentials as a record company boss, real estate owner, and art collector, Geffen now added Broadway producer, although the term was somewhat misleading. Bernard Jacobs would jokingly tell the *New York Times* that Geffen was really just an investor in these plays, but he gave so generously and so often that they let him wear the title of producer. By late 1982, he had five plays running simultaneously on and off Broadway, he'd sold twenty-five million albums since Geffen Records opened two years earlier, and his real estate holdings now included a six-story office building in Santa Monica, one block of land and buildings on Sunset Boulevard, a shopping center in Sylmar, California, and a two-hundred-unit apartment complex in Palm Springs. He was netting nearly a million dollars a month.

While his initial venture into films at the Warner studio had not been very successful, he was still drawn to the motion picture business. It was where the real power lay in Hollywood, and if he could locate the right property, he was ready to make a move. In 1980, he found that property and became involved in one of the most entangled projects in the industry, *Personal Best,* a lesbian love story about two track stars, played by Mariel Hemingway and Patrice Donnelly.

Robert Towne, the author of *Personal Best,* had gained fame in Hollywood by writing the Academy Award–winning script for *Chinatown.* Towne also wrote *Shampoo,* but *Personal Best* was to be his directing debut. Things went well enough until July of 1980, when the production was unfinished and the Screen Actors Guild called a strike. Warner Bros. had been financing the picture but now closed it down in order to keep a united front with the other major producers. The content of *Personal Best* had always been controversial, and in the midst of the work stoppage, Warners decided to drop the film. Once the strike ended, *Personal Best* remained in production limbo.

Because of his Warner connections, Geffen was aware of this situation and intrigued by the unfinished movie. He went to his friend Barry Diller, who was running Paramount, and asked if he would like to pick up the picture. Diller wanted to see what had been shot, but Geffen was reluctant to show him without getting a commitment from Paramount first. It was at this delicate moment in the film's history that Towne's agent, Michael Ovitz, contacted Diller and told him that the director needed more money to complete the movie. Geffen felt that Ovitz was interfering at a particularly bad time, and this was the start of the men's long and uncomfortable professional relationship.

By 1980, Ovitz had begun to emerge as the entertainment executive to watch. The eighties would be his decade, and as surely as Ronald Reagan would set the political tone for America in these years, Ovitz would dictate the atmosphere for all of Hollywood. Five years earlier, he and four other TV packaging agents— Ron Meyer, Bill Haber, Mike Rosenfeld, and Rowland Perkins—had been tossed out on the street by William Morris. They quickly formed Creative Artists Agency (CAA) but had no clients, no office, no furniture, not much money, and no immediate prospects for generating any. Perkins and Rosenfeld were the oldest of the group, at forty, and Ovitz was the youngest, at twenty-eight. While the others worried about their immediate future, Ovitz began laying his strategy for reinventing the agenting business. During his firing, Mike Rosenfeld had admitted to the Morris brass that the five men were going to open a competing office in Beverly Hills; his former superiors were fearful that the renegades would try to raid their client list. Rosenfeld assured them that any damage they did to William Morris would be the equivalent of "a flea shitting on an elephant." The executives were not amused and Rosenfeld was dead wrong.

Ovitz's strategy at CAA was quite simple: the agency would sign all the directors, producers, movie stars, and screenwriters that it could, then present a group of CAA clients to the film studios as a "package deal" for a particular movie. TV packaging agents had been working that way for years, but it had never effectively been tried in the film business. If CAA could accumulate enough clout, it could offer the studios a take-it-or-leave-it proposition: work with all of our people, and pay us a 10 percent commission on each of them, or you won't get the star you want in your picture. It was a revolutionary idea. In past decades in Hollywood, the studios had dictated who would be in which films and who would produce, direct, and write them. Ovitz's plan reversed the rules. The studio system had crumbled, and he was there to replace it with a new order of his own.

By 1980, CAA had signed Dustin Hoffman, Paul Newman, Robert Redford, and Bill Murray. The agency already had scores of screenwriters turning out scripts for these luminaries, and during the next few years Ovitz's concept gathered more and more momentum. Once CAA had top-name talent in its stable, and once the other stars began to see how well Ovitz and his people were doing, they naturally wanted to become Creative Artists clients themselves. Once they'd signed with CAA, it was easier for the agency to put together more packages and wield even more power vis-à-vis the studios. That, in turn, meant more work for CAA's clients and more money for each project. Within ten years of CAA's founding, it not only was the most potent talent agency in Hollywood, just as Ovitz had once predicted, it was also gutting the motion picture department at William Morris, by luring away both agents and clients. The flea had stunned everyone.

The rise of Michael Ovitz had another dimension, unlike anything seen in previous Hollywood eras. Long before becoming an agent, Ovitz had studied and absorbed the teachings of Sun Tzu, the ancient Chinese philosopher who wrote *The Art of War* some twenty-five hundred years ago. This military handbook was the first document devoted to the practice of psychological warfare, as it applies to hand-to-hand combat on the field of battle. Sun Tzu's essential interest was not in the battle itself but in everything that preceded it. He believed that if you could cripple your opponent before the fighting commenced, you were going to win with a minimum of bloodshed.

The Art of War advocates using deception, manipulation, and elite shock troops with maximum flexibility and loyalty to their leader. The text embodies the belief that war is necessary and significant, with its primary goal not killing for the sake of killing but killing efficiently in order to hasten your triumph. The fastest and best way to do that is through controlling your enemy's mind and emotions. Make him doubt himself, or his own power, and you can control and defeat him using less physical force. Make him think that you yourself, or your troops, have mysterious powers of your own. Turn his doubt against himself.

Military leaders had long been aware of these teachings, but when Ovitz began, he wondered if Sun Tzu's writings could be successfully applied in Hollywood in the last quarter of the twentieth century. Could he make film executives throughout Los Angeles believe that if they did not do business with him and use his movie packaging concept, they might not be able to do business at all? Could he convince them that he'd become the smartest and most potent force in town? Could he make them think that he was someone to be genuinely frightened of—and that things went on inside CAA that gave it an aura approaching the supernatural? Would intelligent, well-educated, middle-aged men (for the most part) be willing to swallow this newly created Hollywood myth and give him what he wanted? Could he exploit their essential weakness—their suspicion that they needed him to survive—and make everyone play his game?

The answer to all these questions was a resounding yes. No one before him had perceived how much insecurity lay at the heart of the entertainment business—and how easily it could be manipulated.

Ovitz was much more than a Sun Tzu devotee. He was a superb negotiator, an excellent handler of talent, and a brilliant executive, who took care of the details and made colossal sums of money for his clients, most of whom swore by him. Studios paid his stars more and signed them to longer-term deals. In the early eighties, for example, CAA got Sylvester Stallone, whose career had gone flat, an unheard-of guaranteed five-picture, $15,000,000 deal with MGM/UA Communications and Carolco Pictures. By generating more money for CAA, Ovitz made more money for the entire industry. Under these circumstances, most people learned to respect him and kept quiet about their personal feelings toward the man.

"Mike was always ruthless," says one film executive, "and always waging a kind of strategic warfare. He was built to do this, just like other military generals were, and if he couldn't do it, he would die. He had very conscious objectives, and people got sacrificed in the pursuit of those objectives. If you took drugs at CAA, you were gone. If you wanted to fool around in the office late at night, you were fired. If you talked about his business with the media, you were history. A cruel man will cut off your balls for sport. A ruthless man only does it when it's necessary. From the start, Ovitz was extremely good at setting clear boundaries and being able to control people who are out of control. That's how he got where he is."

The more powerful Ovitz grew, the more he was surrounded by a sense of invulnerability, mystique, and fear. He cultivated the image of the ultraefficient warrior who arose at six each morning, practiced the martial art of aikido at home, slipped into a dark Armani suit, and drove his sleek, dark BMW to work, where he closed every deal quickly. Some people referred to him as a samurai agent. Others called him less flattering things, but not to his face. He was not to be crossed, people said, or careers might be squashed.

Barry Diller and Paramount eventually turned down *Personal Best.* At that point, Geffen, along with Warner Bros., decided to finance what was needed to bring the movie to completion. Geffen himself came up with between $4 and $5 million, and in the fall of 1980, Robert Towne and his film crew went back to work. Almost immediately, there was conflict between Towne and Geffen. In the lawsuit that resulted from the turmoil—Towne sued Geffen, Warner Bros., and Steve Ross for $155 million—the director-screenwriter claimed that Geffen "repeatedly interrupted and interfered" with the production and made "long harassing" calls to Towne, during which Geffen was "abusive and belligerent." Geffen denied all the accusations, saying that he'd visited the set only once and that if his calls were so disruptive, Towne should have just hung up. The movie had become far more expensive than initially budgeted, and Geffen wanted the director to absorb any cost overruns—another issue in the deepening dispute.

In January of 1981, with some filming still left to do and the cost of *Personal Best* now exceeding $12 million, Geffen and Warner Bros. decided to shut the movie down. Workers were dismissed, and security personnel put padlocks on the editing rooms so Towne could not enter them. Armed guards were stationed in front of these rooms, in case the director tried to break in. During this period, Towne later contended, Geffen was boasting in Hollywood that he would "completely destroy" the fledgling director through defamation and character assassination. Despite the padlocks, Towne was determined to get the picture done. In order to bring it back to life, he promised to give Warner Bros. the rights to one of his other scripts, *Greystoke* (about the original Tarzan legend), and let them have first negotiating rights to the screenplay of *Tequila Sunrise*. The filming of *Personal Best* resumed on June 10, 1981.

During the next six months, Towne and Geffen assiduously avoided one another, and the picture was completed. It opened in February of 1982, but not before Towne generated another brouhaha by refusing to put the film's credits at the opening (as was the norm) and insisting they go at the end. Geffen found this action intolerable and seized the final prints of the movie, took them to an optical company, and had the credits inserted, including his own, at the start of the film. Towne then accused Geffen of using more armed guards to prevent him from entering the production booths at theaters in New York and Los Angeles when the film had its bicoastal debut.

The film's final cost was estimated at $16 million. Ten weeks after being released, it had sold only $4.6 million worth of tickets. Although it got several decent reviews, it would be remembered as neither a box office hit nor a highly successful movie but as a bold attempt to bring a lesbian relationship to the screen. Geffen labeled the picture "a stiff" and "a nightmare for me" but also said that he liked parts of it. The film's release did not end the conflict between Geffen and Towne, or Geffen and Ovitz. Years later, as part of Towne's divorce proceeding, Geffen would give a sworn deposition suggesting that Towne had been using cocaine during the shooting of *Personal Best*.

David Geffen, people in Hollywood had begun saying, was the best friend one could possibly have, but the worst enemy. He loved settling scores, and he had a very long memory. Towne had learned these things and so would Ovitz.

In his $155 million lawsuit against Geffen and Warner Bros., Towne said, "This is not an isolated instance of Geffen using libel, slander, and other vindictive and coercive tactics to punish and coerce those with whom he deals and has disputes. Indeed, it is Geffen's practice to launch vicious, defamatory attacks and to employ other coercive tactics to gain his end in such situations."

The lawsuit was settled out of court, and Robert Towne's reputation was not destroyed. He went on to become a well-respected and highly-paid Hollywood "script doctor." Warner Bros. survived as well, and the most remarkable thing to come out of this imbroglio was Geffen's new movie deal with the studio and Steve Ross, which closely resembled his record label's arrangement with WCI. Under this five-year agreement, he would form a new entity—the David Geffen Film Company—which would make four pictures a year. He would select the movies, but Warner Bros. would help finance, distribute, market, and promote them. In spite of his recurring difficulties in the motion picture business, Ross was again willing to bet on Geffen. For the third time since 1972, he'd given the younger man virtually free reign with Warner's financial assets. In 1983, Geffen repaid Ross for his support by pledging, during media magnate Rupert Murdoch's unsuccessful attempt to take over WCI, that if Murdoch were running the company, he would bolt. Ross was grateful for the backing.

As Geffen did more deals in the film world, the tension between him and Michael Ovitz would increase, although it would not be acted out for years to come. By the mid-eighties, public criticism of Ovitz had fallen to a whisper, and even the irrepressible Geffen did not share his feelings about the agent with reporters. Ovitz and his many junior employees at CAA, who'd also read and absorbed *The Art of War,* had simply become too powerful and fearsome. Unlike Geffen, Ovitz did not encourage heated debate within the office, and almost no one inside the walls of CAA or beyond them raised his voice to the man.

One L.A. veteran, however, would prove not to be so reticent. Julia Phillips, a film insider who'd worked as a producer on *Flashdance* and *The Sting,* had developed a well-earned reputation as the official Hollywood Bad Girl. She was full of venom and liked nothing better than exercising it on the male-dominated movie industry. She was delightfully, at times irresistibly, vicious. In her book *You'll Never Eat Lunch in This Town Again,* she turned her sights on almost everyone, including Geffen and Ovitz. She characterized the former as a "little prick," whose "collagened face" made him look like a "middle-aged baby." Then she called him a "bad Jewish mother" and an "asshole."

Ovitz didn't fare as well. She labeled him the "Valley viper" and drew a comparison between him and the head of a rival talent agency, Jeff Berg of International Creative Management. Berg was known as a chilly presence, an intellectual who quoted William Wordsworth in meetings (terribly gauche in L.A.), and a lousy schmoozer. Naturally, his nickname became "Ice." "Jeff Berg," Phillips wrote, "was a caring person compared to this motherfucker" —Ovitz.

When show biz figures wanted a more human touch at CAA, they turned to Ovitz's first lieutenant, Ron Meyer. A handsome ex-marine with the ability to make both regular folks and superstars feel at ease, Meyer played the role of good cop at CAA to Ovitz's bad dude. Everyone got along with Meyer. Everyone called him "Ronnie" and said he was the real glue in the agency. Ovitz had the vision, but Ronnie had the heart, and everybody wanted to do business with him. Geffen found him charming.

CHAPTER 17

After an initial burst of publicity and sales at Geffen Records, it was becoming apparent that some of the older stars were not happy at the label. Neil Young felt that Geffen was seriously interfering with his creativity, and a lawsuit would follow, releasing Young from the company. Elton John and Geffen had had a spat after John refused to show up for the New York opening of *Cats;* he too wasn't long for the label. At the same time, it was clear that some of the newer acts—(Quarterflash, Was (Not Was)—were going to be short-lived. Geffen had used his past connections in the music world to sign this first wave of talent, but many industry people now felt that he was simply too out of touch with current trends to be able to find or sign a second wave.

In 1980, as Geffen Records was being launched, Patrick Goldstein became a rock critic for the *Los Angeles Times*. Goldstein had previously attended film school at Northwestern and worked for the

David Geffen sold his Asylum label to Steve Ross and MCA for the biggest number he could think of: $7 million. (AP/Wide World Photos)

In the early seventies Geffen had a mad fling with Cher, who dumped him for Gregg Allman. (Archive Photos)

While Geffen was recovering from his debacle with Cher, for a short time he moved in with Warren Beatty, seen here with wife Annette Bening. (Reuters/Fred Prouser/Archive Photos)

In the 1970s, before deciding he was gay, Geffen briefly lived with Marlo Thomas. (UPI/Corbis-Bettman)

Actress Kate Capshaw and husband Steven Spielberg, with a playful Geffen peeking his head through, arriving at the Carousel of Hope Gala, October 28, 1994. The event would raise $5 million for research into a cure for childhood diabetes. (Reuters/Fred Prouser/Archive Photos)

In the 1980s, Walter Yetnikoff, head of CBS Records, was the most powerful man in the music business—until Geffen brought him down. (AP/Wide World Photos)

Ahmet Ertegun, founder of the Atlantic label, recorded Geffen's first supergroup: Crosby, Stills, and Nash. (AP/Wide World Photos)

1990, CAA head Michael Ovitz
okered the sale of MCA/Universal to
e Japanese giant, Matsushita. The
ansaction made Geffen a billionaire.
.P/Wide World Photos)

In *L.A. Magazine,* Geffen called Michael Eisner, CEO of Disney, "a liar" and "a little bit woo-woo." (AP/Wide World Photos)

In the spring of 1995, Seagram's CEO Edgar Bronfman Jr. bought MCA/Universal, a move that ultimately changed the power landscape of Hollywood. (AP/Wide World Photos)

Katzenberg (*left*), Spielberg (*center*), and Geffen announcing plans to build a state-of-the-art studio at Playa Vista. (Reuters/Fred Prouser/Archive Photos)

Geffen, seen here with Joan Tisch, has given millions to AIDS causes. (Reuters/Mike Segar/ Archive Photos)

Geffen has not only been a huge contributor to the Clinton campaigns, he has also spent several nights in the Lincoln bedroom. From left to right: Barry Diller, Hillary Rodham Clinton, David Geffen, and Barbra Streisand. (Reuters/HO-APLA/Alan Berliner/Archive Photos)

After years of est, Lifespring, and other spiritual disciplines, Geffen has achieved a surprising inner peace. (Reuters/Sam Mircovich/Archive Photos)

Chicago Daily News. When he came to L.A. to start covering rock 'n' roll for the *Times,* one of his first articles was about the new record label in town. He went over to Geffen Records to meet the boss.

"I was totally charmed and captivated by David," says Goldstein, who is tall and has thinning reddish hair. Something in his long face and serious eyes evokes the self-portraits of Van Gogh. "When he wants to be, he can be extremely seductive. I wrote a very laudatory story about his goals and ambitions. Then I wrote a number of other pieces about him. Whenever you did a story on him, he made you feel that you were a part of this very attractive, exclusive club—the music business. You were an insider, and this club was his world. He let me come to his office, watch him at work, and listen to him on the phone. That's very unlike what a lot of Hollywood executives would do.

"For years, I wrote a Sunday music column, and at the end of each year, I'd rate the record companies in the column and report on how they'd done. Toward the end of 1982, I wrote about Geffen Records. I was being flippant and trying to be entertaining, so I wrote that the only difference between Geffen Records and the *Titanic* was that the *Titanic* had better bands. It was a pretty bratty thing to do, but I didn't give it any thought. I'm forty-four now, but fourteen years ago, I was just a punk, and that was an adolescent remark. Frankly, I didn't realize how much impact something you said in print could have on others.

"David reacted very badly. He interpreted it as a mean-spirited, negative comment that made his company look bad. He had this ongoing feud with Irving Azoff, who'd once worked for Geffen and been David's protégé. Irving, being a very mischievous person—that's the nicest word I've ever used to describe him—apparently began taking credit inside music circles for my remark. He was saying, 'I told Patrick to use that line. I gave it to him.' He thought that would aggravate David even more, and it did. David got real pissed off and didn't call me up, but various intermediaries did call me and let me know what he was feeling.

"Irving and David had this weird, complicated thing going on. During the eighties, they both liked to feed it. It's part of what kept them going—the action and the tumult. It was inevitable that they would feud, because they're so similar. When David doesn't want to deal with people he doesn't like, he always says, 'Life's too short,' but he's had too many fights not to enjoy it on some level. He almost always had a falling out with his various father figures in the business. He would gravitate toward them and then be disappointed.

"About nine months after I wrote the remark about his company, I ran into David at a movie premiere. There were a lot of big shots there talking to one another. I was standing and speaking with a very powerful rock manager who had at least one band on Geffen's label. Before the lights went down, I heard someone scream out my name. I looked around, and there's David three or four rows away, and he's shouting at me, 'You idiot! What kind of a thing is that to write?' I'm, like, totally embarrassed. The rock manager I was talking to dived under his seat, so David wouldn't see him with me. David kept yelling at me. I let him do this for a while, and then he got tired and sat down. I was too stunned to say anything.

"After that, whenever I needed to talk to someone from his company, I contacted other people there. Time passed and I finally called him up for something. He got on the phone and spoke to me. We were civil with each other. I never apologized to him, but I said that if I had it to do all over again, I might have handled it differently."

Throughout the next decade, Goldstein wrote stories about the record company, and in 1993, he interviewed Geffen for *Rolling Stone*. Two years earlier, Geffen had referred to him in *BAM* magazine, an L.A. music publication, as an "idiot," clearly establishing that all was neither forgotten nor forgiven. The testy atmosphere that existed for the *Rolling Stone* interview was palpable enough to come through in the article itself. Pat Goldstein is no doubt many things to many people, but when he reflects on events and individuals, he does not remotely conjure up an "idiot."

"David is very controlling and very guarded with his emotions," he said one morning in a delicatessen on the west side of Los Angeles, where he was having oatmeal and coffee. "He can be outspoken about public issues or Hollywood personalities, but he's very quiet about his private life. His connection to his family is fascinating. He seems to have had a very distant and disappointing relationship with his father. I think that may be the key to him, instead of his relationship with his mother. His mother was, in many ways, an archetypal Jewish mother. She clearly had a big influence on his work ethic and his sense of being a pragmatist. She gave him his drive and ambition. What's more difficult to figure out is his father's influence. His father was sort of a withdrawn academic, but David doesn't celebrate him as a great thinker or a cerebral man. He focuses on the fact that he was not especially good at making a living. He was not a realist, and I think that's the clue to what shaped David. Because he is, above all, a realist.

"He saw his father as someone who was impotent, and David didn't want to go down that road. He wanted to be what his father wasn't. He wanted to be in the real world, not the ivory tower. And he wanted to have power, like his father never did. When you look at the background of a lot of powerful men, you see them trying to please their fathers or live up to their expectations. But in David's case, he just didn't want to end up like his father."

After emerging from the *Personal Best* contretemps, Geffen soon put together a number of other movie deals. Working with two of his employees, Eric Eisner and former *New York Times Magazine* editor Lynda Obst, Geffen created a "ministudio" within his company. His first production was *Risky Business,* about a teenager who, as part of his sexual awakening, decides to turn his parents' home into a bordello. The movie introduced a new young star, Tom Cruise, who did a dance routine in his underwear that had both sexes jumping in their seats. Paul Brickman had written the script, and its original ending had the Cruise character failing to achieve his main goal—getting accepted into Princeton University.

As is common practice in the film industry, *Risky Business* was tested on audiences before its release, and only 38 percent of the viewers said they would recommend the movie (the average recommendation rate is 44 percent). Over the protests of Brickman, Geffen, ever the realist, insisted that they add two minutes to the ending and allow the young man to be accepted into Princeton. In Geffen's view, this would let "the nerds in the audience" feel they'd won something. Since most people had at least a small element of nerdism lurking within them, and since Geffen himself was highly sympathetic to nerds everywhere, he felt certain that this change would have a dramatic impact on the film's popularity.

With a new ending, fit to his specifications, the movie's approval rating shot up to 70 percent. *Risky Business* grossed more than $120 million, and Geffen had produced his first genuinely successful film.

And yet, his feel for motion pictures was not quite as predictable or assured as his touch with the recording industry. He leaned toward the offbeat and went against the grain of the big-budget, star-driven pictures CAA and other Hollywood agencies were now making the norm. Geffen's next few pictures included *After Hours,* director Martin Scorsese's black comedy about a couple's all-night journey through the SoHo district of Manhattan, *Lost in America,* an Albert Brooks movie that constantly seemed in search of a purpose and a theme, and *Little Shop of Horrors,* which featured a people-eating plant. Geffen's next real hit was several years away, with the outlandish *Beetlejuice.*

With all these deals in the air, it was inevitable that the national media would start to drift back to Geffen. It was also inevitable that all sorts of rumors would surround his personal life. A sliver of gossip in the early eighties had him marrying the actress-director Penny Marshall. When Geffen's mother called up and asked her son if this was true, he said no, and she expressed disappointment. (On the other hand, when he finally told her that he was gay, Batya, a realist herself, shrugged and said, "We'd known.")

Near the end of 1982, the courageous editors of *Esquire* decided that it was time to ask one of their intrepid reporters to call the man up and ask if he would like to be profiled once again in their pages. The general public may have forgotten some or all of *Esquire's* 1975 cover story on Cher and Geffen, but the memory of the article was seared into his mind and the wounds were not yet closed. When journalist Robert Sam Anson phoned Geffen and made the offer, the entertainment exec instantaneously went from calm to crazy, thereby providing Anson with one of the great leads in the history of magazine writing:

David Geffen is on the phone [the story began], and he is not happy.... David Geffen is batshit.

"'*In-ter-view?* he screeches. You interview *me?* You have *got,* you know, I mean, you have *got* to be kidding.... Do you *know* what your magazine did to me the last time? Do you *know?*... Reading that article was the *worst single moment of my life.* Do you *know what I did after I read that article?* Do you *know?* I threw up, that's what I did. *I threw up!* And then do you know what I did? *I left the country!* I went to *Brazil! Brazil!* Do you know that? For *six months!*

That article nearly caused a breakdown! Do you hear that? *Breakdown!* Now you want me to do it *again!* Do you think I'm crazy? Is that what you think? That I'm *crazy?*'

"He doesn't wait for an answer. In a rush, he is reciting how busy he is, the film deals he has pending, the trips he is taking, the artists he is signing, a million impossible mouths all begging to be fed. He doesn't *want* publicity, David Geffen is saying. Doesn't *need* publicity....

"'David,' you finally say, 'what time do you want to see me?'

"'*Oy,*' he sighs. 'Four o'clock. Thursday. My apartment. Next to the Pierre.' The line goes dead."

Geffen had long conjured up the kind of radio talk show host—loud, abrasive, tempestuous, comic—who was becoming more and more popular on the national airwaves. He was in essence a performer, who despite all his protests could not quite resist the opportunity to see what his next performance might be. His style combined that of a New York screamer with a Southern California seeker of enlightenment. His roots were always warring with his desire for a higher state of grace. It was a pitched battle, and he came across as disjointed in the Robert Sam Anson *Esquire* article. He was a more interesting man than he'd been seven years earlier, before his cancer scare, but he was still going in all directions at once, pursuing his next dollar. Geffen had more money now, more fame and more art, but the subtle underlying challenge remained the same: How does anyone really grow up?

Cash was everywhere, but more intangible things remained elusive.

After Neil Young bolted Geffen Records over creative differences, he joyfully celebrated his leaving the label, he once confessed to *Rolling Stone,* by smoking a huge joint. It was a very pointed slap at Geffen, who years later said that the two biggest disappointments in his career came from his breakups with Laura Nyro, after she spurned Asylum for CBS Records, and with Neil Young. Young had a shaky voice, and his guitar playing was never polished, but he represented something in the world of rock—a commitment to his music and a refusal to conform to anything—that made up the defining spirit of the art form. As much as anyone, he had the heart of a rocker. He was grating and insinuating, especially during the eighties, when America was enmeshed in materialism, and he haunted people who wondered if they'd sold themselves cheap.

Throughout his years in the record business, Geffen was vulnerable to the charge that he was more concerned with money than with music. As he got older and grew more distant from his own bands, this accusation took on more substance. For him, critics said, the deal was always the art form, not the album (or the film) itself. He knew nothing about making records or shooting movies, knew far less about the creative process than, say, an Ahmet Ertegun or a Louis B. Mayer. He was a mediator between talent and commerce, who'd seen a great opportunity and seized it.

Following their breakup, Neil Young said bitterly that he did not fit in with David Geffen's marketing plan. For once, Geffen did not lash out at someone who'd ripped him but tacitly acknowledged that without spirits like Young, there would have been no rock 'n' roll and no business for Geffen to enter when he was just starting out at William Morris. Young had something that Geffen was still groping for.

"David always wanted legitimacy," says George Trow. "My essential criticism of him was that he found his sense of legitimacy only where the next hit is, and that's not good for an important American man. If you go back to someone like Louis B. Mayer, you'll see that there was a style to MGM, and a standard that was maintained there. Mayer wouldn't make just anything or just go wherever the next hit was. He stood for something.

"But I try to give David his due. He has a genius for making money. He isn't just another guy in show business, any more than Rockefeller was just another guy in the oil business. Yet Geffen, like many rich people, is insecure about his cultural tendencies. When people like this get to the top, they just want to buy the best of everything to cover up those insecurities and tendencies. He has taste and understands our generation of the sixties very well. He has a magical instinct for the commercial side of that, so I'm not surprised by his success. But he has no sense for what has meaning."

CHAPTER 18

In his sarcastic reference to the *Titanic* in his *L.A. Times* music column, Patrick Goldstein turned out to be prophetic about the Geffen Records bands. Geffen himself would later confess that the label didn't turn a profit during its first twenty-four quarters. By the mid-eighties, he was faced with a tough decision: either pull back or make a strong commitment to doing something differently. His contract with Warner Bros. expired in 1985, and if he wanted to renew his agreement with Steve Ross—or sell the company to him—he needed a better bottom line. If Geffen Records was going to become a genuine success, he also had to confront the reality that he was no longer on the cutting edge of the music field.

In a word, rock had gotten harder, while Geffen's ears, like those of many in his generation, had grown softer. Baby Boomers who'd once cherished the sound of Jimi Hendrix's exploding guitar had trouble understanding the loud, harsh racket that newer bands were making. In the past, Geffen had not generally recorded groups whose material he didn't like, but he was over forty now and had ceased being the target audience for his own products; at night, he went home and listened to Mozart or Ella Fitzgerald. It was a time of transition for him—not something every executive can survive, especially in a field as relentlessly hip as the music business. No one can ride the trends forever, and if his label was going to prosper in the future, Geffen realized, he needed outside help. He needed younger people in A&R.

In the forties and fifties, the artists and repertoire arm of record companies had been crucial. A&R was not only responsible for deciding who recorded what songs on LPs but occasionally commissioned tunes from composers for an upcoming album. Many A&R people, such as Mitch Miller, Percy Faith, and Hugo Winterhalter, had once performed in big bands and were trained as arrangers. They'd played a hands-on role in the studio until the end of the fifties, when rock took over and the new bands wrote and arranged their own material. In the new era, only producer George Martin, the "fifth Beatle," had risen to prominence in this capacity. Since most rock groups had little use for A&R types, conflict became inevitable. By the mid-sixties, the joke in the music industry was that A&R now stood for "arguments and recriminations." In the seventies and eighties, A&R evolved into the branch of the business that signed new bands, handled them for record companies, and "broke" them on the pop charts.

At Geffen Records, the A&R department had recently consisted of Eddie Rosenblatt, Carol Childs, and—because he was a born spotter and signer of talent—the owner himself. Now Geffen brought in John David Kolodner, who wore long, flowing white robes around the office and collected exotic firearms. He had a rock-'n'-roll ear and was soon handling singer Sammy Hagar and an English heavy metal group called Whitesnake, comprised of former Deep Purple, former Thin Lizzy, and former Juicy Lucy members. Kalodner also wanted to sign Aerosmith, a formerly hot act that had turned stone cold.

This East Coast band, which had long evoked a kind of poor man's Rolling Stones, had had great success a decade earlier, before enjoying themselves too much and descending into rock decadence. Kalodner felt he could resurrect them and went to Geffen for his blessing. Although Aerosmith had created a sound that was beyond Geffen's ken—(too hard and insistent)—he told Kalodner to follow his gut. Kalodner signed them, Geffen invested a million dollars in recording and promoting the band, and the pronounced lips of their lead singer, Steven Tyler, were suddenly all over the MTV screen. Their 1985 album, *Done With Mirrors,* and their 1987 disc, *Permanent Vacation,* both went multi-platinum.

In 1986, Kalodner wanted to sign another washed-up singer: Cher. When he went to his boss with this suggestion, Geffen told him that Cher was catlike and had at least nine professional lives. She was just starting to become known as an actress, so it was the right moment to make her a revamped recording star for their label. And nothing in Geffen's tormented past with Cher was going to stand in the way of business. Never mind how terrible their parting had been for him. Forget how she'd called him short and ugly in the vaunted pages of *Time.* In the grand Hollywood tradition, the two of them made up and then made a deal. Cher was soon gracing the rock video market as a high-stepping, barely clad, chart-climbing phenomenon, who'd reincarnated herself as an indefatigable rocker. Kalodner had been right again.

Geffen also hired A&R man Gary Gersh, one of the industry's most sought-after talent scouts, who'd lately been working at EMI with the Stray Cats and the J. Geils Band. At Geffen Records, he began handling Peter Gabriel, Robbie Robertson, and Rickie Lee Jones; in years ahead, he would land one of the biggest acts at the label. Gersh and Kalodner were great additions to the company, but the star A&R hire turned out to be Tom Zutaut, who'd grown up playing the tuba and reading magazine articles about a young record exec named David Geffen. As a teenager in Illinois, Zutaut decided that's who he wanted to be when he grew up.

At twenty-two, while working at Elektra, "Zut" had talked some dubious record executives into signing a vivid heavy metal band called Mötley Crüe. The Crüe, following a style embraced by the New York Dolls, wore high heels and makeup onstage. They had once been considered a laughingstock on the L.A. music scene but when they hit big at Elektra with *Shout at the Devil,* a Top Fifty album, Zutaut was launched as a prophet. At twenty-three, he moved to Geffen Records and began handling Edie Brickell and the New Bohemians, plus Tesla and Enya. More important, he went down on the street and hunted for undiscovered L.A. bands. He walked along Melrose Avenue, certainly the coolest stretch of pavement in America, and slipped into the small clothing or music shops where young people were making cottage industries out of nose rings and tattoos. He asked around for tips: Who were the kids running these stores listening to? What did they want to hear on CDs or on the radio? What new bands hadn't been recorded yet? Then he went out and found the groups they'd told him about.

In his *Rolling Stone* interview with Pat Goldstein, Geffen returned to one of his favorite themes when describing Kalodner, Gersh, and Zutaut. They were, he said, "fabulously talented nerds...I love nerds. I was a nerd and I feel good about that. There's a nerdy part in all of us—the part that has turmoil, neuroses, angst, desire, and dreams. These people [in his A&R department] get to be exactly who they are."

Geffen still negotiated contracts, massaged the sales numbers, and occasionally romanced new acts before signing them, but he'd learned to step aside and let these younger men work the streets. He didn't have to listen to the bands they were bringing him, and he didn't have to like their sounds; he just had to sell their products.

The increasingly harsh new music of the 1980s was not occurring in a vacuum but symbolized a number of things that were unfolding during the Reagan presidency. With a true believer in unfettered capitalism in the White House, American business had now returned to the business of expanding its own business. The eighties were go-go years for many corporations and private individuals, especially in Southern California, where real estate prices were escalating by the month. For those who already owned land, homes, or commercial buildings, the local cliché was that you could fall out of bed in the morning and earn a bundle. Consumption was high, and appearances were exceedingly important. You didn't go shopping on Rodeo Drive now without being dressed to the nines—or you'd get the bum's rush. Money filled the air, and for hundreds of thousands of people, it was a time of fiscal abundance. In the mid-eighties, David Geffen's net worth, for example, was estimated at more than $200 million.

Beneath and behind all that cash came the loud, grinding sound of young people trying to discover something new in the world of rock, while other developments indicated that all was not well below the surface of the well-dressed eighties. Some people were growing richer, but others were being left behind. Men were dying by the thousands from AIDS, the baffling disease that had visited itself mostly upon the gay communities of big cities across the nation. A few homosexual activists had raised their voices toward the Reagan administration, in the hope that it would pay more attention to this problem, but their early efforts had gone nowhere.

In L.A., under the leadership of police chief Daryl Gates, race relations between blacks and whites were growing meaner, but conventional wisdom said that adding more cops to the force would probably defuse all this. Homeless people were living on the streets of all metropolitan areas, but you could move many of them along by taking away park benches in public spaces or not allowing them to sleep on the sidewalks. Couples were getting divorced in record numbers, juvenile crime was rising, and cocaine had taken a nasty turn, being transformed into the more addictive drug known as crack, which was permeating the black community. Crack-peddling gangs were taking over inner-city neighborhoods, killing one another over money or murdering those who ventured onto their turf. And some people saw a creeping meanness everywhere.

Music had definitely gotten meaner. Black rap was edged with violence, and some elements of white rock or heavy metal were simply ugly—screaming lyrics and guitar work that made the sixties seem acoustic. AM radio was getting nastier as well. Talk show hosts were becoming wealthy by insulting people and hanging up on them, while several notable comics were gaining fame by insulting gays, women, minorities, and most everyone else. Tastelessness and bad manners were growth industries. Movies were increasingly blood-filled, with new revenge heroes like Chuck Norris, Steven Seagal, and Sylvester Stallone replacing the older ones like Charles Bronson and Clint Eastwood. Despite all that money in the air, everyone seemed to be afraid of something.

With President Reagan in the White House, the media took a brusque turn to the religious right. In 1979, the Reverend Jerry Falwell of the Thomas Road Baptist Church in Lynchburg, Virginia, started the Moral Majority, a lobbying and political action group. The Moral Majority began campaigning nationwide against abortion, pornography, homosexuality, and other forms of "immorality." The group soon had 6.5 million members. By the mid-eighties, one thousand of the nation's 9,642 radio stations and two hundred local TV stations were broadcasting programs affiliated with fundamentalist Christianity. To cite the popularity of only one of those programs, 16.3 million of the country's 80 million television households watched Pat Robertson's evangelical show, *The 700 Club,* at least once a month. In 1985, the Christian Broadcasting Network of Virginia Beach, Virginia, estimated that half of all Americans with a TV set watched one or more of the sixty nationally syndicated religious programs currently being aired. Fundamentalists opened and ran ten thousand day schools for small children and thousands more grade schools across the country. The American Coalition for Traditional Values, a collection of evangelical groups, lobbied in Washington, D.C., for a quota system that would legislate having at least 25 percent of the government's employees share the fundamentalist faith.

All of this activity revealed a spiritual hunger that was permeating the American public, but it also revealed a set of beliefs. While each of the various sects that made up the religious right had certain unique convictions, they generally had one thing in common: they found homosexuality to be a sin, and many of them were convinced that it was not a biological precondition but a "lifestyle choice." If one wanted to stop being gay, went this reasoning, one could simply select another kind of sexual behavior. And if one didn't make this change, the argument concluded, one could look forward to more devastation from diseases such as AIDS. God was punishing people for their sins. It was a grim time to be gay, and a grimmer time to be sick. The gay community, which had flexed its social and political muscles in the seventies, was now trying to cope with its own frustration, anger, and death.

Geffen himself had many friends who were dying of AIDS. He'd begun keeping a card for each one who perished, and the stack was getting thicker all the time. In 1986, he went to get his own HIV blood test, convinced that he was already infected with the virus and in danger of losing his life, yet he did not test positive for HIV and was in good health. Greatly relieved, he recommitted himself to the practice of safe sex. That same year, he received a letter from Bill Miller, another friend of his who'd recently died from AIDS. The letter had been mailed posthumously by a Miller acquaintance, and in it the dying man told Geffen that because of his enormous success, he'd become a role model to young gay men and had a responsibility to set a good example for them. Geffen was moved by this sentiment and felt that Miller's words were appropriate. He would try to do what his late friend had suggested, but he would do it quietly, the way he'd always done things in this arena, because his sexuality was no one else's business.

Under the crust of America in the 1980s, there was a war going on, although it rarely flared into outright violence. More time would pass before those who opposed abortion would take up arms and kill doctors; or before racial animosity would explode into rioting; or before gang drive-by shootings would be commonplace in some urban landscapes. More time would pass before gay activists decided that they had nothing to lose and should start making some bitter noise.

The war was being fought on many fronts and over many issues, but it was largely a struggle over what kind of a country America was going to become: a land of immense diversity, where tolerance prevailed, or a land where fear of the present and the future, fear of differences and of the unknown, would render people even angrier and more intolerant. The war was being fought in bodies and souls across the nation, while people went about the business of earning a living. And there was loud, angry rock building in the background.

Up in America's Northwest, strong coffee and "grunge" music were about to become synonymous. The grunge phenomenon erupted in the early nineties and was strangely reminiscent of the sixties, but this time neither marijuana nor LSD would be the drug of choice. Geffen Records, naturally, was scouting the scene in Seattle and would land one of the biggest bands there, when Gary Gersh signed Nirvana.

"In the late eighties, only the local people knew about groups like Nirvana, Pearl Jam, Soundgarden, Mud Honey, and Alice in Chains," says a young woman named Amy Amatucci, a Generation X music fan who lived in Seattle in those years. "Everyone followed these bands and was real close. The music was all about attitude, dress, and coffee. And being a slacker, where you could fake your way through anything. We were real cynical kids back then. I was only seventeen, eighteen, nineteen. A lot of us had come from broken homes and had been on our own for a long time. By the time we were twenty, we were burned out. We didn't really believe in anything.

"You drank, you did drugs, you hung out on the streets of Capitol Hill and downtown. That's where the music scene was and the coffee shops. The music was a mixture of punk and heavy metal. There was big hair, and the music had a hard-core edge. No one called it grunge. That was coined later by the media. The word 'grunge' got tied in with the laid-back attitude in Seattle. People don't dress up there, and there's this apathy in the air. You wanted to wear dirty clothes or thrashed clothes and have colored hair or dreads and look scruffy. You didn't want to bathe. People weren't very clean.

"I hung with punks, street kids, drug dealers, and gays. The music was for everyone. The bands played in warehouses and small venues. It was a very local, intimate scene for a while. It was just our way of life, not something we thought the whole country wanted to get in on."

When Geffen himself first heard Nirvana, he admitted to his A&R department that he couldn't make out a word the band was singing or make any sense of the music. But he signed the act, and

Nirvana's first album, *Nevermind,* contained the single "Smells Like Teen Spirit," which became the anthem for the grunge movement. It was the number one song in America, Greece, and several other countries.

"The publicity hit Seattle when Nirvana came out with *Nevermind,*" says Amy. "That blew the doors off the music scene and opened the way for everyone to go mainstream and make money. The movie *Singles* came out of our scene. It's mostly Hollywood bullshit. Once Nirvana hit MTV, we knew it would never be the same. The drugs got more intense. It was no longer so safe."

Nirvana's lead singer was Kurt Cobain.

"I heard that Kurt was a junkie," says Amy. "Heroin was completely available but not necessarily acceptable. But no one was gonna say anything to you if you were a junkie. Everyone else had their own problems. Seattle's a depressing place. It rains all the time, and you have to drink coffee all day to keep yourself going. That's why it's the caffeine mecca. They don't call it the suicide capital for nothing."

In the early nineties, Kurt Cobain married Courtney Love after she became pregnant.

"Nirvana had a definite dark side and cynicism," Amy says. "It wasn't heavy metal, but more like angst, depressed, morose. Angry angst. That's what we felt about everything going on around us. Angry about the adult world and the way things were. Angry about all the opportunists. Courtney Love wasn't around until Nirvana got popular. She was out of L.A., and her music sucked. Seattle people didn't want people like Courtney Love coming around and riding our wave. That's when you knew the scene was pretty much over and it was time to move on."

In 1994, Kurt Cobain committed suicide by shooting himself in the head.

"When Kurt died, it was a very big deal in Seattle," Amy says. "People were stunned, devastated. He killed himself because of all that heroin and because he dropped their baby when it was very small. People were angry that he shot himself. He was one of our own. He exemplified what we were all feeling: burned-out and hopeless, but that's also what kept you going. You were muddling through the mess, the anger and sadness all around you. You got through it by listening to the music and going out and partying with your friends. Then for someone that public to kill himself..." Amy pauses briefly. "He did it in his house, outside of Seattle. An electrician found him.

"We saw ourselves as an alternative to the mainstream, because the mainstream sucked. We listened to loud, obnoxious music and did a lot of drugs and didn't want to be what our parents wanted us to be. It was a useless rebellion, and we were rebels without a clue. We thought we were being so different, but when all the other people started copying us, it ended up looking like everything else. It became the mainstream, and then passé. I moved to Tulsa and haven't been back."

CHAPTER 19

The spiritual hunger that was motivating the religious right was also playing a role in Geffen's life and business affairs. By the mid-eighties, the New Age movement, as this phenomenon had labeled itself, was becoming pervasive in Southern California. Its most popular figurehead was Shirley MacLaine, the author of a book about her own inner journey, called *Out on a Limb*. The mass media seized upon MacLaine's ideas about reincarnation and visitations from outer space, and she became the butt of myriad jokes about past-life experiences and other unprovable events. The New Age was often reported on as if it were one large bazaar, where people bought and sold crystals or astrological charts, because the more subtle aspects of the movement were harder to penetrate. While Geffen himself was not a New Age devotee, his ongoing exploration of things like est, Lifespring, intensive psychotherapy, and Marianne Williamson's Course in Miracles placed him under the emerging spiritual umbrella.

If there was truth in some of the media's characterizations of the New Age movement as flaky, there was also truth in another direction. On an individual level, the New Age phenomenon was about the attempt to interpret reality in nontraditional ways and to explore hidden aspects of one's consciousness without the use of drugs or other stimulants. Surrounding the movement were also some very practical principles, often lost in the talk about reincarnation. Geffen, being a highly practical man, was drawn to such things and applied them to his business.

The credo of the New Age businessman might go like this: You are honest with yourself and very clear about what you are trying to create. You make and keep agreements. You do not allow yourself to be a victim or a victimizer of others. You learn to separate your emotions from your creations, so that you are not controlled by how others respond to what you do and are free to go on and create again. You acknowledge, but do not allow yourself to be controlled by, fear. You have a sense of inner freedom. Geffen was born with some of these qualities, but learning to hone them only helped him in the workplace.

"Early on, David had a real reputation as an asshole," says one Hollywood observer. "A screamer and a nasty little guy. There was a story about a rock manager named Brian Rohan punching David at the Beverly Hills Hotel during a luncheon that was being hosted by Clive Davis. Rohan supposedly got forty congratulatory telegrams from other people in the music business for doing this. The anecdote has been exaggerated—maybe Rohan got ten telegrams—but the point still stands. If you're as aggressive and volatile as David Geffen, you're going to anger your share of people. I think David's always wanted to learn more about himself and his behavior, in order to find freedom from himself. I admire him for going into these self-help courses and trying to change. That isn't easy for any of us.

"In our culture in the past twenty years, especially growing out of rock 'n' roll and out of Southern California psycho-speak, another way of doing business has evolved, and David is the best example of it. He has great flexibility and adaptability, but it goes beyond that. It's about being able to reveal to people who you really are while doing deals together. Someone like Michael Ovitz could never do this, but Geffen can say to you, in effect, 'Hell yes, I'm insecure and neurotic, but I'm gonna find strength in that and see how far I can go.' For others to do this would be a sign of weakness and vulnerability, but Geffen has made it work for himself."

▪ ▪ ▪

When Geffen's initial five-year record company agreement with WCI was nearing expiration, he went to Steve Ross to renegotiate their deal. He asked Ross for $5 million now, against future profits. For once, Ross declined to do as Geffen asked and made a counterproposal. He wanted to renew their deal for six more years, until 1990, but instead of giving Geffen a $5 million advance, he offered him 100 percent of the label. In the past, they'd shared ownership, but under this new arrangement, the company would be Geffen's free and clear. The younger man wasn't used to being told no, especially by Ross, and this offer rankled him. Despite these feelings, he agreed to Ross's idea and assumed full ownership of Geffen Records. It was the smartest—or luckiest—move he ever made.

If Ross wasn't willing to bet on the label boss now, Geffen continued to gamble on himself, expanding his assets in several directions at once. Late in 1984, he sold eighteen pieces of Tiffany glass at auction at Christie's in New York. They included three leaded-glass and bronze lamps, two bronze-framed mirrors, and thirteen vases, for a total sale price of $1.2 million. Geffen used the money to buy more modern paintings by Magritte and David Hockney, also paying $770,000 for a Sam Francis canvas at Christie's. He'd developed a routine of rewarding himself for a deal well done at the office with the purchase of a new piece of art. The major auction houses in New York were always glad to see him arrive, even if their other patrons were in suits and ties and he was clad in blue jeans and a T-shirt, and sporting a couple of days' worth of stubble. Looks aside, he knew how to handle a bidding paddle. Several months after selling the Tiffany glass, he was named one of six new trustees at the Los Angeles County Museum of Art.

He had three motion pictures in the works—*Lost in America, After Hours,* and *Little Shop of Horrors*—and was putting together the deal for *Beetlejuice*. This 1988 film, directed by Tim Burton and starring Michael Keaton, also featured a promising young actress named Geena Davis. Its offbeat story, about a hyperactive dead man who rises from the grave and torments the living, didn't initially seem to hold much mass appeal. Geffen felt otherwise, and the film had the largest opening ever for an Easter weekend.

On Broadway, *Cats* was still running, while Geffen had several other plays on the boards. The comedy, *Social Security,* ran for eleven months in 1986 and 1987. *M. Butterfly* opened in March of 1988 and ran for nearly two years, winning three Tony awards, including the 1988 honor for best play. Geffen would also help finance two upcoming musicals, *Miss Saigon* and Stephen Sondheim's short-lived *Assassins*.

On the real estate side, he purchased two more properties in Beverly Hills. The largest one would eventually hold the 287,000 square-foot building that housed the film company Castle Rock Entertainment; in 1995, its assessed value would be more than $71 million.

David Geffen, the miniconglomerate, was growing monthly, but by far the most significant work being done within this empire was at his music label. One of Geffen's leading A&R men, the hefty, baby-faced Tom Zutaut, was as interested in developing new bands and getting them to write better material as he was in discovering an overnight success. One afternoon, he ventured into Vinyl Fetish, a Melrose Avenue record shop, and asked the clerk if he'd heard anything good lately. The answer was yes, and the band was called Guns n' Roses. Zutaut listened to the group, then brought them into the office one afternoon, leaving them in the reception room while he attended to some other details. Geffen walked into the room and saw four young men lounging there, a long-haired, slovenly, badly dressed quartet, even by rock's standards. They appeared broke and disreputable. They even smelled funky.

Geffen found Zutaut and asked who they were. When the A&R man said, "Guns n' Roses," the boss shrugged and replied that they looked as if they didn't have a nickel.

"They don't," Zut said.

In 1987, Guns n' Roses released *Appetite for Destruction*, which sold nine million copies. Geffen Records had just broken one of the biggest acts of the decade and made $13 million on sales of this album alone. Guns n' Roses' next disc sold five million copies, and the band's lead singer, Axl Rose, became one of rock's new bad boys, with a huge gift for self-publicity and stepping in trouble.

"It's a miracle," Geffen once told *Rolling Stone*, "that certain people can survive the fame they get at an early age. I mean, Axl Rose—one minute he's sleeping in doorways, a minute later he's a multimillionaire and every girl wants to fuck him. That's very hard to deal with."

In addition to Guns n' Roses, Geffen Records now had Whitesnake, Aerosmith, Cher, Don Henley, and Peter Gabriel, all of which added up to 8 percent of domestic LP sales. The label's A&R department now became even more aggressive. In 1987, Zutaut hired twenty-eight-year-old Vicky Hamilton as a full time talent scout—a radical move in a field dominated by men. Hamilton had lately been known on L.A.'s music scene as a hard-rock den mother, who got bands gigs, fed them, put them up in her home, gave them money, and kept them going. She followed groups named Poison, Darling Cruel, Salty Dog, and Faster Pussycat from club to club, and when she heard someone new and worth pursuing, she immediately phoned or faxed Zutaut. Late at night, while Geffen was sleeping in his beach house, or watching a video, or out on a date, Hamilton was scouring the darkness for talent, doing the kind of legwork many larger record labels had gotten away from.

The company hired two more twenty-something "street scouts," Mio Vukovic and Anna Statman. Vukovic had been working at Scream, an underground club, while Statman had been at Slash, a tiny independent label. Both were given full signing power, meaning that they could commit $200,000 to $400,000 of Geffen Records capital to a group, for recording, touring, video, and promotion expenses. The company hired tape listeners—Mario Niles and Todd Sullivan—who passed judgment on the endless flow of tapes that came into the office on Sunset Boulevard.

Then Geffen hired a pair of "undercover agents," whose names were never given to the media and who went to clubs incognito, so that no one would associate them with the label. The agents went out five evenings a week, hitting Gazzari's on Sunset Boulevard, the Whisky on the Strip, Bogart's on the Pacific Coast Highway, Club Lingerie, and the Coconut Teaszer. While their boss was on the phone arranging Broadway financing or raising money for films, the "Geffen Night Patrol" was busy turning his company into the best independent label in the business.

"In the mid-eighties, David was smart enough to realize that Geffen Records had to sign bands that did not speak to him personally," says *L.A. Times* rock critic Patrick Goldstein. "He kept total control of the promotion, marketing, and distribution deals with the new bands, but he let the younger people find the new acts and bring them in. David would always tell you that he might not know the names of the songs his bands played, but he could tell you their positions on the charts and the air play they were receiving.

And when his A&R staff needed someone to impress a new artist to get him signed, David knew how to woo musicians, even when he understood nothing about their music.

"What he understood, really, was the rock-'n'-roll game. Geffen Records wanted cutting-edge bands in the late eighties, and part of being on the cutting edge was being angry and rebellious. Guns n' Roses were always misbehaving in David's office, and there are stories of them trashing Geffen Records and breaking windows." Another L.A. rock band had a lead singer who was "apparently crazy," Goldstein says. "Tom Zutaut signed her, and they had a disagreement, and she jumped up on his desk and peed on it. What was intriguing was that the record company didn't try to cover this up but used it as a publicity gimmick. It gave the singer a cachet and made her seem outrageous."

Goldstein concludes, "A lot of music executives are great in only one era, but David could move from the sensitive rock of the seventies to the hard rock of the eighties and on into the grunge sound of the nineties. He could do this because he surrounded himself with good people and gave them power and responsibility. In the eighties, Geffen Records had the best rock executives around. Eddie Rosenblatt was the best president of a record company, and the A&R staff was the very best in the business. You surround yourself with these people, throw in a little magic and luck, and you're going to be successful."

The talent scouts were expected to fight for their bands, and heated arguments were commonplace. Geffen encouraged the heat and always acted as a final arbiter in serious disputes, labeling himself "the keeper of the asylum." As Lynda Obst, who worked on Geffen's film production side, once put it, the boss was "hipper than his staff." He didn't try to protect employees from conflict or talk them into staying with his company if he felt they would be better off elsewhere. People who looked to him as a parental figure were often disappointed. Years later, however, some of them realized that they'd benefited from the way he'd handled them.

"In retrospect," Obst wrote in her Hollywood autobiography, *Hello, He Lied,* "I am profoundly grateful to David Geffen for having been, for me, so hard to please. At the same time, he gave me something he was uniquely qualified to give: the highest standards. I never felt, at any given moment I worked for him, that I was living up to his expectations. Had he been easy for me to please, had I seen him as an approving father, I might have stayed there forever, locked into the powerful hook of perfect daddy and performing-seal daughter. But I was afraid that there were no tricks I could perform for David that would make him flip. In the end, the withholding father I turned him into turned out to be better for me—he helped push me out of the nest. Otherwise, I would have been afraid to fly."

After leaving Geffen, Obst went on to form her own production company. There she made *The Fisher King* and *Sleepless in Seattle.*

CHAPTER 20

By the late eighties, Michael Ovitz had consolidated his grip on the film business in Hollywood. His list of directors included Rob Reiner, Oliver Stone, John Hughes, David Lynch, Ron Howard, Richard Attenborough, and Jonathan Demme. A few of his actors and actresses were named Robert De Niro, Whoopi Goldberg, Glenn Close, Bette Midler, Demi Moore, Sean Connery, Danny DeVito, Michael Douglas, Robin Williams, Val Kilmer, Tom Cruise, Sally Field, Dennis Hopper, and Al Pacino. In the music field, CAA represented Barbra Streisand, Michael Jackson, and Madonna. Among Ovitz's assets were megaselling authors Stephen King and Michael Crichton, plus 250 of Hollywood's most prominent screenwriters, plus seven or eight hundred other clients.

CAA was now filled with young men who dressed like Ovitz, in Armani, who came to work like Ovitz, in BMWs, who studied *The Art of War,* just as Ovitz had once done, and who drove deals as hard as their boss did. Some industry observers called these young men "clones," but others labeled them "samurai warrior ants." Many people believed that CAA was not especially female-friendly and was also homophobic, because gay agents did not fit in with Ovitz's long-range strategy.

His triumph over Hollywood was symbolized by the spectacular new CAA headquarters, being constructed at the western edge of

Beverly Hills. Designed by the world-renowned architect I. M. Pei, the structure occupied one corner of the intersection of Little Santa Monica and Wilshire boulevards. From the outside, the building's marble-and-glass curves conjured up a black-and-white seashell. Inside, the fifty-seven-foot-high atrium had travertined walls, a ficus tree, and a twenty-seven-foot-high painting by Roy Lichtenstein, entitled *Bauhaus Stairway: The Large Version*. The canvas cost $2 million. Other artists represented in the building included Jim Dine, Claes Oldenburg, Chuck Close, and Andy Warhol. CAA had its own curator.

In order to do business in Hollywood now, one had to come to this remarkable edifice, stand in the huge lobby, take in the objets d'art, and gaze at what one thoroughly driven and talented executive, along with his hardworking employees, had achieved through applying a comprehensive, unwavering plan for amassing power. The new CAA building, though quiet and tasteful in most ways, was also like a loud boast—a constant reminder of what others had not done. When David Geffen went there to talk about movie deals, he couldn't help but know that he was standing in the House That Michael Built and living through the Age of Ovitz. Geffen's mother had once told him that he didn't need to do anything in order to see his enemies falter; he just had to watch and wait, because time would take care of everything else. It was a noble sentiment, but Batya's son was not so passive (or, perhaps, so noble).

A film executive who's dealt with both men says, "Geffen and Ovitz basically couldn't stand each other. They were total opposites. Ovitz was a frat president at UCLA. Geffen lied about attending school there. Ovitz was so straight that he never wanted to be photographed with a drink in his hand. Geffen once got naked in front of the Beverly Hills Hotel. Ovitz calculated everything very coolly, every move and decision, based on his long-term goals. He used a classic economic plan of capturing the supply side of the business—the talent—and then driving the prices up and up. Geffen was exactly the opposite. He lived on instinct and laid his feelings on the table.

"It galled David, and other people in the business, that someone had risen from the William Morris mailroom to Ovitz's level. But give Michael credit. He was the best at what he did. On the other hand, it was like having a king in town, and when you went over to CAA, you had to pay homage."

Hollywood insiders had begun saying that Ovitz had bigger things in mind than agenting, and many felt that he coveted one thing in particular. Back in the thirties, Lew Wasserman, a skinny young gentleman with his hair parted just off center, had gone to work for the Music Corporation of America, the largest band-booking agency in the nation. MCA soon expanded into the film business, where Wasserman put together the first-ever million-dollar contract, for a young actor named Ronald Reagan. In the mid-forties, the agent became the head of MCA and the master of the "back-end deal," in which a motion picture star got paid both a fee for services and a percentage of film receipts. MCA kept expanding, until the federal government enforced its antitrust laws in 1962, and made the conglomerate leave the agency business. Since then, MCA had grown to include TV production, book publishing, international film rights, music, and theme parks.

In the late eighties, the aging Wasserman was still in charge at MCA. He wasn't just another accomplished executive but one of those rare men who could bridge differences in the entertainment community. He was, after all, a former business associate of Republican President Ronald Reagan, and he now ran the fund-raisers for his overwhelmingly Democratic industry. He'd become the titular Hollywood godfather, because he projected precisely the image that Hollywood wanted for itself: a reasonable man, a family man, a man connected to the past, a man who transcended the nasty, petty side of the business, where everyone squabbled with everyone else about money.

Wasserman looked out for the industry and it looked up to him. When American senators or presidents visited Hollywood, they paid their respects to Lew and his wife, Edie. Everything was orderly with Wasserman at the helm, although that couldn't last forever. Someday he would have to be replaced, and not just anyone could sit in his chair. People said that's where Michael Ovitz wanted to be, and he would find a way to get there.

Ovitz had lately been branching out from agenting, representing corporate executives in their negotiations with management. One of his new clients in this role was Walter Yetnikoff. It was a perfect marriage. The "most powerful man in Hollywood," as the entertainment press had dubbed Ovitz, was now aligned with the head of CBS Records, whom *Rolling Stone* had recently called "the most powerful man" in the music business. Two behemoths—two men whom

Geffen increasingly could not abide—had come together and joined forces.

After some bad years in the early eighties, CBS had rebounded brilliantly under Yetnikoff, due largely to the efforts of two young men. From his first appearances at small Greenwich Village clubs, Bruce Springsteen created an excitement and expectation that would take another decade to fulfill. John Hammond had originally signed him to CBS, and his 1973 debut album, *Greetings From Asbury Park,* drew favorable comparisons with Bob Dylan. Springsteen followed with two more successful albums, *The Wild, the Innocent, and the E Street Shuffle* and *Born to Run,* but then management problems kept him out of the studio for the next three years. During this hiatus, he toured constantly and tirelessly, with concerts that lasted three to four hours apiece. By now he'd inherited James Brown's old mantle as "the hardest-working man in show business" and was being heralded as the last rock star in America. He didn't fully arrive with 1978's *Darkness on the Edge of Town* or 1982's *Nebraska.* But two years later, *Born in the U.S.A* was the number one album in America for seven weeks and sold eighteen million copies. The thirty-five-year-old rocker was now the Boss, the biggest white music star in the world.

As a small boy in Gary, Indiana, Michael Jackson began singing with his brothers, and in 1969–70, the Jackson Five (who were briefly repped by a young Michael Ovitz at William Morris) had four number one hits in a row. Michael Jackson was still only twelve years old. In the late seventies, his voice changed, and he began a solo career and a connection with music producer Quincy Jones. Jackson signed with Epic, a CBS subsidiary, and in 1979, with Jones at the controls, he recorded the album *Off the Wall.* It contained four Top Ten hits, went multiplatinum, and reached number three on the American charts. By any standard other than the one Jackson was about to set, *Off the Wall* was a huge hit. In 1982, he and Jones created *Thriller,* which had seven number-one songs ("Billie Jean" and "Beat It" were the standouts) and became the bestselling album in the States and England—the best-selling record ever. It was Billboard's number one LP for thirty-seven weeks and sold nearly forty million copies.

If Walter Yetnikoff had been irascible and irreverent before the megaearnings of Springsteen and Jackson for CBS, their overwhelming success did nothing to blunt his tongue. He became even more outspoken and politically incorrect. When his recording artist Cyndi Lauper (somewhat) jokingly called him a male chauvinist pig, he told her to go sit on a bale of straw until her period was finished. Yetnikoff referred to Bob Dylan as "an old Jew." When Laurence Tisch purchased CBS and began his reign of tight-fistedness at "Black Rock," Yetnikoff called him "the goy upstairs." Then he called him "the kike upstairs."

Yetnikoff's drinking was getting worse, and he'd developed a nose for cocaine. He liked being on the edge, being the man with the jitters. He liked, as he put it, "schmingling and bingling." He was now "Velvo"—"Little Walter" in Yiddish—and he was having a great time, even when his company came under fire. In the mid-eighties, charges of corruption flew around CBS because of reports that Yetnikoff had spent $12.5 million in 1985 alone to get independent record promoters to play his discs on the air. Some of those "indies," it was alleged, had ties to organized crime. Yetnikoff laughed off these charges, the same way he laughed off rumors that Larry Tisch loathed the way he talked about him.

Yetnikoff openly told the press that he was a friend of Joey DiSipio, an indie promo man who'd been singled out in an NBC-TV payola investigation, which was being driven by Rudolph Giuliani, the future mayor of New York, and by Senator Al Gore, the future vice president of the United States. Joey DiSipio was a known associate of John Gotti, the head of New York's Gambino crime family. Yetnikoff acknowledged that he also owned part of a race horse with Morris Levy of Roulette Records, who hung around with Sal "The Swindler" Pisello, a reputed Gambino soldier, and Thomas Eboli, the alleged head of the Genovese mob. Levy was about to get ten years in a federal penitentiary for extortion.

Yetnikoff admitted doing all these things, but so what? Rock 'n' roll liked having a bad-boy image, and why couldn't this apply to the top executives as well as the musicians? Yetnikoff was riding so high that Larry Tisch couldn't fire him for being obstreperous, couldn't even rein him in. He went to clubs in the Village with Mick Jagger, after luring the Rolling Stones away from Ahmet Ertegun and Atlantic Records with a four-record deal worth $28 million. He went to mob joints in Little Italy with one of his new best friends, Tommy Mottola, the manager for the hit duo Hall and Oates. After hours, he went to the Mayflower Hotel, in midtown Manhattan, with some rockers and a companion from his "shiksa farm." Yetnikoff was running the hottest label in the world—in 1984, CBS had grossed $1.265 billion—so why worry? Wasn't he favored by the gods? In his office, Yetnikoff kept a personal message from Pope John Paul II. It read: "The Holy Father Paternally Imparts His Apostolic Blessing to Walter Yetnikoff as a Pledge of Continued Success and Favors."

The only thing he didn't have at CBS was access to the movie business, and that annoyed him. Walter Yetnikoff, the undisputed "king of the grooves," was not associated with a major film studio the way his two main rivals were. As the head of MCA Records, Irving Azoff was affiliated with the MCA/Universal studio; David Geffen kept churning out pictures in conjunction with Warner Bros. To compete, Yetnikoff needed a good Hollywood agent, so he'd become connected with the best one in L.A.: Michael Ovitz. Yetnikoff soon had a deal with Disney's Touchstone Pictures and was producing *Ruthless People,* starring Bette Midler and Danny DeVito. For the film's soundtrack, Yetnikoff got Daryl Hall of Hall and Oates, Mick Jagger, and Dave Stewart, the lead guitarist of the Eurythmics, to record for him. He was now a legitimate Hollywood player, just like Azoff and Geffen.

Throughout the second half of the eighties, Yetnikoff, Azoff, and Geffen, the "Big Three" of the music business, did a curious and colorful dance with one another. Sometimes they were pals, but at the same time, they couldn't stop gnawing on each other in the media:

In *Esquire,* Geffen said that Yetnikoff "is an absolutely honorable man who keeps his word, and that's more than you can say about the Irving Azoffs of the business."

In the same article, Azoff called Yetnikoff "Dennis the Menace as Attila the Hun."

Yetnikoff told *Rolling Stone* that Azoff had "a genetic defect. Irving lies when it's to his advantage to tell the truth. He just can't help it."

Azoff told *GQ* that Geffen "is intensely difficult if you piss him off."

And Geffen told *Rolling Stone,* "I feel like every time Irving is embracing me, he probably has a knife slated for my back."

Azoff had angered Yetnikoff by luring away from CBS the megasuccessful band Boston. Yetnikoff annoyed Geffen by refusing to let Michael Jackson appear on the *Days of Thunder* soundtrack being released by Geffen Records. When Yetnikoff heard rumors that Geffen might try to steal Michael Jackson, or grab Bruce Springsteen, the CBS label chief was seriously annoyed.

Yetnikoff's concerns were not completely unfounded. For years Geffen had been nurturing a friendship with Michael Jackson, and in 1984 he'd approached the singer with a movie deal. He wanted to put the twenty-six-year-old Jackson in a Geffen Films property called *Streetdandy,* which would showcase his gifts as a performer. Tom Hadley, the creator of *Flashdance,* had written a screenplay with Jackson in mind and Geffen Records planned to market the film's soundtrack. *Streetdandy* was never made, but Geffen remained close to Jackson. While running Asylum, Geffen had also met Bruce Springsteen's manager, Jon Landau, who'd developed great respect and admiration for the label boss. Landau sought Geffen's advice on many issues and even referred to him as his "rabbi."

The Big Three seemed to enjoy fighting with one another, and their jousting was humorous until it ventured into one arena: Geffen's sexuality. Then the stakes rose and the feelings became more exposed and raw. Azoff, according to some reports, had a habit of referring to Geffen as "she" around L.A., and the irrepressible Yetnikoff was said to make jokes about Geffen's prowess at fellatio.

All this remained a very delicate subject with Geffen, who did not like having people draw any conclusions about his erotic identity; he was maintaining his stance as a bisexual with all his options open. Homosexual jokes were off-limits.

CHAPTER 21

Over time, Yetnikoff had grown increasingly unhappy working for "the goy upstairs," Laurence Tisch at CBS. Seeking a new boss, Yetnikoff contacted the Sony Corporation of Japan to see if their executives might be interested in purchasing his record label, the most profitable division of CBS. Sony was delighted at the prospect. For years, the electronics giant had wanted to get into the "software" side of the entertainment industry, since it had already mastered selling the hardware: the audio tape players, radios, and video cassette recorders that were so popular in American and worldwide markets. Now Sony wanted to duplicate its success by peddling the music or movies that record labels or film studios turned out.

Early in 1988, Sony purchased CBS Records for $2 billion, only one of the mergers and acquisitions taking place throughout the music business. Two years earlier, Germany's Bertelsmann conglomerate had purchased RCA Records for $300 million. The following year, Warner Communications, Inc., paid $125 million for Chappell and Company, one of the world's largest music publishers. That same year, MCA and Boston Ventures purchased Motown Records from Berry Gordy, Jr., for $61 million. In 1989, Polygram, a unit of the Dutch corporation N. V. Philips, would pay $300 million for Island Records, and within a few months, Britain's Thorn EMI, which owns Capitol Records, paid $104 million for 50 percent of Chrysalis Records. Then Polygram bought A&M Records for $450 million and MCA bought GRP Records for $40 million in common stock. Following all this activity, only one thriving independent label was still standing alone: Geffen Records, the most successful indie of them all, with fifty gold albums and twenty-two platinum LPs. By 1989, the company had 110 employees and was doing $225 million in annual sales.

After purchasing CBS Records, Sony turned its attention to the Columbia/TriStar studio, whose recent past had been troubled. In 1978, David Begelman, the head of the studio, left after a check-forging scandal. Four years later, Herbert Allen, the New York investment banker who'd become Columbia's chairman of the board, sold the studio to Coca-Cola. Coke soon proved that although it had a brilliant understanding of the soft-drink business, it was lost in the dreamworld of Hollywood. Five years after buying Columbia, Coca-Cola executives were ready to bail. They approached Sony with the idea of selling the studio to the Japanese conglomerate, and Herbert Allen was brought in as an adviser on the deal. One of Allen's foremost Hollywood contacts was Michael Ovitz. Power, Ovitz had learned, followed money, and money was in the hands of the investment bankers who brokered the sale of huge corporations. Allen, who'd lately been tutoring Ovitz on investment banking, now included the agent as a consultant on the Sony-Columbia negotiations.

Ovitz was a minor player in Sony's eventual purchase of the studio, but he met the Japanese executives involved in the sale and had a superb camaraderie with them. As someone who'd spent decades investigating Far Eastern manners and mores, he was a devout disciple of some aspects of Oriental philosophy and knew when and how to bow in front of older Japanese men. In addition, his timing for impressing Sony's honchos was perfect. After years of struggling with a variety of scriptwriters and other film talent, Ovitz was about to see one of his most successful movie packages reach the screen. He'd worked tirelessly to bring *Rain Man* to fruition, and it premiered during the Sony-Columbia negotiations. It starred CAA clients Tom Cruise and Dustin Hoffman; it was directed by CAA client Barry Levinson and produced by CAA client Mark Johnson. The picture won four Oscars, and Levinson, Johnson, and Hoffman all thanked Ovitz for his efforts from the stage of the Academy Awards ceremony.

Ovitz had predicted to the Sony execs that the film would be a smash, and it was. He'd struck them as a prophet, a guru in a thoroughly unpredictable business. Inadvertently or not, he'd made it seem that selling films wasn't that different from marketing radios or VCRs. Sony's people were said to be in awe of him and, after closing the deal for the studio, they offered him the job of running it. He was flattered by their attention; as a master romancer of others, he enjoyed being romanced himself. Hollywood was full of rumors that he wanted to leave CAA and oversee a studio, like Michael Eisner at Disney or Lew Wasserman at MCA, who'd also started out in the business as an agent. Becoming a studio head was a natural transition for Ovitz, the next step in consolidating his hold over the industry.

Sony put together a deal for the head of CAA, to whom they'd begun referring by the code name "Superman." The corporation was willing to pay him around $100 million to leave Creative Artists and come to work for them. Ovitz countered by asking for nearly twice that much and also wanted control of CBS Records, the moneymaker on the company's software side. Sony balked. Some people said that Ovitz had overplayed his hand, but others contended that he had no intention of leaving agenting, at least right now, and had never wanted the new job.

Sony soon hired two of Yetnikoff's pals, Jon Peters and Peter Guber, to run their studio. The duo would cost the company billions, and in retrospect, they would make Ovitz look like a much better choice.

CHAPTER 22

In the final month of the 1980s, *Vanity Fair* ran a series of photographs of people who were rising stars on America's celebrity scene. One of the featured individuals was "Music Maverick" David Geffen, captured shirtless outside his Malibu home, with the Pacific Ocean spread out behind him. His backyard is a soft, sandy beach, the water a rich blue, and he looks utterly delighted with his surroundings and himself. He's gotten about as far away from the cramped streets of Brooklyn as one can get in the continental United States. As the breakers roll onto the beach, Geffen is on the telephone, taking yet another call, making another deal.

He seems intent on showing off his body. The formerly scrawny man is now filled out and fit. Not quite muscular, he does look solid and tanned. All those workouts with his private trainer and his dedication to a Pritikin diet have clearly changed his physique. It's a picture worthy of the Hollywood moguls of half a century earlier—

but they would never have posed bare-chested or conveyed quite the same manner of self-satisfaction.

In the photo, Geffen's lips are lightly pursed. He looks sensual and serene, almost seductive. It is the face of a sybarite, of someone who's discovered the California good life and relishes it so much that he cannot quite suppress his glee. It is the expression of every person who was ever hurt or put down by bigger, richer, or smugger high school classmates—and then went on to achieve things unimagined by his teenage competitors. Now that he has more than enough money and freedom to do anything he pleases, his mouth conveys more than a little smugness.

When *Vanity Fair* ran this photo of Geffen, the magazine could not have known two things that were rumbling on his horizon, as surely as an undertow was rumbling beneath the waves landing on the beach near his home. The periodical could not have guessed that 1990 would be the year of Geffen's leap into megariches and fame—but also the year when he would be challenged, from the other side of the American continent, as never before. His discreet life was about to be attacked and disrupted in ways that even some of his enemies found vicious. He would emerge from all this a different man, and never look so smug again.

Seventeen years after Batya Geffen gave birth to her second son in Brooklyn, Michelangelo Signorile was born in the same borough of New York City. Signorile lived his first eight years in the Prospect Park neighborhood, just north of where David Geffen had spent his youth. The two Brooklyn natives were separated by nearly a generation, but some things hadn't changed much since Geffen's boyhood.

"Brooklyn," Signorile wrote in his 1993 book, *Queer in America: Sex, the Media, and the Closets of Power*, "isn't the easiest place to grow up, especially if you're a homo."

Born Italian and raised a Catholic, Signorile was called a sissy, a queer, and a fag early in life, both in Brooklyn and then later, when his family moved to Staten Island. He got into fistfights with kids who taunted him about his sexuality, and he once tried to prove his masculinity by throwing basketballs at the head of a boy perceived to be more effeminate than he was. The balls knocked off the boy's glasses and drove his head into a wall.

Signorile was removed from one Catholic school after he tried to tell the officials about his homosexual feelings. He attended Syracuse University, where he studied journalism, and went to work covering the party scene in Manhattan for several periodicals, while enjoying the city's nightlife as a gay man. Younger and brasher than David Geffen, he did little to conceal his sexual identity in the office or elsewhere. At the same time, he didn't talk about it easily, for fear of making others uncomfortable. He had sometimes thought about committing suicide.

Signorile was never interested in politics until 1987, when he became aware that gay activists in Manhattan were starting to organize protests around the spread of AIDS, just as they'd organized eighteen years earlier around the Stonewall rebellion in the West Village. In late June of 1969, two hundred gay men had been evicted from a bar on Christopher Street, the Stonewall Inn, in a routine police raid on a homosexual establishment. During the raid, the cops had physically harassed the men, as had happened before at other local gay bars. This time, the men fought back, resisting arrest with violence, setting the bar on fire and pelting police with cobblestones.

People on both sides were hurt, and the cops took refuge in the Stonewall until backup support arrived. The resisters' actions triggered three days of demonstrations and street fighting, with the protesters shouting "Gay Power!" as they marched through the West Village. A turning point had come in the history of homosexual rights in America. The Gay Liberation Front grew out of this resistance, and the site of the actions has been commemorated by a sign in the neighborhood.

Now, in the second half of the eighties, another revolt was fomenting on the narrow, winding streets of Greenwich Village. All of New York's sidewalks have an in-your-face edge, but this neighborhood carries a special flavor. The West Village makes up one of the original "gay ghettos" in the United States, and it conveys the feeling of homosexuals not as a victimized minority, but as a serious political force, ready to exert their power for an appropriate cause. By 1988, with AIDS having killed nearly fifty thousand Americans, including many from these streets, the West Village was full of anger and resentment toward President Reagan and a government which the gay community felt had done almost nothing to stop the spread of the disease. Some gay militants had begun burning the president in effigy and had created a protest flag that read SILENCE = DEATH.

The most radical group was known as ACT UP: the AIDS

Coalition to Unleash Power. ACT UP met at the Lesbian and Gay Community Services Center on New York's West 13th Street and soon had several hundred members. It began selecting targets for its attacks. In 1988, Michelangelo Signorile joined ACT UP, which contained several former public relations experts who knew how to manipulate the media and grab attention.

"I was the gossip columnist on the [ACT UP] committee," Signorile wrote in *Queer in America*, "a *People* magazine free-lancer and a former 'column planter' who had worked for a PR firm guaranteeing its clients mentions in columns like Liz Smith's. I dealt in sleaze and dirt and I spoke the language of the masses, which was where... ACT UP's message had to go."

ACT UP was committed to whatever outrageous behavior would bring it coverage and bring more awareness to AIDS issues. The group wanted more funding for AIDS research, more testing of new anti-AIDS drugs by the Food and Drug Administration, more drug trials using people of color, and more overall governmental response to the illness that had struck their community. A favorite tactic of the group was the "zap"—a guerrilla assault on their targets. One occurred during a speech by Josef Cardinal Ratzinger at St. Peter's in Manhattan's Citicorp Center. The cardinal, a German prelate who'd written a paper for the Vatican decrying homosexuality as "intrinsically disordered" and "moral evil," was encouraging the Church to fight against the gay movement. Signorile and his friend Michael Musto, a columnist for the *Village Voice,* decided to attend Cardinal Ratzinger's talk.

In St. Peter's, sitting at the altar with Cardinal Ratzinger, was New York's highest Catholic official, Archbishop John Cardinal O'Connor. In the audience were Wall Street businessmen, rejected conservative Supreme Court nominee Robert Bork, Mrs. William Buckley, and some other wealthy East Side women, plus other Catholic functionaries. Signorile looked around at the gathering and told himself that he hadn't seen this many priests since leaving parochial school. He stood in the back of St. Peter's, not knowing what to expect, although he was aware that some other gay activists were scattered throughout the crowd. Cardinal O'Connor introduced Cardinal Ratzinger, who received a great round of applause.

At the end of Cardinal Ratzinger's first sentence, eight people stood up and began chanting, "Stop the Inquisition!"

One man pointed at the prelate and yelled, "Antichrist!"

"Nazi!" another screamed out.

Counterprotesters now stood and tried to shout down the activists. St. Peter's was suddenly filled with echoing, angry voices. All hell was breaking loose—inside the building and inside of Michelangelo Signorile, who'd come to the speech mostly to watch.

"It was electrifying," he wrote in his book. "Chills ran up and down my spine as I watched the protesters and then looked back at Ratzinger. Soon, anger welled up inside me. This man was the embodiment of all that had oppressed me, all the horrors I had suffered as a child. It was because of his bigotry that my family, my church—everyone around me—had alienated me, and it was because of his bigotry that I was called 'faggot' in school. Because of his bigotry, I was treated like garbage. *He* was responsible for the hell I'd endured. He and his kind were the people who forced me to live in shame, in the closet. I was livid."

The police had arrived, but Signorile ignored them. Something within him snapped, and he leaped up onto a marble platform, aiming a finger at Cardinal Ratzinger.

"He is no man of God!" Signorile cried out. "He is the Devil!"

A gasp shot through the church, and handcuffs were slipped onto Signorile's wrists. He was thrown against a wall and frisked. He was taken to jail but released later that evening, in time to join Michael Musto and some other friends for a late dinner. The meal seemed irrelevant; so did some of his friends. It was the end of Signorile's life as a nightlife reporter and the beginning of his new existence as a gay revolutionary.

"I'd lost the desire to sit through boring dinner parties," he wrote. "I'd lost the desire to attend affairs where talking about being queer was considered gauche. And, somehow, I'd gained the desire to scream at the top of my lungs that I was homosexual. For the first time, too, I was excited to see something in the *New York Post* the next day besides the gossip columns: a headline—GAYS RATTLE POPE'S ENVOY—next to a photo of an anguished Cardinal Ratzinger."

Late in 1988, Michelangelo Signorile helped coordinate a ten-hour demonstration at the FDA headquarters in Bethesda, Maryland, where ACT UP was protesting the inaction over the spread of AIDS by this governmental agency. One group of activists lay down next to cardboard tombstones in front of the FDA building and had "die-ins." Another group wrapped themselves in rolls of red tape. Another charged the FDA building and knocked a police officer through a window. Another marched around in lab coats covered with red paint, chanting, "The FDA has blood on its hands and we're seeing red!" Many were arrested.

"I am here today—we are all here today—because we all have AIDS," John Thomas, the head of the AIDS Resource Center in Dallas, told reporters at the event. "Some of us have AIDS in our bloodstreams. And some of us have AIDS in our minds. We look into the mirror and see a sore that won't go away, and we are fearful that we are going to be diagnosed. And we all have AIDS in our hearts. All of us have lost people we love."

Ann Northrop, a media organizer for ACT UP, pointed at the FDA building and said to the assembled press, "You think they're doing all they can? They're not. They're sitting on drugs that can save people's lives. Their message is very simple: 'We're trying.' They're not. They're *lying*. That is the message of ACT UP."

Media outlets called the protest "the largest act of civil disobedience since the storming of the Pentagon over twenty years ago." The story was front-page news across America and made the NBC evening news. The AIDS movement was officially out of the closet.

"A turning point," Signorile wrote in *Queer in America*, "was reached in a decades-old movement that had previously feared the homophobic media or, at best, courted only the elitist press, such as the *New York Times*. Before, we had tried to change the minds of politicians. Now, in the aftermath of the FDA demo, the potency of the *popular* press—and the possibility of manipulating it through sophisticated means in the same way that Democrats, Republicans, Hollywood corporations, and the right wing always had—was realized. The desire to effect massive changes in social thought could be fulfilled."

Headline-grabbing demonstrations were effective, but Signorile's more significant role in the movement would come from his training as a journalist. In June of 1989, Kendall Morrison, a successful Boston businessman with AIDS, started a periodical called *OutWeek*, published in a small room on lower Lexington Avenue. *OutWeek* was available every Monday morning in New York, and for some it became a must read. This was because it was the first journal that had ever focused solely on the most controversial gay issue within both the homosexual and the straight media. *OutWeek*, or at least its most outspoken writer, Mike Signorile, was now insisting that because of the AIDS epidemic and other political concerns in the era of Ronald Reagan and his successor, George Bush, all gay people must come fully out of the closet. And if they didn't, he would drag them out in print—kicking and screaming.

One of the oldest unwritten rules in journalism had just been savaged, and Signorile set off a ferocious debate. In the past, people's sexuality, especially if they were famous and homosexual, had been untouchable as a subject for reportage. Those days were ending, as Signorile began targeting the people he wanted to "out" the most. He would have several big targets, but the largest was another Brooklyn native who was running a record company in L.A.

For Geffen, nothing could have been more excruciating.

"David always did things quietly," says one of his acquaintances. "He kept his private life private. In the eighties, David, Sandy Gallin, and Barry Diller—the so-called Velvet Mafia—were discreet. They usually went out with younger men and didn't get too involved. David is not a dramatic character in a motion picture, the way some people envision the wealthy to be. He's a very real man. He works extremely hard and likes to socialize with a few intensely loyal friends. It's the people on the edges of the Hollywood game that go to wild parties, take drugs, and have a lot of tumultuous relationships. Those with real power are often homebodies, who close a deal and then retreat to their bedroom. David never, ever wanted his sexuality to become a public issue. If you bragged about sleeping with him, you would probably never do it again.

"Sex isn't very well understood in our culture. People want it to be simple, and it isn't. There are men who like women but don't want to be around them all the time. There are men who don't care much for women but love sleeping with them. There are men who are physically attracted to men but don't feel emotionally attached to them at all. Their own emotions flow more toward women. There are men who really don't care about anything but momentary sexual pleasure, with either sex, and then they want to be left alone.

"Sexuality is much more fluid than our society is comfortable with. We have a terribly strong need to pigeonhole everyone into being straight or gay or whatever. Geffen's life and his career are testaments to things that go beyond pigeonholing. He's always doing something different, always changing and creating something new. Where others have stopped, he's just kept going. He's a complex human being, with all kinds of impulses, and that just naturally makes some people nervous. He knows that you can't really explain yourself to others or get them to understand who you are. Many people are fearful of complexity. So you keep quiet and try to live your own life."

CHAPTER 23

At the start of 1990, when Geffen's contract with Steve Ross was nearing expiration, he began looking at his options for selling his label to a larger entity. In recent years, every time a conglomerate had absorbed a smaller record company, the price of the remaining independents had been driven up. Half a decade earlier, Ross had felt that $50 million was too much to pay for Geffen Records. Now the ante had been wildly inflated—and Geffen owned 100 percent of the label himself. He contacted Ross, and they talked about Warner buying the label, but Geffen was insulted by the man's offer—or perhaps he was more insulted by other developments.

Ross and Geffen's relationship, after nearly twenty years of cooperation, generosity, and mutual profitability, had lately been jolted. Throughout 1988 and 1989, the purchase of a record label had been a very low priority for Steve Ross, who had been working on the biggest deal of his life: the acquisition of Time, Inc., and the merging of Time and Warner into the largest media conglomerate in the world. In February of 1989, the deal was consummated, and Ross stood at the apogee of his career. The former funeral parlor director had lashed together two vast companies, and the Time Warner empire now reached around the globe. In a decade that had featured and honored such men, he'd become the deal maker par excellence.

Only one or two details had slipped past (or not slipped past) Ross on his way to the merger. He'd informed his closest business associates and some of his celebrity friends about the upcoming corporate marriage, but he'd told the head of Geffen Records nothing. To Geffen, known for working the phones in a bicoastal frenzy from six A.M. to midnight, information was breath itself. He prided himself on being aware of everything before anyone else, in part because he wanted to be able to position himself for the next round of business, in part because he was an inveterate gossip, and in part because serious players had to be included in every loop in the media mergers and acquisitions that were now unfolding in the realms of music, film studios, and TV networks. Everything was getting bigger and bigger, and while this may not have always worked to the advantage of shareholders or corporate employees or the workers creating the products, vast amounts of money could be made by those swinging the deals. Ross, for example, received $74.9 million for the Time Warner merger. Staying informed was crucial.

Geffen was livid at not knowing about the merger before it occurred. He was equally livid when he learned that some of Ross's celebrity pals, including Barbra Streisand, Clint Eastwood, and Steven Spielberg, had received a piece of the merger action, in the form of stock options, while he himself had been left out. Following the merger, there were rumors that Ross had intended to tell Geffen about the deal before it hit the front page, but someone had leaked the story to the media, and by then it was too late. There were other rumors that Ross had not told Geffen precisely because he was concerned that the younger man would gossip to others and undermine the impending deal. And there were still other rumors that Ross felt he'd been generous enough with Geffen over the years and wanted to reward others.

Geffen's feelings weren't assuaged when Ross made a lowball offer for his record label, an offer that seemed to make a lot of economic sense. Time Warner now had a collective debt of $12 billion, and this was simply not the time to buy another business, especially one whose value many financial experts felt to be greatly inflated. In the aftermath of the Time Warner merger and Ross's refusal to give Geffen what he wanted for his company, only one thing was certain: Ross and Geffen's relationship had been damaged. Geffen's actions during 1990 would make that damage permanent.

With Steve Ross no longer a player, Geffen put out feelers to other potential buyers. One was Paramount, which Ross regarded as a Time Warner enemy. Another was Thorn EMI, the British concern that already owned the Capitol label and part of Chrysalis. Cash rich and in an extremely acquisitive mood, Thorn EMI was reportedly willing to offer $750 million for Geffen Records, a colossal sum and, according to some in the music industry, vastly out of line with the company's worth. Yet Geffen did not leap at the money. Foreign tax laws would have lowered his profit from the sale, but he also remembered something his mother had told him: "The devil," Batya had said, "always arrives with the biggest check." On this occasion, he listened to her advice and then floated the idea of selling to Disney, where he had a long-standing ally in that company's studio head, Jeffrey Katzenberg.

Fifteen years earlier, when Barry Diller was running Paramount and Katzenberg was his assistant, Geffen had made the young man's acquaintance. In the mid-seventies, Geffen and Diller were returning to the States from a vacation abroad and had to pass through customs before reentering the U.S. Neither of them was looking forward to this tedious process, and at exactly the appropriate moment, the third man in their party, young Katzenberg, charged forward and took on the customs officer. Although Geffen himself was known for his aggressiveness, he'd never seen anyone as bold or effective as Katzenberg in plowing through bureaucratic hindrances. The assistant blew them through customs and on the spot convinced Geffen that he was a born winner. Nothing in the intervening years had changed his mind.

A native New Yorker, Katzenberg had dropped out of college and worked briefly as a talent agent before joining Paramount in 1975. Nine years later, when Paramount chief Michael Eisner left that studio to run the Walt Disney Company, he took Katzenberg with him. At the time, Disney was a tired and faded kingdom, whose best years clearly seemed behind it. Both Eisner and Katzenberg were hardworking, but stories of Katzenberg's drive soon took on the aura of legend. He arrived at the office before seven A.M. and made a hundred phone calls a day, with gusts up to 120. He read twelve scripts a weekend; Eisner called him a "golden retriever" for finding and bringing him the best new screenplays. When he visited his barber for a haircut, he was so busy thinking about impending deals that he said nothing except "Long," "Short," or "Medium."

With Eisner as CEO, greatly expanding the merchandising of Disney products, and with Katzenberg as studio head, overseeing a series of enormously successful animated films, Disney recaptured its magic and exploded in the marketplace. The company that was worth $2 billion in 1984 was worth ten times that much a decade later. By the early nineties, some people in the industry had begun referring to the birthplace of Mickey Mouse as "the Ravenous Rat."

Eisner and Katzenberg, along with Lew Wasserman and Sid Sheinberg over at MCA/Universal, were considered among the greatest one-two-punch combinations in show biz history. By 1990, Geffen had built a long-standing friendship with Katzenberg, although his relationship with Eisner was touchier. Geffen took a certain pleasure in tweaking the noses of those at the very top of the entertainment world, and in the future he would not spare the Disney chief. He also felt that his friend deserved more credit for Disney's revival than his boss did.

Katzenberg did the dirty work at Disney, and in the 1980s that included taking on the town's superagent, Michael Ovitz. Disney had never had a reputation for flinging money around, and in the late eighties and early nineties, the studio was determined to hold the line on film costs. That meant scrapping with heavyweight talent agents, who were just as determined to get megamillion-dollar deals for their clients. Upon arriving at work, Katzenberg was fond of announcing, "I'm going to kick movie star butt today." That also meant kicking some agents in the tail. Michael Eisner, for his part, never discouraged this kind of talk, but in public he made a point of saying that he and Ovitz vacationed together and were very good friends.

As Ovitz had grown more powerful, Katzenberg had become more critical of his methods of strong-arming studios into a position where they had to lay out twenty or thirty or forty or fifty million dollars for a single picture, which in turn caused the moviegoer out in Middle America to part with four or five or six or seven dollars to take in a film. The Disney studio head was virtually the only executive in Hollywood secure enough, or brave enough, to hint that the reign of Ovitz might not be good for the business in the long run.

The fact that Katzenberg and Geffen had a common enemy over at CAA gave the men another bond. Geffen occasionally said that he'd never seen the level of fear in any industry that was now rampant in the movie business. The higher the prices, the greater the fear of failure on all sides. One bomb, Geffen often remarked, could get you fired, something that would never happen in the music industry. And fear generated mediocrity.

Despite Geffen's friendship with Katzenberg, Disney did not buy his record label. Geffen had recently had his eye on another Hollywood conglomerate in the San Fernando Valley, not far from the Disney headquarters in Burbank. Geffen was intrigued with MCA, not so much because it had a stellar reputation in the music field but because it was run by Lew Wasserman, who turned seventy-seven years old in 1990. Everyone knew that he would be stepping down from "the Octopus" in the near future, but no one knew who would become the next head of MCA or take his place as the patriarch of Hollywood. Geffen himself was interested in replacing the godfather, although virtually no one in L.A. would have given him a chance.

"Until 1990," says a film executive, "no one in this town thought much about Geffen."

Part of the reason for this was because of his sexuality, which rankled people of both genders.

"He just wasn't the sort of person you wanted representing your industry," says a studio exec in the Valley. "Too unpredictable."

A female TV producer puts it more pointedly: "Geffen is damn lucky that he isn't dead from AIDS."

Everyone in Hollywood knew Geffen's predilections, and although few people genuinely cared what he did in bed, others thought it could prove problematic if he assumed control at MCA and replaced the redoubtable Wasserman. True, Barry Diller had run Paramount and then 20th Century Fox, but this was not quite the same thing as Geffen sitting down in Wasserman's chair. Diller was a self-possessed, mature man in a way that many others in the business were not. One rarely thought of him as anything other than a hard-nosed executive, and his personal life managed to stay in the background. But Geffen....

He was still a rock-'n'-roll wheeler-dealer sitting over on Sunset Boulevard making money off sex and drugs and funky music. His tendency to say controversial things and to settle scores verbally in public made some people jumpy. Whoever succeeded Wasserman would be following a legend and taking on a symbolic role in the industry. Under these circumstances, in the land where image was everything, one's off-hours activities really did matter.

Wasserman's number two man and potential successor at MCA was Sid Sheinberg, but many observers felt that when Wasserman left, Sheinberg would go with him. Nearly twenty years Wasserman's junior, Sheinberg had the reputation in Hollywood for being too prickly and rough-hewn to represent the massive operation. He was a good soldier but lacked his superior's ability to move gracefully through all events and opportunities. One of Sheinberg's greatest contributions at MCA/Universal was discovering and supporting a young man who'd come to the studio in the late sixties and said he wanted to be a filmmaker. He'd put together a little movie called *Amblin'* and wanted Sheinberg to look at it. The older man watched it and immediately signed the younger one to an MCA/Universal contract. Since then, Steven Spielberg had become the most financially successful filmmaker in Hollywood history, creating *Jaws, E.T., Jurassic Park,* and *Schindler's List.* He'd made billions for MCA.

If Sheinberg was considered a long shot, the more likely scenario was that when Wasserman was ready to retire, Michael Ovitz would leave the agenting business and take over the MCA helm, following almost exactly in Wasserman's own footsteps. Ovitz was doing nothing to discourage this kind of speculation. After Sony had bought the Columbia/TriStar studio for $3.4 billion in 1989, another Japanese giant, the Matsushita Electric Industrial Company of Osaka, a $65 billion producer of fans, light bulbs, and other appliances, decided to dive into the prestigious field of American entertainment. Its executives went to Sony's honchos and asked them who in Hollywood was the best person to educate and guide them toward purchasing their own studio and media conglomerate. Only one man came to mind at Sony: the one they'd dubbed "Superman."

Matsushita hired Ovitz to help them select a Hollywood property and broker the entire deal. The agent would be responsible for bringing in the investment bankers and the public relations experts; more important, he would designate for himself the role of being the only significant liaison between the Japanese buyer and the American seller, two groups that were literally and figuratively an ocean apart. Throughout his career, Ovitz had exercised his gift for positioning himself in exactly the right place at precisely the right time. His timing in this situation was again perfect, and early in 1990 he gave the Matsushita executives a crash course in the history of the film business. Then he carefully steered them away from two other studios that were on the block, Orion and Paramount, and straight toward MCA. Once he'd brought off this deal, went the best-informed Hollywood scuttlebutt, the Matsushita execs would naturally want him to leave his Beverly Hills office, move over to the Valley, and run MCA himself.

On Thursday, March 8, 1990, Sid Sheinberg contacted Geffen and said that he'd heard the label boss was shopping his company around. Was Geffen Records, Sheinberg wanted to know, still available? Geffen said it was, very pleased that Sheinberg had called. Only one obstacle at MCA—having to report to label boss Irving Azoff—would have kept him from considering their offer, but Azoff had left the company in late 1989 to go to Giant Records. The path was now clear.

Geffen told Sheinberg that he was interested in receiving an offer from MCA, and the older man replied that he would send it over by messenger in a day or two. Geffen countered by saying that this was 1990, the fax machine had become the supreme tool for swift negotiations, and he wanted the numbers now. Minutes later, his fax began whistling with two paragraphs from the Valley. MCA was offering Geffen a million shares of a new stock that paid a $6.80 annual dividend, or he could convert them into ten million shares of common stock of MCA, which amounted to 12 percent of the company. Taking his buyout in common stock, as opposed to cash, would provide some tax protection. This option would also give him nearly as much equity as Lew Wasserman, who had 11.3 million shares. MCA was currently trading at $54.50 a share.

If Geffen accepted Sheinberg's bid, he would continue running the label and retain ownership of his stage and film subsidiaries. And under the conditions of the "standstill agreement" that was part of the deal, Geffen could not buy any more MCA stock for twenty years, could not sell all of his stock for seventeen more years, and could not sell it to any one individual. The entire package was worth a fortune—$545 million to him at the moment and not a penny to Steve Ross or Time Warner—but the way it was constructed left Geffen with essentially paper wealth. He would be fabulously rich, in terms of his stock portfolio, but his cash flow would not be greatly changed.

On Sunday, March 11, Geffen spent part of the day with an old friend, producer Ray Stark, who then drove him over to the Beverly Hills office of MCA. Geffen sat down with Lew Wasserman, who again spelled out the terms. Each time Wasserman listed a condition of the agreement, Geffen said yes without resistance. In less than one hour, the deal was done. Geffen now had ten million shares of MCA's common stock, but it would take a very unlikely ally to make him cash rich beyond his craziest dreams.

CHAPTER 24

Some financial analysts felt that Geffen's sale to MCA was a blow to his oldest ally, Steve Ross. Others said that Wasserman and MCA had been badly taken in the deal (MCA's stock fell three points on news of the sale, to $52 a share), and that Time Warner was wise to have passed up the chance to pay half a billion dollars for a label with less than one-tenth of the market. Geffen told the *L.A. Times* that in his "hearts of hearts" he'd wanted to stay with Ross and Mo Ostin, the head of Warner Records, but he'd simply had better offers coming from other quarters. Ross himself did not publicly comment on the situation, except to wish Geffen well. As co-CEO of the world's foremost media enterprise, Ross had countless other things to focus on, and his health had been failing for a decade, with a heart attack in 1980, surgery for prostate cancer in 1985, and a 1990 prognosis that the prostate trouble was likely to recur. Any regrets he had about Geffen were more likely personal than professional.

"The two men had had a long and complicated relationship," Connie Bruck wrote of Ross and Geffen in her book *Master of the Game: How Steve Ross Rode the Light Fantastic From Undertaker to Creator of the Largest Media Conglomerate in the World*. "While Geffen, years later, would say that Ross had taken advantage of him in the deals they struck, the prevalent view in the upper strata of WCI was that David Geffen did better in his negotiations with Ross than anyone else in the company did; that, as several said, he 'had Steve's number.'"

Jack Warner, who died in 1978, had been the most flamboyant of the four original Warner brothers. He favored yachting blazers and crude jokes. On meeting Albert Einstein, he is said to have told the scientific genius, "I have a theory about relatives too. Don't hire them." Warner and his brothers produced fifteen hundred movies and won three Oscars for Best Picture: *The Life of Emile Zola* (1937), *Casablanca* (1943), and *My Fair Lady* (1964). In March of

1990, Jack's widow, Ann Page Alvarado Warner, also passed away, after living alone for the past dozen years in her and her late husband's Bel-Air estate. Following Ann's death, her two daughters, Barbara and Joy, decided to put this property on the market as quickly as possible.

The Warner estate, built in 1937, sat on ten hilltop acres on Angelo Drive, and many in the entertainment community regarded it as the last great "mogul's residence" left in Hollywood. The grounds held a fern garden, a waterfall, tennis courts, a golf course, a caddy shack, a swimming pool, a maids' quarters, a pergola, and an esplanade rife with fountains and statues. The house, neoclassical in design with gingerbread curlicues under the eaves, had five bedrooms, a nursery suite, a screening room, and Jack Warner's old office, which was lined with cracked leather. One room had paneling that had been carved by a son of Chippendale. One floor had been imported from a French palace—the same floor that Napoleon had knelt down on to propose to Josephine; the estate inevitably drew comparisons with Versailles. In the halcyon years of the motion picture industry, Jack and Ann Warner had held elaborate parties in the mansion, once throwing a birthday bash for Cole Porter. He sat next to the piano in the second-story playroom, while Judy Garland sang his songs as a tribute to the aging composer.

David Geffen revered the golden era of Hollywood. He'd grown up reading about it, watching its films, and wanting to emulate Louis B. Mayer. Geffen loved to hear the older men, like Swifty Lazar and Ray Stark and Sam Spiegel, talk about those days; he loved just spending time with the *alter kuckers*. They connected him to his business and spiritual roots. They reminded him of a different time in Hollywood, when fear was not the overwhelming mode of operation in the movie business and the art of filmmaking was at least as important as the art of cutting the deal. Maybe that era had been corny, but it had also produced some world-class entertainment. Geffen knew that he hadn't yet made any pictures that rivaled such Sam Spiegel productions as *Lawrence of Arabia, The African Queen, On the Waterfront,* and *The Bridge on the River Kwai,* but that didn't mean he wouldn't do such work in the future. The old guys were inspiring.

When Geffen, now feeling flush after the sale of his record label to MCA, heard that the Warner daughters wanted to sell their parents' property, he immediately contacted them and asked for a favor: if they would promise not to list the house with a real estate agent for ten days, he would buy the mansion and everything within it. The museumlike residence held millions of dollars worth of porcelain objets d'art and exorbitant pieces of furniture, including two George III gilded mirrors (worth $200,000 to $300,000), a Dutch tulipwood-and-engraved-glass cabinet ($70,000 to $100,000), a marble-and-lapis-lazuli fireplace ($30,000 to $50,000), and a portrait of Ann Warner by Salvador Dali ($600,000 to $800,000). The house also contained valuable movie memorabilia, such as leather-bound Warner Bros. film scripts and eight golden Oscars.

Ten days after Geffen had contacted the Warner daughters, the deal was sealed. He paid $47.5 million cash for the property, the largest price tag ever paid for a home in L.A., if not in the entire United States. He was suddenly the owner of the grandest old house in town, but he didn't quite know what to do next, as he still preferred being in his beach house in Malibu.

"I bought it because I was seduced by the deal," he later told *Vanity Fair* about this purchase. "I got caught up in the gestalt of something. I got caught up in the *Jack Warner* of it all. He was this legend to me, and this was his house. Now I'm worried about how I can ever live in this house."

His first act was to sell $9 million worth of antiques and memorabilia that had come with the property. Then he called Rose Tarlow, a highly fashionable, highly selective L.A. interior decorator with her own shop on Melrose Avenue, and asked her to redo the stodgy old structure. Tarlow said no at first and then no again and then no once more, much as Bob Dylan had first responded to Geffen's efforts to sign him to the Asylum label. After a while she broke down and said yes. Before long she had a construction crew tearing up the plumbing, knocking down walls, slicing holes in the ceiling for skylights, and staining the floors. She decreed that the garden statuary had to go. She turned the nursery into a gym and significantly enlarged the bathrooms. A perfectionist not known for sparing expenses, Tarlow intended to be finished with the place within a few months, perhaps a year at the most, so Geffen could move into his refurbished mansion.

Seven years later, Tarlow was still redoing the estate, and Geffen remained at Malibu. By then he'd purchased and begun remodeling the late Claudette Colbert's "Belle Rive" home in Barbados.

▪ ▪ ▪

In May of 1990, two months after Geffen closed his deal with Lew Wasserman and MCA, Michael Ovitz flew to Osaka, Japan, and made a four-hour presentation to the Matsushita Electric Industrial Company brass. In Osaka, the agent gave his final recommendation for which entity he felt the conglomerate should pursue in its quest for an American entertainment giant. To no one's surprise, he selected MCA. Matsushita agreed with Ovitz's choice, and the agent now began the intricate task of bringing together the buyers from the Far East and the sellers in Hollywood. There were ticklish issues everywhere. During the Sony-Columbia deal, officials in the U.S. government had raised serious questions about a foreign corporation buying a piece of America's cultural history; a congressional hearing had even been held on the matter. Some Hollywood people had not been enamored of Sony's purchase, and they were now less pleased with the prospect of a second Japanese corporation owning another film studio.

On the California side of the Pacific, it was generally believed that the Japanese were much better at manufacturing and selling electrical products than they would ever be at mastering the slippery slope of the movie industry. The same thing could be said of most U.S. corporations. If Coca-Cola had had no clue in Hollywood, what chance would Sony or Matsushita have? Many American businesspeople also found these huge Far Eastern corporations hard to do business with; they acted by consensus, tended to move much more slowly than U.S. companies, and were known for sending "shadow" executives to the States to oversee the activities of their American employees. That was not the sort of thing, of course, that would sit well with Wasserman, Sheinberg, or anyone else in Hollywood who'd spent years working in the industry. Finally, many in the entertainment field believed that Japanese corporations were less than open-minded about homosexuality. That also didn't play well in certain corners of L.A.

Ovitz was undeterred by such concerns. The intrepid power broker, who'd now assumed an international role never undertaken by a talent agent before, was used to being in uncharted terrain. Nothing excited him more than uniting disparate parties, placing himself at the very center of the action, and doing the kind of deal that no one else had quite envisioned. His strength had always been in selling others his version of the future. What was the difference, really, between packaging a daytime TV show or a movie like *Rain*

Man and finding just the right elements to close the multibillion-dollar sale of an American corporation to people on the other shore of the Pacific? His finest hour was about to occur.

In November of 1989, Ovitz had traveled to Hawaii and first met with Matsushita's executive vice president and director, Masahiko Hirata. The agent had then worked diligently to keep Hirata and his people informed, as well as keeping Wasserman and Sheinberg apprised of all his moves. Going out of his way to offend no one, Ovitz assured the Japanese that they could buy MCA for a reasonable price and assured the Americans, and the volatile Sheinberg in particular, that they had nothing to fear from this deal. Following the transaction, Wasserman and Sheinberg would keep their jobs and receive enormous compensation from the new owners. Ovitz would handle the details, and the Americans just needed to trust him.

One detail Ovitz avoided in the spring and summer of 1990 was bringing together the Matsushita executives and the MCA brass. Nearly five months would pass, after the agent had recommended that Matsushita buy MCA, before Masahiko Hirata and Keiya Toyonaga, the corporation's managing director, flew to Los Angeles and sat down in Wasserman's home for a face-to-face meeting on October 7. It was a stiff introduction, and little more than pleasantries were exchanged before the electronics execs returned to Osaka and waited for the next word from Ovitz.

During those five months, the agent had been extremely busy laboring behind the scenes and doing what he did best. He decided which information should go west across the ocean to Matsushita and which should flow back east into the San Fernando Valley. Using the kind of stealth that had long given CAA a nearly mystical air of secrecy and power, Ovitz held surreptitious meetings in Manhattan hotel rooms. He flew to Osaka out of San Francisco instead of L.A., so that no one would see him boarding a plane at LAX. He kept his car parked in the CAA garage so that his own employees would think that he was up in his office taking care of business, instead of halfway around the world in Japan. He called himself "Mr. Nelson," his code name in these furtive negotiations. He stayed up all night in Osaka so that he could return phone calls to people in Hollywood, who thought he was sitting over on Wilshire Boulevard.

At Creative Artists, Ovitz had always stressed teamwork and shared many of the spoils with his employees. According to Mike Rosenthal Jr., the son of one of the agency's founders and a longtime

CAA TV agent, Ovitz's people made 10 to 15 percent more than other top-level agents in L.A. But as he'd become a larger and larger force in the industry, Ovitz's natural inclination for working alone and working undercover began to surface, and he did things that even his closest associates knew nothing about. For example, he told them that he flew to meetings in a private jet belonging to film director and CAA client Sydney Pollack; the jet, in fact, was Ovitz's, but he didn't want his employees to know that. For years, Ovitz's methods had been startlingly effective, because of the unique position he'd created for himself in the consciousness of people worldwide who monitored the entertainment business. If you wanted to get things done in Hollywood, you went through Michael Ovitz.

He'd made a reported $11 million by being a less-than-vital consultant on the Sony-Columbia deal. He would make as much as $40 million on the Matsushita-MCA transaction (the actual number would never become public). Ovitz's CAA would go on to create the successful "polar bear" TV ads for Coca-Cola and become an adviser to Nike. Most remarkable of all, Ovitz did all this and remained accountable to no one—no board of directors inside his own firm, no shareholders, no studio heads, and no media representatives, because he refused to give interviews. In all transactions, he collected his fee and moved on, just as talent agents had always done, leaving others to carry out the day-to-day operations of running their own businesses. He did not brook conflict or opposition within his own building, or outside it. If you bucked Ovitz, people said, you were finished in Hollywood.

In an industry known for spinning myths, he'd become the greatest mythmaker of them all.

CHAPTER 25

By early 1990, Michelangelo Signorile was finding his legs as an *OutWeek* columnist. His anger was still bottomless, but it had evolved; it was no longer directed so much at the Cardinal Ratzingers of the world as it was at the media and some prominent gay figures themselves. Signorile, like many other people now, had his own crises to deal with, very close to home, and his emotions were overflowing into his work. He wrote in *Queer in America:*

> I found myself avoiding my family, not returning phone calls and not visiting. Finally, my mother mailed me a letter asking what the problem was and why I was ignoring her. I was filled with so much frustration and anger that I fired off a diatribe and mailed it back.
>
> I wrote that I couldn't deal with visiting because I was sick of hearing all the wonderful, great, suburban things going on in their lives while my life, and the lives of so many people I loved, were in turmoil. I said that I felt I couldn't even discuss these problems with my family. I told her I was gay and that I had been involved in a relationship with someone who was HIV-positive and that it was very stressful.
>
> I received a letter back. My mother was very upset. I called her, and we got into a yelling match. I treated her unfairly, expecting her to come to terms with my life overnight. This was all very difficult for her to take, and there weren't many people with whom she could talk about it. And yet, I was in such a state of grief and despair that I couldn't be the one to help her.
>
> I got off the phone angry and upset. I'd lost my mother. I'd lost my lover. Because of this fucking crisis, I was losing my friends. I was filled with rage.... I saw that the entertainment-fashion-art-media industry, which shaped mass culture, was violently homophobic in spite of the fact that gays dominated it. I felt a surge like the one I had experienced at St. Peter's Church when Cardinal Ratzinger spoke. I was to feel it often. It would

take over my body. When it did, I sat down at the keyboard to write columns for *OutWeek* and the anger simply came out in the form of capital letters:

"DOES ONE HAVE TO TAKE A C.I.A. CODE-BREAKING COURSE IN ORDER TO FIGURE OUT WHAT THE FUCK IS BEING SAID IN THE PAPERS THESE DAYS? IT'S UTTERLY HOMOPHOBIC OF US AND THE MEDIA TO CONSTANTLY BEAT AROUND THE BUSH, SPEAK IN CODES, AND TREAT HOMOSEXUALITY AS SOME SCANDALOUS SECRET, THE NAME OF WHICH WE CAN'T INVOKE...."

I was going through something and tens of thousands of people would soon be going through it with me, as I targeted those I saw as the perpetrators of the sham:

"YOU SLIMY, SELF-LOATHING, HYPOCRITICAL MONSTERS. YOU GO TO OUR PARTIES, YOU WHIRL WITH BIGOTS AND MURDERERS, YOU LIE AND ENGAGE IN COVER-UPS, YOU SELL YOUR SOULS—MEANWHILE, WE'RE DYING!"

In his book, Signorile compared homophobia in Hollywood in the early nineties with anti-Semitism in America during the heyday of the old movie moguls:

> In many ways, outing represents a maturing of the gay community. As Jews and blacks did many years ago, queers are now calling to account members of our community who have power and privilege. The new generation is saying that those individuals...also have a civic duty to the community in which they reside at least part of the time and thanks to which they enjoy the benefits of the liberation that has so far been won. And we're saying that the time has come for them to be known....Forty years ago, most people who were Jewish in Hollywood had to change their names to escape anti-Semitism; and much of the media participated in their subterfuge. But times have changed; the Jewish community has reached a point where it abhors such hiding and chastises those who encourage or participate in it.

In January of 1990, the *Star*, a tabloid newspaper, wrote that Chastity Bono, the grown-up daughter of Sony and Cher, was gay. This was the first major public "outing," as *Time* magazine would dub the process of naming the names of alleged homosexual celebrities.

Signorile now began attacking one of his primary targets, syndicated columnist Liz Smith, who he contended was gay. He lambasted Smith for her flattering coverage of Ronald and Nancy Reagan when Reagan was president and for her similar treatment of the new occupants of the White House, George and Barbara Bush.

"Am I supposed to just let Liz write her ass-kissing bullshit without saying anything?" he fulminated. "Fuck her!...I realize you're oppressed just like the rest of us (which is why you're hiding in the first place). But don't react to it by oppressing *us*. It's much easier for you to break the chain of homophobia than it is for me. You are in enormous positions of power. Use that. This is a crisis!"

As a result of Signorile's diatribes, *W*, the women's fashion periodical, now put *OutWeek* on its "In" list. No one, its editors said, should miss its offering of "culture, politics, and vicious gossip."

But Signorile was also unleashing a backlash. Amy Pagnozzi, a columnist for the *New York Post,* compared Signorile to Senator Joseph McCarthy, who had led witchhunts for Communists four decades earlier. James Revson, the nephew of Revlon founder Charles Revson, was a columnist for another New York daily, *Newsday*. Revson and Signorile had earlier gone on a couple of dates, but Revson was now appalled by Signorile's actions, and in *Newsday* he called the *OutWeek* writer "truly frightening and offensive....Outing only creates fear and fear creates more repression." In 1991, Revson died of AIDS.

Andrew Sullivan, the openly gay editor of the *New Republic,* wrote that homosexuals, despite their differences over the years, had always been on the same side—until now. Proponents of outing, he went on, "have attacked the central protection of gay people themselves....The gleam in the eyes of the outers, I have come reluctantly to understand, is not the excess of youth or the passion of the radical. It is the gleam of the authoritarian." Randy Shilts, the celebrated gay author of *And the Band Played On,* wrote in the *San Francisco Chronicle,* "As for the nastiness of outing...it's still a dirty business that hurts people." Signorile's tactics were also lambasted by the nation's original alternative weekly, the *Village Voice*. Some labeled what he was doing "fascism."

The gloves were now off, the battle joined. Signorile's logic regarding outing was reasonably subtle. He was not interested in who was sleeping with whom; that was still off limits. People only needed to be outed, went his argument, if their sexuality was connected to larger social issues.

In *OutWeek,* Signorile wrote of Revson and his wealthy gay friends, "It doesn't matter to them that their coming out of the closet might help other queers. THEY HAVE TO PROTECT THEIR OWN FRAGILE, LITTLE, PRIVILEGED WORLD."

In March of 1990, Signorile reported that Malcolm Forbes, the recently deceased founder of *Forbes* magazine, had been gay. Before printing this, Signorile wrote, he'd spoken with a dozen men who'd been "intimately involved with Forbes." In his *OutWeek* article, Signorile also claimed that because Forbes had felt the need to remain in the closet, he'd sexually harassed and abused his male employees. If Malcolm Forbes had purposefully deceived the public by creating the impression that he was intimate with Elizabeth Taylor, Signorile contended, that was news. If Forbes had mistreated other men at his magazine, because of his own predilections, that was bigger news and needed to be exposed.

Deliberately hiding people's sexual orientation in the media, Signorile believed, was just another form of homophobia on the part of the straight press and another form of self-loathing by the gay community. Three times as many gay youth committed suicide as heterosexual kids, and it was Signorile's conviction that they did so in part because they lacked successful role models in the adult world. Until sexual orientations were treated equally in the media, he concluded, the problem would only deepen.

Gabriel Rotello, the editor of *OutWeek,* also wrote in the publication, "In 1990, many of us in the gay media announced that henceforth we would simply treat homosexuality and heterosexuality as equals. We were not going to wait for the perfect, utopian future to arrive before equalizing the two: We were going to do it now. That's what outing really is: equalizing homosexuality and heterosexuality in the media."

This struggle for equality, Signorile was quick to point out, was not occurring in a political vacuum. The Christian right had assumed enormous power in the media in the 1980s, and its stance against homosexuality was as strong as its position against abortion. In 1990, religious conservatives claimed to have a coalition of sixty million Americans, and their message constantly saturated the marketplace. The Reverend James Dobson, who led the Colorado-based Focus on Family, had a radio program that aired three times a day and five days a week on 1,450 stations in the United States. The Coral Ridge Ministries broadcast a weekly TV program to 309 stations in two thousand American cities. Pat Robertson's *700 Club* was reaching twenty-nine million homes daily. The Christian Coalition would send three hundred delegates to the 1992 Republican National Convention in Houston; and for that election, it would distribute forty million voter guides lauding "family values."

The religious right was also paying very close attention to which Hollywood executives were sympathetic to gay or lesbian causes—then naming the names of these suspect characters in their publications. When Disney brought out *The Lion King,* some fundamentalists charged that this animated children's film had a subliminal, detrimental, underlying homosexual theme.

Initially, the mainstream press refused to report on Signorile's outing of Forbes. New York's *Daily News* killed a story on the subject, and the TV program *Entertainment Tonight* canceled a segment concerning the issue. Yet Signorile was causing journalists to debate among themselves the whole matter of an individual's "right to privacy." The unwritten rules of the media game were changing, and Signorile had set off something like panic in the celebrity field.

Liz Smith, for one, felt compelled to defend herself against Signorile's broadsides. After being attacked in *OutWeek,* she spoke to the publication and Signorile quoted her remarks in *Queer in America.*

"I don't want to make a statement about my mythical sex life," she said. "Millions of people don't want to be defined by their sexuality. I'd like to be defined by my work, my life.... I'm a divorced woman. I spent my adult, mature life married for ten years. Let people speculate. I'll lead my life the way I choose to."

In late March, London's *Daily Mail* reported that longtime TV star Richard Chamberlain was gay. Although Signorile had not played a role in this outing, he did call Annette Wolf, Chamberlain's publicist, to discuss this story. She was livid.

"I am in complete disagreement with the whole philosophy of what you do...," she told Signorile. "I am not going to have Richard Chamberlain talk to you and lower himself to have this conversation. You're doing yourself a major disservice and also doing the same to your community. You cannot invade people's privacy. You have absolutely no right to disclose anything about anyone."

With articles on Chastity Bono, Malcolm Forbes, and Richard Chamberlain having appeared in recent months, the *Los Angeles Times* began reporting on the "outing" phenomenon taking place in the entertainment business.

"What began as a gay political tactic has heated up the tabloids and shifted to the mainstream press," the *Times* wrote in the summer of 1990. "Now Hollywood is grappling with the ethics, emotional impact, and economic consequences of publicizing the alleged homosexuality of celebrities.... Names have been named, photos published and details of sex lives discussed.... Not surprisingly, it's causing anger, anxiety, and fear in Hollywood, where a sexy, heterosexual image seems crucial to many lucrative careers."

Signorile, now confident that he had the media's attention, turned his bile against David Geffen and his record company. In 1988, the label had brought out the second Guns n' Roses album, *Lies,* which also went multiplatinum and sold five million copies. (According to music industry analysts, the success of Guns n' Roses, more than anything else, had led MCA and Thorn EMI to make such huge offers for Geffen Records.) A track on *Lies,* entitled "One in a Million" had ignited Axl Rose's first major controversy. The song contained the lyrics "Immigrants and faggots... think they'll do as they please / Like start a mini-Iran or spread some fucking disease." Before the disc was released, Geffen had approached Rose, the band's lead singer, and told him that the song would generate controversy and cause Rose trouble. The singer was unperturbed; he wanted "One in a Million" on the album, and it stayed. Geffen did not seem to have considered the possibility that the lyrics could bring him worse problems than Rose.

Signorile was looking for blood and had now found it. The man in charge of Geffen Records, who called himself bisexual and claimed to be more than sympathetic to gay causes, a man who was worth hundreds of millions of dollars even before the recent sale of his label, was putting out songs that, to Michelangelo Signorile, did nothing but reinforce homophobia. In addition to this, Geffen's label also distributed the recordings of Andrew Dice Clay, a comedian whom many saw as a gay basher. In 1989, the columnist had criticized Geffen in *OutWeek* for his support of Guns n' Roses. In 1990, after Geffen had become a much more public figure because of the media coverage of the sale of his company, Signorile began turning him into his primary villain.

"I met a man the other night in a club," Signorile wrote in his column. "[He] had disagreed with me a year ago, but now was saying that he understood, shared and supported many of my motives and tactics. He brought up a sad thought: If Rock Hudson, Perry Ellis, Barry Diller, Liz Smith, David Geffen and Malcolm Forbes had held a joint press conference back in 1982 at the beginning of the AIDS crisis, think of the effect it would have had. Think of the power it would have unleashed. Think of the visibility it would have created. THINK OF THE LIVES IT MAY HAVE SAVED."

In the same column, he said the "revolution" had started and then issued an ultimatum to "closeted queers" in New York and Hollywood: "EITHER YOU JOIN US OR WE WILL BEGIN IMMEDIATELY TEARING DOWN EVERY WALL, EXPOSING YOUR HYPOCRISIES. . . . IT'S YOUR DECISION WHICH WAY YOU WANT TO GO. BUT DON'T THINK TOO LONG. TIME IS RUNNING OUT."

Signorile himself was now under attack from all angles: the telephone, the fax machine, on the street, and in what other media outlets were saying about him. He seemed unfazed by the criticism and began preparing for his most personal assaults yet.

Thus far in this controversy, Geffen had reined in his tongue. But now, intensely aware that he was becoming the outing movement's whipping boy, he decided to fight back. In 1989, he'd begun serving on the board of governors for AIDS Project Los Angeles and had also become a member of the American Foundation for AIDS Research. In the spring of 1990, the Gay Men Health Crisis (GMHC) in New York, the largest and oldest AIDS organization in the country, was holding a fund-raising concert, called "A Rock and a Hard Place." Geffen offered them Guns n' Roses as one of the acts. In the aftermath of the "One in a Million" brouhaha, this choice struck many as outrageously inappropriate, but Geffen believed, despite Axl Rose's lyrics, that the singer was not homophobic. He'd merely been expressing some feelings he'd had long ago, and the band, Geffen contended, could help dissolve any lingering hostility by appearing at the benefit. GMHC was not receptive to this suggestion and turned the group down flat. Geffen blew up.

"I don't care what their [Guns n' Roses] record is," he told *Entertainment Weekly.* "If you need a blood donor and the only person who can give you a transfusion is Hitler, you take the blood."

Michael Musto, another Brooklyn native who was Signorile's friend and a gay *Village Voice* columnist, now jumped into the fray. He called up Geffen and asked him about the GMHC controversy.

"Guns n' Roses volunteered to do the benefit," Geffen told him with the same defiance he'd used with *Entertainment Weekly.* "GMHC are a bunch of assholes for dropping them."

When Musto asked the man if he was gay, Geffen refused to answer the question.

In his next column in the *Voice,* Musto excoriated the label boss, writing that the Geffen Records coffers were filled with "blood money" that had been made by Guns n' Roses. For monetary reasons alone, Musto charged, Geffen wouldn't do anything to change the racial or sexual attitudes of the enormously successful band. The column ended on a very personal note: "David, the way to fight AIDS is to extinguish stupidity, not excuse it. Stop hiding behind checkbooks and hurt feelings and do something that will really help the fight. My friends are dying. We don't have time for this bullshit."

Signorile went further. After learning that Geffen had called the GMHC a "bunch of assholes," he printed the phone number for Geffen Records in his next column, urging his readers to "zap" the office with their protests.

"GEFFEN, YOU PIG," Signorile wrote, "WE DEMAND THAT YOU IMMEDIATELY STAND UP FOR YOURSELF AND THIS COMMUNITY AND DENOUNCE AND DROP GUNS N' ROSES. We demand an apology for their gross, violence-inciting statements—both from you for not saying anything as they spewed such venom and from them for their ignorance.

"I don't care how much blood money you've given to fight AIDS. You slit our throats with one hand and help deaden the pain with the other. You, David Geffen, are the most horrifying kind of nightmare."

A week later, Geffen told the *L.A. Times* that the charges against him were "a bogus issue. Homosexuals see homophobia everywhere. They have such a 'victim' mentality. I see so little homophobia in Hollywood."

Then Kevin Sessums, a reporter for *Vanity Fair* and a friend of Geffen's, wrote Signorile a letter, which Signorile printed in his next

OutWeek column. The letter said that because of Signorile, Geffen's office had received "threats of bombings and even death." Sessums called what Signorile was doing "blood journalism," "terrorism," and "tantrum politics."

Signorile was not dissuaded.

CHAPTER 26

During his career, Geffen had used a number of lawyers in his business affairs, but the two most potent ones were currently in his employ: music attorney Allen Grubman on the East Coast and entertainment barrister Bertram Fields in L.A. Grubman was merely known for being effective and highly successful, while Fields also had a reputation as an intimidator. A stock saying in the City of Angels went, "You just don't want Bert Fields calling you up on behalf of his client."

Allen Grubman had grown up in Geffen's old Borough Park neighborhood. He'd gotten into the music business by working on an early Hall and Oates contract with Tommy Mottola, currently the number two man at Sony Music under Walter Yetnikoff. More recently, he'd helped Thorn EMI buy a stake in Chrysalis Records and assisted Polygram in its purchase of Island Records. Yetnikoff himself had Grubman handling extensive legal work for Sony, partly because he liked doing business with ambitious younger men from Brooklyn. The only thing Yetnikoff didn't like about Grubman was that he was professionally aligned with David Geffen. When the Sony Music chief told him to break off this connection, Grubman refused, but Yetnikoff still regarded him as an ally. Lately, he needed all the allies he could muster.

In September of 1989, Yetnikoff's drinking and drug dependence had grown so severe that he'd checked into the Hazelden Clinic in Minnesota to dry out. Between running his business, slipping behind Warner Records in their fiercely competitive battles for the domestic market, struggling through a crumbling marriage, and negotiating with Sony to install Jon Peters and Peter Guber as the coheads of its new Columbia/TriStar studio, Yetnikoff had been under enormous stress. In October, fresh out of Hazelden, he became the head of a steering committee that would oversee both the studio and his record label—thus overextending himself as he tried to cope with his dependency problems. In a sense, Yetnikoff had never been more powerful, but in another sense, he'd never been as vulnerable to the forces gathering around him.

In 1988, his second-biggest recording act, Bruce Springsteen, had agreed to participate in a fund-raising tour for Amnesty International. Yetnikoff was annoyed by this decision because he had extremely strong convictions about Israel and felt that Amnesty International was prejudiced against the Jewish state. He let Springsteen and his manager, Jon Landau, know of his displeasure, but the rock star went ahead with his plans for the tour. Yetnikoff stopped taking Landau's calls, but Geffen and Landau still regularly communicated with one another.

On the film side, Yetnikoff had wrung an astoundingly lucrative deal for Peters and Guber out of Sony, getting them a $200 million buyout of their production company, $50 million in deferred compensation, annual salaries of $2.7 million apiece, and an 8 percent share of the studio's equity appreciation. Sony's brass, who were now being soaked in Hollywood's strangely intoxicating waters, went along with this package and relied upon Yetnikoff for advice and direction about their studio purchase. It is a truism about Hollywood, and the entertainment field in general, that many business skills are simply not transferable; the ability to run a music company successfully doesn't imply anything at all about one's capacity to master the far more expensive and tricky world of motion picture making. Sony was still a virgin in L.A.

While Yetnikoff was trying to manage several realms at once, his second-in-command, Tommy Mottola, began minding more of the record label's day-to-day affairs. He hired his own people and was soon working with Allen Grubman on a new contract for Michael Jackson, the biggest client on their list. Jackson was one very large reason that Yetnikoff wanted Grubman to end his professional association with Geffen. Before releasing the *Days of Thunder* soundtrack, Geffen had asked Jackson to write a single for the album. Yetnikoff protested, so Geffen eventually used an outtake from Jackson's *Bad* LP. This had left Yetnikoff aggravated because he simply did not want Geffen anywhere near Jackson's material. One day, he decided to vent his feelings.

He called Eric Eisner, one of Geffen Records' key executives, and indulged in his special kind of humor. According to Fredric Dannen in *Hit Men,* Yetnikoff told Eisner that Geffen was having oral sex with a male executive at 20th Century Fox. Then he said that he would pay Geffen handsomely to give his new girlfriend fellatio lessons. When these remarks were passed along to Eisner's boss, Geffen's response was reportedly the same as Yetnikoff's had been fifteen years earlier, when he took over the CBS label and declared to his troops that it was time to crush their primary enemy, Warner Records. This was no longer business, Yetnikoff had said, but war.

For years Geffen had been building an alliance with Michael Jackson, going back to his 1984 effort to put the singer in the film *Streetdandy.* Ever since then, rumors had surfaced that Geffen was trying to lure the performer away from Yetnikoff. This hadn't happened, but other recent developments had shaken Sony's hold over Jackson. In 1989, the singer had dismissed his manager, Frank Dileo, a strong Yetnikoff supporter. John Branca, Jackson's lawyer and another Yetnikoff ally, assumed the managerial role. In mid-1990, Geffen began communicating more intensively with Jackson, telling the superstar that his record company had cost him money on his *Moonwalker* video and that he should be earning more royalties. In early July, Jackson dumped Branca and was left with neither a manager nor an attorney. Geffen introduced him to Sandy Gallin, who managed Dolly Parton and Roseanne Barr. A longtime friend of Geffen's, Gallin also had a beach house in Malibu and was a charter member of the so-called Velvet Mafia.

In August, Jackson hired Gallin as his new manager. With Gallin advising him, the singer now made another move, hiring Bertram Fields and Allen Grubman as his legal team. When Yetnikoff learned of these maneuvers, he was enraged. Jackson owned two music publishing companies, and Yetnikoff was further angered to discover that the larger one, ATV, was dropping its parent organization, EMI, and replacing it with Geffen's new corporate boss, MCA. With Jackson now surrounded by Gallin, Grubman, and

Fields, Geffen began schmoozing Tommy Mottola and Michael Schulhof, Sony's American head of operations.

Yetnikoff again told Mottola to get rid of Grubman, even ban him from the premises, one of Yetnikoff's favorite tactics for those who were persona non grata at his company. Instead of following his superior's order, Mottola went over Yetnikoff's head and spoke to Schulhof. Yetnikoff finally realized that his problems had become serious, but rather than soberly considering his position, he presented the Sony honchos with an ultimatum: stand by him and get rid of Mottola, or vice versa.

On August 17, 1990, the *Wall Street Journal* reported that Yetnikoff, whose relationships with both Michael Jackson and Bruce Springsteen had lately deteriorated, had reached an agreement with Sony. According to the *Journal,* the corporation was moving him away from managing the record group and would most likely replace him with Mottola. The source of this article was never determined, but most knowledgeable people felt that it had been planted by Mottola, along with his new ally in his struggle to take control from Yetnikoff: David Geffen. On August 20, Sony president Norio Ohga released a statement of support for Yetnikoff, saying that the company "could not be more pleased with... Walter." Four days later, *Billboard* published an interview with Yetnikoff, in which he insisted that he would stay on as head of the label. Accompanying the story was a sidebar containing a statement by Jon Landau. It read:

"Walter Yetnikoff was a good friend to Bruce Springsteen and me for many, many years. We enjoyed a superb professional relationship and a pleasant social one. For reasons that remain obscure to us, that relationship ended not long after CBS was purchased by Sony. Neither Bruce nor I have had a significant conversation with him in nearly two years."

It was a quiet, yet public, slap in Yetnikoff's face, filled with foreboding.

Alienated from Michael Jackson and Bruce Springsteen, embattled in corporate infighting with Tommy Mottola, and under siege from several directions by David Geffen, Yetnikoff had nowhere to turn. Even the pope couldn't save him now. If Yetnikoff was expecting more support from the Sony brass, he was severely mistaken. Japanese executives loathe bad publicity and media squabbling among their employees. On the day the *Billboard* article was published, Norio Ohga met with Yetnikoff and gave him a warning, but Ohga's decision had already been made. Two weeks later, Sony announced that Yetnikoff, the king of the grooves and the master of schmingling and bingling, was out. The most powerful man in the record business in the 1980s had fallen hard.

When Geffen heard the news, he picked up the phone and called his friend-of-the-moment, Irving Azoff.

"Ding, dong," Geffen said into the receiver, "the witch is dead."

After his dismissal, Yetnikoff tried to return to his office at CBS headquarters to conclude his affairs, but he was ordered not to trespass at Black Rock or visit its employees at work. He was banned from the building, and the locks were quickly changed on his old doors.

While Yetnikoff was slipping, Michelangelo Signorile had kept up his assault on Geffen. In addition to the Guns n' Roses controversy, the columnist attacked Geffen's label for distributing a live album by Andrew Dice Clay (Def American Records put out Clay's albums and was about to release the debut LP by the Geto Boys, a black Houston rap group whose lyrics graphically depicted rape and murder). Using his trademark capital-letter style in *OutWeek,* Signorile also went after Barry Diller, who'd made a three-picture deal with Clay at 20th Century Fox, and Sandy Gallin, who was Clay's manager. Signorile felt that Geffen, Diller, and Gallin were all acting unconscionably by doing business with the "viciously antigay" comedian.

Signorile was starting to make an impact and to find some West Coast allies for his guerrilla activities. When he called Geffen Records for a comment on Andrew Dice Clay, he was told by PR spokeswoman Byrn Bridenthal that the label was now distancing itself from the comedian; the Geffen logo would not appear on Clay's upcoming live album. A number of prominent Andrew Dice Clay billboards around L.A. were spray-painted—with insults to Barry Diller scrawled across them. In July, Diller killed the three-picture pact with Clay. In August, Geffen Records announced that it was dropping its distribution arrangement with Def American Records regarding the Geto Boys album, stating that the material by this group "possibly endorses violence, racism, and misogyny."

This decision pleased Signorile but angered others. Rick Rubin of Def American told the *L.A. Times* that he was "shocked and disturbed by Geffen's decision." *Times* rock critic Patrick Goldstein raised the issue of the Geffen label having a double standard based on race, as the company was still putting out material by Slayer, a heavy metal white band, and by Andrew Dice Clay, a white comic. Many people found Slayer and Clay to be at least as offensive as the Geto Boys. Geffen Records president Eddie Rosenblatt attempted to counter this argument by saying that one cannot "equate a comedy record to the Geto Boys." Doug Morris of Atlantic Records, which had brought out the hugely controversial and successful rap album *Banned in the U.S.A.* by 2 Live Crew, told the *Times* that Geffen had been faced with a tough call on the Geto Boys and had made the right choice. But Russell Simmons, the head of Def-Jam Records, said that because Geffen supported Slayer and Clay, he had an obligation to stand behind the Geto Boys. A month later, Geffen ended his distribution agreement with Def American, dropping both Slayer and Andrew Dice Clay in the process.

When charges of censorship were now raised against Geffen, he said that he was not opposed to the marketing of the offensive material; *he* just didn't want to be the one selling these albums.

"I'm not going to make money," Geffen told *Rolling Stone* with typical bluntness, "off records that talk about mutilating women and cutting off their tits and fucking their dead bodies."

After Geffen dumped Andrew Dice Clay, Signorile praised him for the first time in his column, but the attacks were not finished. In September, the names of Geffen, Diller, and Gallin were placed on the benefit committee for the AIDS Project Los Angeles (APLA) Commitment to Life Awards ceremony, to be held later that year. An L.A. protest group, Artists Confronting AIDS, took exception to the names and wrote a letter to APLA.

"In looking over the ill-conceived list of notables chosen to promote the benefit," it read, "we noticed a startling number of closet-case celebs alongside some of Hollywood's most notorious homophobes. Is this an AIDS fund-raiser or a monument to show-biz self-hatred?...Commitment to Life? Honey, next year, call it what it really is: Commitment to the Closet."

The L.A. chapter of another gay activist organization, Queer Nation, showed up at the APLA benefit carrying signs depicting Geffen, Diller, and Gallin. The signs read MISS GEFFEN, THE RECORD PRODUCER; MARY GALLIN, THE AGENT; LA DILLER, THE MOVIE MOGUL.

The three men were mortified.

CHAPTER 27

By September of 1990, Michael Ovitz had made significant progress in his efforts to convince the Matsushita Electric Industrial Company to purchase MCA. He'd lined up American lawyers to represent Matsushita in the negotiations that were scheduled to begin soon in New York. He'd brought in his friend Herbert Allen to act as the deal's investment banker, and he'd hired a public relations firm, Adams and Reinhart, to handle the press during the coming months. Matsushita itself had insisted on adding to the mix Robert Strauss, the former national chairman of the Democratic Party and a respected figure on the international political scene, who knew people on both sides of the table.

Throughout the past summer, Ovitz, the master of secrecy, had managed to keep most of his activities surrounding the sale quiet, but Hollywood insiders had long known that MCA was on the block and that Ovitz was brokering the deal. In fact, David Geffen had in fact sold his company to MCA in part because he believed that Wasserman was about to step down or sell the corporation—developments that could greatly redound to his benefit. Now that Ovitz had selected a buyer for MCA and negotiations were about to commence, Geffen realized that he was in a position to become extremely wealthy in real terms, not just on paper. If Matsushita purchased MCA, the conditions of his selling Geffen Records for common stock would no longer apply. He would now be able to cash out his ten million MCA shares for hundreds of millions of dollars.

In recent months, the forty-seven-year-old had been publicly bruised and battered by gay activists, and this had left him feeling more introspective. In mid-September, he traveled to New York, and one Saturday afternoon he and his lawyer and friend Allen Grubman returned to their old Borough Park neighborhood to remember where they'd come from. It was here that Geffen's sexuality had first become an issue, here that he'd first been labeled a fag. The neighborhood was different now—yet somehow the same. Fewer Italian families lived there than in the 1940s. Orthodox Jews from the former Soviet Union had lately been immigrating to Brooklyn, and many of them had settled in Borough Park. Flyers, written in Russian, hung from lampposts, and wary old men walked along the sidewalks in black coats and hats, the uniforms of their fathers, moving past the iron-grated kosher shops and other small stores. Thirteenth Avenue, the business district for the local Hasidim, was quieter on Saturdays than other days but evoked some of the feeling of a Middle Eastern bazaar. The el rattled overhead, and Manhattan—not to mention Malibu—seemed more than a world away.

You work on yourself throughout your lifetime, Geffen liked to tell people, but you die unhealed. Whatever in him that was not healed came from this modest neighborhood, where laundry hung on lines and graffiti covered the subway stations. The streets held the same movement they'd always held, the same sense of worn dreams and permanent change. Hispanics and Asians shared the sidewalks now, along with people from Eastern and Western Europe, all of them trying to make the place feel like home. The air was damp and cool, smelling of aging food from cramped shops, and the early autumn light carried just a trace of sadness. Something here sharpened the senses, imparted an edge of endurance.

Almost all of the men in Geffen's life had emerged from this environment, notably Nat Lefkowitz, Ted Ashley, and Steve Ross—the father figures of his twenties, thirties, and forties. Clive Davis, Walter Yetnikoff, and many others in the music business had also come from here, each of them finding wealth and a place in the great history of American entertainment. If the MCA-Matsushita deal went through, Geffen would be richer than all of them, perhaps all of them combined. The small, slight, curly-haired boy who'd been insulted and hustled on the playgrounds of Brooklyn would vault into a realm virtually unexplored by entertainment executives. Richer than Barry Diller, richer than Michael Eisner over at Disney, and far richer than Michael Ovitz.

One other important figure in Geffen's life came from the streets of Brooklyn, but he was more like a profoundly unruly son than a father figure: Michelangelo Signorile.

As they rode out from Manhattan to Borough Park, Geffen told Grubman that he wanted to show the attorney where he'd been born and raised. They drove by the row house where Geffen had grown up. They drove by the storefront that had been his mother's corset shop (Batya had recently passed away). They drove around the neighborhood, reminiscing about the past, and then drove down to Coney Island, where they got out of the car and strolled to the end of the boardwalk. They talked for hours about the old days and the new ones, before climbing back into the car and making the return trip to Manhattan. Grubman dropped Geffen off at his apartment, and when the attorney got home, his friend called him to add one more remark to their long conversation. After this upcoming sale, Geffen said, things would never be the same again.

In September, when Ovitz first met with MCA's investment banker, Felix Rohatyn of Lazard Frères, he told Rohatyn and Sid Sheinberg that Matsushita was willing to offer MCA between $75 and $90 a share for its stock. Since MCA was now trading at $36 a share, down from $54 the previous March, this bid looked colossally generous. Along with many other stocks, MCA's had recently plunged, in part due to international political fears. On August 2, 1990, Iraq's Saddam Hussein had invaded Kuwait, giving every financial market in the world the jitters. By September, MCA's stock had seriously depreciated, yet Ovitz had convinced the heads of Matsushita that it was worth much more than its current value on Wall Street. And besides, this was merely Matsushita's opening gambit for what might be a very long negotiating ordeal. It was also a secret offer, intended only for the eyes of the handful of key players in Osaka and Hollywood.

On September 25, the *Wall Street Journal* reported that Matsushita was now talking with MCA about buying the media conglomerate for between $80 and $90 a share. Now millions knew about the offer. From New York to Los Angeles to Japan, everyone was asking the same question: Who'd leaked this story to the *Journal?* Speculation was rampant, with some people suspecting that MCA officials had divulged the information to the paper because it made Matsushita's offer for their depressed stock look so good. Others said that Ovitz had spilled the numbers to a reporter in order to move the negotiations forward. The talent agent, went this argument, knew better than most people the tendency of Japanese corporations to engage in months-long consensus-building before they acted on an acquisition; this would cause them to accelerate the process. A third school of thought—by far the most pervasive—

believed that Geffen, who had access to the numbers through his MCA connections, had released them to the *Journal*.

According to this point of view, Geffen had been waiting nearly ten years, ever since his difficulties with Robert Towne and Ovitz over *Personal Best*, for the chance to strike back at the agent and show the world that the head of CAA did not control everything and everyone. The *Journal* article, went this line of reasoning, would publicly embarrass Ovitz and devalue him in the eyes of his Japanese colleagues. On the other hand, Geffen's motivation could have been precisely the opposite. In these circumstances, he and Ovitz were essentially on the same side, and if the agent quickly closed the sale at anything near $80 a share, Geffen would be the greatest beneficiary of the deal. He had the most to gain by nudging the negotiations forward, and by having a story appear in a highly respected paper saying that Matsushita was ready to make a very attractive offer. Perhaps he could even force the buyer's hand.

The Matsushita brass, who placed great value on stealth and silence, did not quite see things this way. They were seriously displeased with the piece in the *Journal*, and reports from Osaka indicated that another such leak might bury the deal. With this in mind, Ovitz brought the two sides together on October 7, in Wasserman's home in L.A., for their initial face-to-face meeting. During the next few weeks, numbers were floated back and forth across the Pacific, while MCA's shares rose to nearly $50 on the New York Stock Exchange. By early November, Ovitz was laying plans for the parties to meet soon in New York, so that negotiating could begin in earnest. On the evening of November 18, Wasserman and Sheinberg met with several Matsushita executives at Manhattan's Plaza Athénée Hotel, where their conversation was conducted through interpreters and rarely moved beyond formalities. The following day, however, Ovitz brought MCA a firm bid: Matsushita was willing to pay $60 a share, plus $3 a share for an equity position in an MCA-owned TV station, WWOR. This was far less than the $75 to $90 Ovitz had mentioned to the leaders of MCA two months earlier, and Wasserman was not impressed. He and Sheinberg turned down the offer.

They did the same thing when Ovitz brought them a second bid, on Tuesday, November 20, of $64 a share. Ovitz was now left with the difficult task of explaining to the Matsushita negotiators, who were lodged at the Waldorf-Astoria Hotel, why the Americans felt they were being lowballed—as well as explaining to the MCA heads why the numbers weren't considerably higher. On Wednesday morning, November 21, instead of trying to resolve this dilemma through another meeting, the talent agent did something unexpected. He announced that he wanted to spend Thanksgiving, which happened to be the next day, with his wife and children in Brentwood, then boarded a plane and flew back to L.A. Some thought his leaving so abruptly meant that the deal was dead. Yet there was strategy behind everything Ovitz did, including his sudden departure. And it worked.

With Ovitz gone, Herbert Allen and Robert Strauss stepped in and quickly resurrected the negotiations. Strauss represented Matsushita and Allen MCA, and on Thanksgiving Day, the Japanese raised their offer by $2 a share, a difference of roughly $200 million if the bid was accepted. By evening, the parties had reached an agreement: MCA would accept $66 a share, plus $3 a share for WWOR. Four days later, on Monday, November 26, the papers were signed in Manhattan and the deal was consummated. Matsushita had bought the conglomerate for $6.6 billion.

After collecting untold millions for his efforts, Ovitz went back to work at CAA and began planning his next coup. The Matsushita purchase of MCA was the largest negotiation he'd ever overseen—the largest ever handled by someone in his profession. Ovitz had entered the stratosphere of public acclaim. The papers were full of praise for the "samurai talent agent" who'd managed to swing the deal in a relatively short period of time, with virtually no glitches. Ovitz had never been more powerful, more respected, or wealthier. Within Hollywood's creative community, there were a few muted cries of dismay. Some MCA employees worried that the Matsushita executives might not give them the same artistic freedom they'd been used to, and other people felt that Wasserman and Sheinberg would have a very difficult time adjusting to being employees of a vast and distant foreign corporation. But for the moment, almost everyone tried to remain optimistic.

David Geffen had great reason for optimism. He was having a stupendous year, despite the nagging criticism of a handful of gay activists. He'd sold his record company for a vast price and seen his most formidable rival in the music business, Walter Yetnikoff, not just fired but barred from his own office. Now, thanks to Michael

Ovitz, someone he'd long regarded as an adversary, Geffen had just made $660 million in cash. He celebrated the 1990 holiday season sailing in the Caribbean with Sandy Gallin and Barry Diller.

CHAPTER 28

Geffen's sudden riches made him a media darling once again. In early December, the editors of *Newsweek* considered him for a cover story but decided against it. Then he turned down the cover of *GQ* but accepted the same offer from *Forbes;* feature articles were written on him in *GQ* and *Vanity Fair* in early 1991. Now that he was being touted as the richest man in entertainment history, he was no longer treated with snickering disdain by reporters but with respect, if not something approaching awe. A stock-and-bond portfolio estimated at $750 million and a net worth of nearly a billion dollars is bound to shift some attitudes. All of the journalists surrounding Geffen lauded his abilities as a businessman and indicated that, with the recent fall of Yetnikoff at Sony, he was an extremely formidable adversary. Even the hyperbolic name of Michael Corleone, the ruthless mob boss on the come in the first *Godfather* picture, was starting to be linked to Geffen. While each of the national magazine stories added to his aura as the smartest, or luckiest, person in America, the most significant one appeared in *Forbes* on December 24, 1990.

The cover showed Geffen lying down with his hands behind his head, looking boyish and very pleased with life. The picture's tag line read, "Music Magnate David Geffen: Getting Rich Is the Best Revenge." In the article itself, the subject of Steve Ross surfaced, as did Ross's long-standing support of Geffen in the music business. Geffen began by saying, "I love Steve Ross," but then mentioned trying to sell his record label to the older man in 1986, for $50 million, and in 1987, for $75 million; each time, he said, Ross kept turning him down.

"I guess he'd kept hoping I'd have a bad year and he'd get the company for less," Geffen told *Forbes*. "Had Steve Ross been a different guy, he could have bought the company for $50 million and I'd be killing myself today."

In what would strike many entertainment people as a completely gratuitous remark, he then said of Ross, "His biggest get-off is when he can sit there after a deal is made and say how he took someone to the cleaners."

Geffen bitterly remembered the $5 million that Ross had not been willing to advance him in 1984, when the men were renegotiating the original WCI/Geffen Records contract.

"Steve Ross," he said, "wasn't willing to bet on me but I was happy to bet on myself."

Geffen was also "really offended" when Ross didn't include him in the stock options that resulted from the Time Warner merger, the way he'd included Steven Spielberg, Barbra Streisand, and Clint Eastwood. When Geffen spoke of how fast he'd accepted the offer for his label from Sid Sheinberg and MCA, he said, "I learned my lesson with Steve Ross about how people blow deals. So I simply said yes."

Seeking a response to these comments, *Forbes* went to Ross, but the head of Time Warner maintained, according to the article, "a dignified, if somewhat hurt, silence." Even the editors of the magazine seemed a bit taken aback by Geffen's vitriol toward his former partner. They quoted Shakespeare to make their point.

"How sharper than a serpent's tooth," the Bard wrote in *King Lear,* "it is to have a thankless child."

For those who place importance on psychological symbols, Geffen's statements in *Forbes* were a perfectly visible slaying of a surrogate father by an unforgiving son. He slammed the door hard, perhaps to convince himself of something that he needed to be convinced of. Ross was the last paternal figure Geffen would have before crossing the threshold into inescapable adulthood, and maybe he had to purge the relationship, and the old pattern, in public—get it out of his system so he could move on. He was nearly fifty and there would be no more benefactors with the stature of Steve Ross, no more men willing to bankroll him in a way that would prevent him from losing a dime in his new ventures. Geffen could conceivably lose a billion dollars in the future, or make a billion more. He cut the cord in *Forbes,* and was now on his own as he'd never quite been before.

If some people were shocked and angered by what he'd said about the Time Warner CEO, others were not. The ritual acted out by the two men was deep and entangled, and it left both of them with wounds around the heart that were still unhealed when Ross died in 1992. For Geffen, business had never been just business when it involved interaction with senior, male entertainment executives. He was always looking for love, as well as money, so he was always vulnerable. For Ross, the goal was to be the all-father to his employees, and he expected love in return. So he was vulnerable too.

"It had been a punishing period," Connie Bruck wrote of Ross's life in 1990 and 1991, in her book *Master of the Game*. "He had been enraged by remarks David Geffen made about him in *Forbes,* after Geffen had sold his record company to MCA and had then made two thirds of a billion dollars when Matsushita acquired MCA. Geffen—the only person Ross had backed to turn on him publicly—was quoted as saying, 'His biggest get-off. . . .'

"Geffen's statement was true as far as it went—although he omitted that the art of it, of course, was to take someone to the cleaners but do it so brilliantly that that person did not know it and went away happy. What Geffen had done, in any event, was viewed by Ross and his most ardent supporters as a kind of sacrilege, attempted patricide. The pact, however implicit, was that Ross supported you and cared for you, he would bolster you when you faltered, he would always be there, he would be the idealized father you never had; and you, in turn, simply had to do your best at the thing you loved and give him your undying fealty. Fealty meant ascribing to the legend: Ross was good, he was honest, he was fair, and he was loyal to death. Geffen had dared to make a very small rent in the veil."

And that rent inevitably left anger in its wake.

"I'm older," says one Hollywood executive, "and I genuinely dislike seeing my generation replaced by men as nakedly ambitious and driven and self-congratulatory as Geffen. In my day, successful business people in the field of entertainment were admired more than feared. But today, things have changed. Long ago, David Geffen got even with the rest of the world. He's won everything there is to win. He needs to realize this and let it go."

A former Warner executive comments, "I doubt if you could

ıyone in Hollywood who would want to trade their own life ıvid Geffen's. I doubt if any of them has as many ghosts as he does. People in Hollywood are envious of his wealth and his smarts and his fame, but I would be stunned if you could find someone who wanted to be him. I defy you to find that person. David must be a very lonely man, and I wonder if he's had one minute of peace in his life. Sammy Glick never stopped running, and I'm sure that David won't either, until the first shovel of dirt hits the top of his coffin."

With his proceeds from the MCA sale, Geffen became the biggest individual taxpayer in America in 1990. He soon bought more clothes for his New York and L.A. wardrobes, purchased paintings by Jasper Johns, Jackson Pollock, Roy Lichtenstein, and Andy Warhol, and paid $26 million for a Gulfstream IV, the jet of choice for the early nineties. He and investor Richard Rainwater would buy a 4 percent stake in Honeywell, and Geffen would consider owning a piece of Paramount Pictures, the Bel-Air Hotel, and the Executive Life Insurance Company, which held more than $50 million of the junk-bond debt of his good friend Calvin Klein. None of these deals came to fruition.

Nor did his newfound fame and riches dampen the attacks by his detractors. Michelangelo Signorile was again upset because amidst all the publicity Geffen had received following the sale of his MCA stock, he'd continued to maintain his stance to the press as a bisexual. In December of 1990, Signorile encouraged his *OutWeek* readers to "ZAP GEFFEN AGAIN!" and they did. The *Forbes* article had described Geffen as "Hollywood's first billionaire" and "a bachelor to boot." It was this last phrase that sent Signorile back to his keyboard.

"My heart," he wrote in *OutWeek,* "goes out to any of those hetero girls who might be reading this.... It's terrible that *Forbes* is once again misleading you poor dears....

"And it is up to David Geffen himself to tell that to the media. HERE IS THIS ALL-POWERFUL QUEER GETTING HIMSELF ON THE COVERS OF MAGAZINES—AND HE CAN'T EVEN STAND UP, BE PROUD AND GIVE VISIBILITY TO THIS COMMUNITY."

Signorile was further incensed when Geffen told *Vanity Fair,* in its March 1991 issue, that he was "bisexual" and then said, "I have not kept any secrets. . . . There's not a person who does not know my story."

In *OutWeek,* Signorile kept pressuring Geffen to come out publicly, while gay activists in L.A. vented their feelings on other issues, most notably their belief that current movies like *Silence of the Lambs* and *Basic Instinct* carried homophobic messages. With the 1991 Academy Awards approaching in early spring, the Los Angeles chapters of Queer Nation and ACT UP sent letters to Academy members asking them to discuss AIDS at the Oscar ceremony, enclosing a SILENCE = DEATH button in each envelope. Only two celebrities—Susan Sarandon and Bruce Davison, one of the stars of *Longtime Companion,* a film about AIDS—wore them to the ceremony, and no one there talked about the disease. But fifty activists protested the event from outside the Dorothy Chandler Pavilion, and one man got inside and charged the stage before being stopped by security at the orchestra pit.

"A hundred thousand dead from AIDS!" he screamed as he was being led away by security guards. "What are you doing?"

Later that evening, one hundred members of ACT UP gathered outside of Spago, Wolfgang's Puck's chic Sunset Boulevard restaurant where agent Swifty Lazar was having an Oscar party. The protesters carried signs that read COME OUT QUEER HOLLYWOOD, THE TRUTH SHALL SET YOU FREE and GAY STARS SHINE BRIGHTEST WHEN THEY ARE OUT.

There was little immediate response by the Hollywood community to any of these activities, but as 1991 progressed, the industry's power brokers began to behave differently, either from embarrassment or a gradual realization that the protesters were not going away.

Barry Diller and Sid Sheinberg formed Hollywood Supports, an organization committed to dealing with AIDS discrimination and homophobia in the entertainment business. Diller gave an interview to the *Advocate,* a gay magazine, and said, "I think it would be irresponsible for a senior executive in this community not to speak to the issue [of homophobia]. . . . We've got to start busting the myth that audiences won't accept gay material. We have no evidence of people running screaming from the theater."

In the August 1991 issue of the *Advocate,* Signorile took his most controversial step yet: He wrote that Pete Williams, the chief

Pentagon spokesman during America's recent Gulf War, was homosexual. This set off another enraged debate over outing, both within and beyond the gay community, but Signorile maintained that because the U.S. military banned gays from service, and because many homosexual men and women wanted to join the armed forces but could do so only by hiding their sexual orientation, Williams's private life was a matter of public concern. Signorile believed that the nation and its leaders needed to confront the fact that one's sexual desires had nothing to do with one's ability to serve one's country.

Once again, many people feared that Signorile's actions might destroy someone's career, but the opposite occurred. In 1993, Williams moved along to *The NBC Nightly News* and became a national correspondent.

The same month that Williams was outed, three hundred of Hollywood's big names gathered at a West L.A. home for a benefit for the National Gay and Lesbian Task Force, an event virtually unimaginable in earlier years. Bob Daly, the Warner Bros. chairman, was there, along with Disney's Jeffrey Katzenberg, ABC's president of entertainment, Robert Iger, MCA's Sid Sheinberg, and, most surprisingly, Michael Ovitz. Several studios were now considering domestic-partnership benefits for their gay employees, and homophobia in the movies was an open topic of discussion. The activists had been seen and heard.

At the close of the March 1991 *Vanity Fair* article, Geffen gave in to introspection, speaking publicly in a way that he'd never quite done before. His old brashness had started to fade; a tone of humility and maturity had entered his voice. He seemed a bit surprised at how much larger his image was now, and it was as if the past year or two had significantly pained him but made him think.

"We want heroes," he said, "and then we want to kill them. We want to see that they have clay feet. I have clay feet. I'm imperfect in every way."

When hints of a new Michael Corleone taking over L.A. were raised in the story, Geffen denied that he had a "Godfather capacity" in Hollywood. He really didn't have the clout to fix things with just a phone call or two, he emphasized. He appeared to want to talk more about his relationship with his innermost self than about his business power plays.

"On the day you die," he said, "you will be the only one who knows what lies you told. And how well, or badly, you behaved at any given moment. How brave you were. That's why you have to forgive people. Because each of us has to live with what we've done."

Then he made a statement—a complex, emotionally charged, disturbingly revealing statement—that echoed across the entire history of show business in twentieth-century America.

"I'm just a boy from Brooklyn who wishes he were six feet tall, with blond hair and blue eyes," he said. "That's who I really am."

ACT THREE

Love

CHAPTER 29

1992 was a pivotal year in American politics—and in the political atmosphere of Los Angeles. Presidential incumbent George Bush was seeking reelection, hoping to extend the twelve-year stay in the White House shared by himself and Ronald Reagan. In the spring of 1992, Texas billionaire and wild card Ross Perot tossed himself into the race, via a series of TV interviews and public opinion polls, then tossed himself out and then back in again, as unpredictable as a Panhandle twister. Bush and Perot were running against one another and against the younger, Democratic governor of Arkansas, Bill Clinton. In his mid-forties, Clinton was roughly the same age as David Geffen, who'd worked for Democratic candidates and causes ever since the nomination of George McGovern for president back in 1972. The 1992 campaign turned out to be the most intriguing national political event in decades.

The race held at least three genuinely startling elements. First of all, there was Perot's obvious appeal to an electorate weary of standard-issue politicians, along with his even more obvious ambivalence about his reach for the White House. He couldn't seem to make up his mind about anything, yet he constantly held around 20 percent of the voters in thrall. Second, the country was gripped for weeks by the emergence of a woman who claimed to have been Clinton's mistress for a dozen years—Gennifer Flowers, who took off her clothes for *Penthouse* magazine and then went on the record in its pages about some of the governor's horizontal aptitudes. Clearly, American politics had added a new dimension. Her allegations caused a great ruckus in the media and the public about Clinton's character flaws and his likely unfitness for the presidency. He was christened "Slick Willie" and soon lived up to his nickname by managing to convey in press conferences that he was genuinely sorry about some of what he'd done as governor, yet had enjoyed himself immensely while in office.

Perot and Gennifer Flowers were lighthearted diversions compared to the third development. The Republicans held their convention in Houston in July, and the gathering featured rabblerousing orations by evangelist Pat Robertson and former Richard Nixon speechwriter Pat Buchanan. In recent years, the two men had been part of the Republican camp but had generally been kept at bay by more moderate segments of the party. Now, in 1992, they were given the chance to vent their feelings and openly talk about the "cultural war" that their America was fighting against the amoral or immoral elements of our society—starting with the non-Christian and non-heterosexual groups within the country. The Republic had reached a critical passage; lines were being drawn, and in some quarters tolerance was clearly evaporating. Robertson and Buchanan had amassed enough power to be taken very seriously inside their own party, and the networks were now providing prime-time nationwide TV coverage of their speeches. Some people were taken aback by their message.

"During the Republican convention, I was in Philadelphia for some meetings," says John Parr, former president of the National Civic League in New York and a longtime Democratic activist. "I remember coming back to my hotel room, turning on the television, and watching Buchanan speak. He was definitely the lead dog in their parade. The overwhelming sense I had was of this incredibly mean-spirited man who was almost spitting as he made his speech. You could feel the fear-mongering pouring out of him. It was us versus them, in an effort to divide America against itself."

Out in Malibu, David Geffen also tuned in these speeches, and his response was similar to Parr's. As he would later tell *Rolling Stone,* "The first day of the Republican convention, I was shocked after hearing Pat Buchanan and Pat Robertson. I couldn't believe this was happening. It made me sad, and it made me angry, and it made me think that it's time to get involved. . . . The kind of government the Republican party was talking about during their convention was a white, male, Christian, heterosexual world. There are lots of other people out there."

Bill Clinton may have had many flaws, but in looking over the field, Geffen, always the realist, found him to be the best and most electable of the three men. He decided to give the Arkansas candidate $100,000, which was in keeping with his recent efforts to donate money to things he believed in (he would give the United Jewish Fund

$1 million in 1993). He'd been at least a partial child of the sixties, because of his interaction with the counterculture and some of the most significant musicians of that time. He'd been a child of the seventies, because of his nights at Studio 54 and his continuing exploration of his psyche and his sexuality. He'd been a child of the eighties, because he'd leveraged $30 million at the start of that decade into roughly $1 billion at the end of it. Now, in the nineties, he was evolving into something in line with the persistent media rumors that during the final ten years of the century, and the millennium, people with a political consciousness would come forward and be willing to work for social change. The "me decade" of the eighties would, at least in theory, be replaced by something less self-indulgent and more noble. The nineties would be a kind of sixties redux, except the new decade would not be saturated with war protests and drug consumption but would be more sober and substantive. Geffen, as usual, was part of this trend.

Lately, numerous things had happened in his life and beyond it that might have made anyone think more about the surrounding political realities. He'd been hammered by members of the most militant wing of America's gay community, who were determined to drag him, kicking and screaming, out of the closet and to make this a public spectacle. He'd resisted their efforts so far, and when asked about Mike Signorile, he referred to him as a "terrorist." Yet there was reason to believe that Geffen had been affected by the militants in ways that went deeper than his decision to stop distributing the recordings of the Geto Boys and Andrew Dice Clay. He'd recently set up the David Geffen Foundation, which was deluged with hundreds of requests for money each week, including some people who just wanted the funds to finish college. He'd hired Bob Burkett, a political adviser, Washington lobbyist, and veteran Democratic activist, to help him lay out a social agenda for his financial donations.

For the past several years, Geffen had been involved with AIDS Project Los Angeles and had given the organization money, but now he increased his efforts. In March of 1992, he gave $1 million to APLA, its largest gift ever, to be used for the food, counseling, and health care needs of three thousand clients. Geffen had begun writing $10,000 checks to individuals with AIDS. In May of 1992, two years after the outcry over his offer of Guns n' Roses for a GMHC benefit concert, Geffen gave $1 million to GMHC, which was the largest AIDS charity in Manhattan, serving forty-five hundred people. In 1992, he donated a total of $5 million, including all the profits from his current movies and plays, to AIDS-related projects. He also underwrote the gay-based Lambda Defense Fund's case against the Naval Academy for dismissing a young man, Joe Steffan, who'd openly acknowledged his homosexuality while in the service.

In April of 1992, after four white Los Angeles police officers were acquitted in the videotaped beating of black motorist Rodney King, L.A. exploded into several days of rioting. Not since the sixties had a major American city witnessed such a spontaneous combustion of racially inspired rage. Although the actual looting and burning had not crept into the fashionable and expensive neighborhoods of L.A.'s West side, or into Malibu, the fear caused by the violence nevertheless shot through everyone in the metropolis. Los Angeles had a long and complicated history of white officers pushing, or breaking, the legal boundaries with black citizens, and the acquittal, by a white jury, in the King case finally lit the torch.

Beneath all the money and glamour of L.A.'s entertainment industry and other wealthy sectors, the have-nots and minorities that make up the "other" L.A. were filled with anger and resentment. More than in most cities, the police were the buffer between these two worlds, and violence was no more than an ugly traffic incident away. The riots put L.A. and the rest of the country on notice: America still had painful racial problems that could detonate at any time. Twelve years of Ronald Reagan and George Bush had not ameliorated these troubles, and any political rhetoric that pitted blacks against whites could only deepen the division.

Geffen, who'd earlier been attacked for his support of controversial recording artists, like the Geto Boys, was now openly critical of Warner Records, his old parent company, for including the song "Cop Killer" on the *Body Count* album by the black rapper Ice-T. Geffen blasted Warner label boss Mo Ostin for putting out the LP and making money from a product advocating the murder of policemen.

"Mo Ostin is more concerned with market share than I am," he told *Rolling Stone.* "I'm willing to give up market share for things that really mean something to me. Mo says this is about censorship, but it has...only to do with money and responsibility."

Geffen also said that he agreed with actor Charlton Heston on virtually nothing but concurred with Heston's position that if the lyrics had read "Jew Killer" instead of "Cop Killer," Warner would not have released the record. At the very least, Geffen contended, Warner should donate the profits from the song to a fund for wounded policemen.

Then another political event landed much closer to home for Geffen, when his own record label was hit with reports of sexual harassment on the job. Twenty-eight-year-old Penny Muck had worked at Geffen Records for several years and helped promote Guns n' Roses and Aerosmith. Having seen her share of coked-out musicians and star-gazing groupies, she was not naive about the industry's underbelly of drugs and sex. But she was unprepared for what happened in the summer of 1991 when, according to Muck, Marko Babineau, a forty-year-old veteran of Geffen's promotional staff, approached her desk, opened his fly, took out his penis, and masturbated in front of her.

"Watch me! Watch me!" he yelled out, before ejaculating on the magazine she was reading. He then told her to clean up the mess and walked back to his office, Muck later said, "as if nothing had happened."

For years at Geffen Records, Babineau had walked the fine line in the rock music business between being a highly effective wildcat and being out of control.

"Marko was really good at breaking Geffen's acts," says Patrick Goldstein, the *L.A. Times* rock critic. "You don't want to believe anything bad about him, but promo men always act crazy. It's a tradition in the industry. One guy at another company used to whip his employees to get them motivated. At a lot of record labels, they don't know what the promo men are doing because they don't want to. Are they making payola payoffs? Are they bringing drugs and hookers to radio stations in order to get air time for their acts? There's been so much of this kind of behavior that it can be difficult to determine when someone is acting crazy and when he's just doing his job. In the record business, when a female artist jumps up and pees on an A & R man's desk that's colorful behavior, but when a promo man starts coming on a woman's desk everyone gets up in arms. There's something of a double standard there.

"Once the Marko situation happened at Geffen Records, David didn't try to cover it up. They handled it better than most companies would have."

Following the incident, Muck felt very isolated at the label, convinced that no one would believe her if she told the Geffen executives what had happened. She enjoyed working at this office because in the music business, as she once put it, the name "Geffen" equaled "prestige." She was making $32,000 a year and needed the job, so she decided to keep quiet—but couldn't. She signed a claim against the company with California's Fair Employment and Housing Commission and with the federal Equal Employment Opportunity Commission, charging that she'd been verbally and physically harassed by Babineau, and further charging that Babineau had threatened her job and her career in the business if she talked about his actions. Her attorney, Benjamin Schonbrun, also stated that Geffen Records "did not take appropriate measures to ensure a safe and sexual-harassment free environment...for years." Two other women who'd earlier complained about Babineau inside the company had been transferred to other departments, Muck alleged.

In her claim, Muck said that the last reported incident with Babineau had occurred on August 20, 1991. Fifteen days later, Geffen Records released a statement that Babineau was taking a six-month "break" after twenty years of promoting music, in order to be with his wife and baby daughter. He quickly resigned. Attorney Bertram Fields, speaking on behalf of Geffen Records, denied that the label had any prior knowledge of Babineau's misconduct.

Babineau had been vanquished, but Muck was not finished. In November of 1991, she filed a multi-million-dollar suit against Geffen Records, MCA, and Matsushita for their tolerance of "outrageous sexually deviant behavior" by a top executive at the label. In a prepared statement that she read from the steps of the county courthouse in Santa Monica, Muck said, "I feel degraded, humiliated, and frightened. But I hope that other women will have the strength to come forward."

Island Records, Capitol, and RCA were soon hit with allegations of sexual harassment or lawsuits by female employees. In mid-autumn of 1991, the *L.A. Times* did a front-page article on the problem, which was said to be five times worse than the "casting couch" associated with the movie industry. Fifty women talked anonymously to the paper and said that they'd been subjected to slaps on the buttocks by record executives, demands for oral sex in limousines on the way to concerts, and being asked to sleep with musicians signed to their label. Middle-aged males, the women said, often acted liked teenaged boys, and promo men were the worst offenders.

In November of 1992, Geffen Records agreed to settle Muck's lawsuit out of court, paying her $500,000. She went on to work at an artist management firm in L.A., while Babineau opened his own promotion company in Bel-Air. Muck's charges and legal actions sent fear through an industry that had long been accustomed to outlandish behavior on the part of its male honchos. Geffen himself told *BAM* magazine in 1991 that Walter Yetnikoff had gotten fired in part because of his habit of going up to women and asking them to "jiggle your tits for me."

With the sale of the independent labels to the straitlaced, no-nonsense conglomerates in the late eighties, and with the recent retirement of old-line recording execs like Capitol's colorful Joe Smith, and with the rise of legal challenges to uncontrolled sexual urges in the office, an era in the music business was passing away. Some would miss it and some would not. After decades of untrammeled adolescence, record labels were being forced to grow up and become just another well-behaved division inside a vast, often foreign-owned corporate structure. Rock 'n' roll had settled into middle age.

Geffen's political activities did nothing to dampen his expanding material desires. He now had a chauffeur-driven Lincoln Continental, with multiple phone lines, and had installed a special $600,000 phone connection in his Gulfstream IV so he could stay in touch while flying over the ocean. In 1991, he bought a $3 million home on Sunset Strip, to go along with his Malibu beach house, the $47.5 million estate on Angelo Drive, his seven-room apartment in Manhattan, and Calvin Klein's former residence in the Fire Island Pines section of Long Island. He began taking financial advice from such heavyweights as New York investment banker Felix Rohatyn and the "Oracle of Omaha," fellow billionaire Warren Buffett. The excitement of meeting Warren Buffett face-to-face in the nineties, Geffen once said, was akin to the rush he felt when first encountering Bob Dylan back in the sixties.

In May of 1992, when Calvin Klein's struggling clothing empire could not meet an interest payment, Geffen stepped in and purchased

$62 million of the fashion designer's junk bonds. After bailing out his friend, Geffen suggested that Klein hire a new poster boy—a rippling nineteen-year-old rap singer from Boston named Marky Mark—and feature him at bus shelters, in magazines, and on TV wearing nothing but Calvin Klein underwear. For $100,000, Klein signed Marky Mark and put his muscles on display. Geffen's instincts were once again golden; within three months, Klein's underwear sales had gone up 34 percent, and the company began to turn around. In June of 1993, Klein borrowed $58 million from Citibank and bought back the bonds from Geffen, whose actions had not been solely altruistic. He sold the bonds for a profit.

During the early nineties, Geffen purchased approximately $120 million worth of art, giving him the largest collection of abstract expressionist and pop art in L.A., if not the country. Edward G. Robinson had been Hollywood's first great buyer of art, with works by Monet, Degas, and Picasso, while in more recent decades actors Jack Nicholson and Steve Martin, producers Ray Stark and Douglas Cramer, and Michael Ovitz had amassed very impressive collections. Now Geffen outstripped them all.

In November of 1991, he created a stir at Sotheby's in New York, when he arrived wearing a T-shirt, jeans, tennis shoes, and a white cap placed backward on his head, while the rest of the gathering favored evening clothes or suits and ties. Geffen took a seat, grabbed a blue paddle, and began bidding on Willem de Kooning's *Woman,* which he bought for $3.4 million, before gliding off into the night. When asked about the man's attire, the auctioneer, John L. Marion, replied, "He can wear anything he wants."

The walls of Geffen's Malibu beach house were covered with paintings, which were set off nicely by the ocean-view windows and the white couches, white chairs, and hardwood floors. For companionship he had a ten-button telephone—"The phone for some people," said a friend, "is kind of like safe sex"—and he also had a parrot named Archie. He taught the bird to speak, and one part of their verbal interaction summed up his entire twenty-year career inside the offices of Asylum and Geffen Records.

In a town and an industry often paralyzed by fear, Geffen had always encouraged his employees to speak up or talk back when they had something to say. In a city where many executives believed that the key to success was always appearing to be larger than you really were, Geffen had maintained himself at a human scale. He may have been a garish consumer in some areas, like the art world or buying Jack Warner's house, but he still lived in a modest residence by the ocean and didn't bother shaving when he visited Sotheby's. In a business filled with people who'd created a false public persona, Geffen worked without a mask. Many people didn't like his personality or couldn't tolerate his level of self-confidence, but they conceded that he was what he was: an unpolished, advice-giving, pesky individual from Brooklyn who said what he felt, regardless of whom he offended, and did most of his business from his gut. He was almost fifty years old and was doing the very hardest thing to do in Los Angeles—attempting to be himself.

When Geffen told Archie to shut up, the parrot looked right at him and said, "Shut up! Shut up! Shut up!"

In early November of 1992, Bill Clinton was narrowly elected president, marking the first time that anyone of Geffen's generation had ascended to this level of political prominence. In the same general election, the voters of Colorado passed Amendment Two, which made it illegal to create legislation based on people's sexual orientation—meaning that the state could not pass a gay rights bill. In his campaign, Clinton had come forward as a rock fan, made numerous appearances on MTV, and used Fleetwood Mac's "Don't Stop Thinkin' About Tomorrow" as one of his theme songs for the next presidency. No one could have imagined Ronald Reagan, George Bush, or Ross Perot doing such a thing; a new set of possibilities had come to Washington, D.C. The president-elect, who understood power shifts in important places as well as anyone, knew that Hollywood was also undergoing significant changes, which would intensify as the nineties unfolded. Paying attention to such things could be very beneficial.

Clinton was grateful to many people who'd supported his campaign, and they included the richest man in Hollywood. The new chief executive would soon give Geffen a guided tour of Air Force One and a phone number where he could be reached. Before long, the record executive who'd grown up sleeping on a sofa would find himself spending the night in the Lincoln bedroom at the White House. Geffen was quite flattered by these gestures, coming as they did from the leader of the world's largest democracy, but he tried not to lose his perspective. One day at Geffen Records, he was on the phone with Robbie Robertson, the renowned singer-songwriter-guitarist for the Band, when his secretary interrupted to say that the White House was on another line. He told her to take a message.

CHAPTER 30

In the past, Geffen had refused awards for his charitable work on behalf of AIDS, but by late 1992, he'd changed his mind. He was becoming more visible and politically involved, he'd donated money to help elect President Clinton, and he may have also wanted to clear up some misconceptions about his sexuality in the media (which had him dating Madonna in 1991, just as it would later have him marrying Keanu Reeves, whom he claimed never to have met). When both AIDS Project Los Angeles and Barry Diller asked him to accept APLA's 1992 Commitment to Life Award, largely because he'd given the organization $1 million earlier in the year, he accepted their offer. Not everyone in the gay community was pleased with his selection, but as an APLA secretary once put it, "Our organization really likes to honor people with money who can bring in other people with money."

On the night of November 18, he and Barbra Streisand received the award at the Universal Amphitheater. Six thousand people were on hand, and Geffen told them, "We are in a health crisis that is overwhelming whole populations of people across the planet, and yet we are still giving awards to people who simply do what they can to help." These remarks drew a lukewarm response, but the audience gave him a spontaneous outpouring of applause and affection when he announced from the stage, for the first time in public, that he was indeed "a gay man."

Some members of the homosexual community instantly forgave Geffen for not doing this in years past and felt that he'd now done everything necessary to silence his critics. Others condemned him for not calling for a boycott of Colorado following the passage of Amendment Two, as gay activists and certain entertainers were now doing, and for not making this pronouncement in 1991, when he'd presented himself as bisexual in an interview with *Vanity Fair.*

Like Geffen, Liz Smith had also felt the wrath of Michelangelo Signorile in his *OutWeek* column. Seven days after Geffen appeared at the APLA awards ceremony, Smith wrote a passionate defense of Geffen in her nationally syndicated column, praising him for his work on behalf of gay and heterosexual organizations.

"A few gay activists," she declared, "...are...just plain jealous that this guy is now one of the richest and most powerful men in the entertainment world....To his critics, I say get over it, get a life, and leave this guy alone."

A month after receiving the APLA award, Geffen was named Man of the Year by the *Advocate.* His face was on the cover and the magazine published a lengthy interview with him. The *Advocate* editors called Geffen "the most powerful openly gay man in the country," adding that they'd chosen him for this honor in part because Geffen had paid for two full-page ads in the *New York Times,* following Clinton's election, reminding the new president not to forget his prior commitment to ending discrimination against gays in the military. (Whenever he was asked about this issue, Geffen replied that he couldn't understand why anyone would want to be in the armed forces, but if they did, their sexual orientation shouldn't make any difference.) Geffen and his political consultant, Bob Burkett, devised the slogan "Live and Let Serve" and organized meetings between members of Congress and military leaders who were in favor of lifting the ban against gays.

The person whom the *Advocate* now presented as its Man of the Year was not exactly the same David Geffen who'd been speaking to reporters throughout the past two decades. Perhaps it was because he'd publicly come out the month before. Or because he was talking to a gay magazine now, instead of one geared toward the heterosexual population. Or because he was more relaxed than ever before, more open, and had discovered that it was "very empowering" to announce his sexual identity in front of a large audience. Once again, Geffen displayed his lifelong ability to turn what initially seemed like very negative events into positive ones.

"I don't think," he told the periodical, "that I would be anywhere near as healthy a person emotionally as I am today or as successful had I not had that experience [of his cancer scare in 1976–80]. I was caught up in a lot of silly shit in 1976 that I simply dropped."

Then he began speaking as very few, if any, highly accomplished American businessmen had ever spoken before for attribution:

"A lot of people think that being fucked-up propels their success. I've learned exactly the opposite. The healthier I've become in my life and the more I have worked on myself, the more successful I've become....

"I'm loving myself more and more.... I highly recommend it [publicly coming out] to anybody even though it took me a long time to get here.... I never elected myself to be a role model, but if I am going to be a role model, I want to be one that I can be proud of....

"I learned long ago that I can't live my life to make other people happy. I have to live my life to make myself happy. We live in a world in which we find ourselves disappointing people we don't even know."

Despite these remarks, he remained deeply unforgiving toward Signorile and other gay activists:

"I think outing is wrong and unconscionable. I think it does not help; it hurts. It makes people more afraid, not less afraid. I think that terrorists like Michelangelo Signorile have not done any good. I think they've done a lot of harm. I think he's an angry, hostile, jealous guy who has his nose pressed up against the window at the party that he imagines is going on but that he hasn't been invited to. And I think that's what motivates his rage rather than the desire to do good for gay people in general. I think people are allowed to have their secrets.... There are people whose lives are tremendously hurt by this sort of thing, who are married or have careers that could be tremendously affected by this, and I think it is an act of cruelty."

Gay activist and writer Larry Kramer had criticized Geffen for not making movies that dealt with gay or AIDS-related subjects. When asked about this, Geffen said, "Frankly, I don't give a shit what Larry Kramer thinks about me or the movies I make or what motivates me to make a movie. I think Larry Kramer is attacking me simply because he's unhappy that I'm not unhappy. I think it's silly to say that because one is gay one should be making movies about gay people. I think that people should aspire to do good work. By the way, we haven't talked about the fact that I'm making *M. Butterfly.*"

Geffen was in the process of turning this Broadway play, which had won three Tony awards in 1988, into a film starring Jeremy Irons and John Lone. *M. Butterfly* was the story of a man who'd lived for years with a person he believed was a woman but turned out to be a man.

When asked if the number of gay characters on TV and in movies would soon increase, Geffen replied, "I think we're moving in a direction in which there are more gays, more blacks, more women—more everything. And I think in a Clinton administration we're going to see that happen more and more. I think we're going to see a government that looks more like the America that we see on the streets. It isn't going to be only white, Christian, male, heterosexual. Finally."

In the future, when pressed to define himself sexually, Geffen would say that he was now "100 percent gay," except on those occasions when he saw actress Demi Moore walk by his beach house wearing virtually nothing. Then anything was possible.

The year 1993 began with great optimism for Bill Clinton and David Geffen, but the hopeful mood soon dissipated for the new president. In April of 1993, under extremely controversial orders from the new attorney general, Janet Reno, the FBI launched an attack on a Waco, Texas, religious compound run by David Koresh. The compound held many of Koresh's followers, who refused to leave their stronghold despite warnings that the FBI was coming in. Both adults and children died in the resulting blaze. It was the first disaster for a new administration that was having a very jittery beginning. Despite promises of ending the ban on gays in the military, President Clinton eventually settled for a compromise: the armed forces adopted a "Don't Ask, Don't Tell" policy about recruits' sexuality, designed to keep virtually everyone from confronting the issue head-on.

Late in 1993, Geffen also became embroiled in controversy, when Guns n' Roses came out with another album, *The Spaghetti Incident?* On the disc, Axl Rose had included a song, "Look at Your Game Girl," written by convicted mass murderer Charles Manson. The felon was not mentioned in the liner notes, but at the end of the song, Rose says, "Thanks, Chas." When law enforcement and victims' rights groups became aware that Manson had composed this tune, they organized a protest at the Geffen Records office on Sunset Boulevard and a nationwide boycott of the label and its film products. Doris Tate, the sister of actress Sharon Tate, who was killed in the 1969 slayings in Benedict Canyon, had founded the Doris Tate Crime Victims Bureau and was leading the protest.

"We've had enough of this anything-for-a-buck mentality," she told the media, "and we're going to fight it on every front. We intend to hurt them in the only place they seem to care about: their wallet."

Geffen was on vacation in Barbados when he turned on the television and saw a CNN report about Charles Manson and his recording label. Until then, he had been unaware of the song's origin, and later claimed that he couldn't have kept it off the album anyway, because of the contractual rights of his artists. Watching the CNN broadcast, he went berserk.

Manson's copyright royalties on "Look at Your Game Girl" were worth $62,000 per million albums sold (consumers bought 300,000 copies in the first two weeks). Guns n' Roses and Geffen Records tried to defuse the controversy by giving all the monies earned from the Manson song to the son of one of the victims of the 1969 slayings, while donating the monies generated on live performances of it to an environmental group. The label pledged other funds to the Doris Tate Crime Victims Bureau.

The boycott faded away, but Geffen was soon enmeshed in another entertainment controversy. Anne Rice had gained great popularity as the author of several novels featuring the character Lestat, a vampire with a long history of biting men, women, and children on the neck. Rice's book *Interview with the Vampire,* set in eighteenth-century France, was published in 1976, and Geffen later acquired the rights to it for $2 million. In conjunction with Warner Bros., he was now producing a film version of the book. On Halloween night of 1993, Anne Rice went to a Houston bookstore and addressed a crowd of her readers who, along with her, were outraged that Tom Cruise had been cast as Lestat. She'd wanted Daniel Day-Lewis or Jeremy Irons or John Malkovich. According to Rice aficionados, Cruise was completely wrong for this darkly dramatic role. He was too cute, too lightweight, and obviously had been chosen for commercial reasons.

Wearing black leather and a wide assortment of nose rings, the author's fans had stood outside in a rainstorm before her arrival at the bookstore, asking passersby to sign a petition boycotting the movie and chanting, "No Tom Cruise! No Tom Cruise!"

While addressing the crowd of a thousand protesters, Rice said of the casting of Cruise, "I wanted to call David Geffen and say, 'How the hell could you do this?'" She also said that Cruise was too short to play her vampire and his voice was too high. With all these difficulties swirling around the picture, wags in Hollywood had dubbed the $50 million film "Geffen's Grave" and "Cruise's Coffin."

Geffen wasn't much perturbed. He'd first worked with Cruise on the successful *Risky Business* and now felt that playing Lestat would be an excellent stretch for the thirty-year-old actor. The producer had initially contacted Cruise with the proposition in December of 1992, when the star was in Australia with his wife, actress Nicole Kidman. Intrigued with the role, Cruise flew to Paris to look at eighteenth-century works of art and began reading about the decadence of French aristocrats. He lost twelve pounds in order to look more gaunt and bloodthirsty. He practiced moves with his jaws.

Cruise was a Creative Artists client, and his agent, Michael Ovitz, also felt that the role suited him. This gave Ovitz and Geffen something, finally, to agree on. During the flap over the casting of Cruise, Ovitz, who never gave press conferences, blessed the film by releasing the kind of stilted statement that he was known for.

Interview, the pronouncement read, "will stand on its own intrinsic quality, which, given the talented people involved, will likely be very high."

Anne Rice was also a CAA client, but Ovitz made no public comments about her. Geffen, however, was not one to take an elbow without giving a forearm shiver back. In the pages of *Esquire,* he called the author "a difficult woman at best" who lacked kindness, discretion, and professionalism. Movie critics were pleasantly surprised with Cruise's performance as Lestat.

CHAPTER 31

1994 would set in motion changes that would ultimately rearrange the power landscape of Hollywood. On April 3 of that year, the president of the Walt Disney Company, Frank Wells, a lawyer and highly regarded film executive, died in a helicopter crash. No one could have predicted the full consequences of this tragedy. During the past decade, three men had primarily been responsible for revitalizing Disney and raising its revenues from $225 million to $4.5 billion a year. Three men had laid the groundwork for making the empire of Mickey Mouse the most successful entertainment enterprise in the world.

Michael Eisner had run the corporation. Jeffrey Katzenberg, the head of the company's $3.7 billion movie division, had worked tirelessly to bring to the screen Disney's recent string of animated hits: *Who Framed Roger Rabbit?*, *Aladdin*, *The Little Mermaid*, *Beauty and the Beast*, and *The Lion King*. It was Geffen who'd told Katzenberg that some earlier failed Disney animations were flat primarily because of the music, so he should hire Alan Menken and Howard Ashman to compose Broadway-like scores for upcoming pictures; Katzenberg took his advice, and the Menken-Ashman team wrote the songs for *Aladdin*, *The Little Mermaid* and *Beauty and the Beast*. Frank Wells was the third executive who'd helped rebuild Disney. As the president and chief operating officer of the company, he was below Eisner, but above Katzenberg, and crucial to the harmony of the organization. He had excellent corporate skills, and no one was better at marshaling the vast forces of Disney to carry out the vision of the boss.

Based on past conversations with Eisner, Katzenberg had long assumed that when Wells stepped down in a few more years, he would ascend to the Disney presidency. Following Wells's unexpected death, he then assumed that Eisner would appoint him the company's number two man. That hadn't happened, because Eisner was increasingly unhappy with some of Katzenberg's recent behavior. The studio head had written a memo criticizing Disney's film division for spending too much money on expensive films like *Dick Tracy* and *Billy Bathgate;* embarrassingly for Eisner and his corporation, the memo had become known to the media. Then, in the summer of 1994, shortly after Wells's death, Katzenberg had spoken negatively about a rival studio, MCA, at a video industry convention in Las Vegas. Backstabbing the competition behind closed doors was business as usual in Hollywood, but this simply wasn't done in a public setting. Both Eisner and the head of MCA, Lew Wasserman, were miffed.

There was one other thing about Katzenberg, who was married and the father of twins, that made some people uncomfortable: he was highly sympathetic to Hollywood's gay community and downright chummy with its most prominent member, David Geffen. In February of 1993, Katzenberg had hosted Geffen's fiftieth birthday party at his home. The guest list for this intimate soiree had included Barry Diller, Sandy Gallin, Ray Stark, and Calvin Klein, the very heart of the much-ballyhooed Velvet Mafia. In the "small world" of Disney, which sold its products worldwide to parents and children, image was an overriding concern and gay issues could be troublesome.

Geffen himself held the opinion that Disney had been progressive in its treatment of gays, but he gave most of the credit for this to Katzenberg. On one occasion, when Geffen felt that Disney had not donated enough to an AIDS charity—the company had chipped in $25,000, while the label boss himself had given four times that amount—he called Eisner and did what he did exceedingly well. Using persuasion and a dose of guilt, he played the same role with the Disney CEO that he'd played two decades earlier with Ahmet Ertegun, when trying to get an advance for Crosby, Stills, and Nash. He adamantly asked for more money, until Eisner threw in another $75,000.

In mid-July of 1994, while attending a conference for corporate leaders at Sun Valley, Idaho, Eisner awoke with pain in his arms and checked into a local medical clinic. The next day he flew back to L.A. and underwent more testing. Doctors rushed him into emergency quadruple-bypass surgery and he spent the next several weeks recuperating. In the immediate aftermath of the surgery, no one from either the Eisner household or Disney itself called Katzenberg to tell him about the operation, and he found out about it only after phoning Eisner at home.

Sensing trouble, Katzenberg set up a meeting with his boss, prepared to resign as the studio head. Eisner surprised him by asking the younger man, whom he'd worked with for nineteen years, to put together a memo detailing his plans for making Disney more successful. Katzenberg did as he was asked. By the last week of August, Eisner had returned to his office and soon requested a meeting with Katzenberg, who thought he was being summoned to talk about his memo. Instead, on August 24, Eisner told him that he would never become the president of the Walt Disney Company. It was, depending on one's point of view, a firing or an invitation to leave.

Katzenberg had just learned what many others were learning about massive conglomerates in the nineties: loyalty and hard work were not necessarily rewarded; diligence didn't guarantee a good future; and even a tremendously successful studio head was just another employee whom the boss could dismiss at will. Katzenberg's departure from Disney was a professional divorce of major consequences, setting off rumors and grumblings throughout the entertainment industry. Geffen instantly came to Katzenberg's defense and the usually mild-mannered Steven Spielberg told the *L.A. Times* that the axing was a "Machiavellian loss" for Eisner. Hollywood pundits began joking that Eisner's next move would be getting rid of Mickey Mouse.

In the aftermath of the Eisner-Katzenberg split, only three things were clear: the ex-studio head did not have a job, the Walt Disney Company did not have a president, and Michael Eisner, who'd carried a gargantuan workload even with a second-in-command, had just had open-heart surgery (the Disney CEO was known for his obsessive attention to detail, such as personally selecting the carpet for the corporation's hotels). Katzenberg, who was known for moving at "warp speed," as he liked to say about his friend David Geffen, was not the sort of man to go plop on the sand in Hawaii for a month or so and think about his options.

Rumors had him going to MCA or Microsoft or running CBS, but he was a fighter, and his instinct now was to strike back, both directly and indirectly, at the man who'd let him go. From the direct angle, he began tabulating how much money he felt Disney owed him as compensation for his work on the studio's recent animated films.

He calculated it at about $250 million, or 2 percent of those movie profits. He would sue Disney for that amount in the future, but right now, he began making other plans.

Just three hours after his fateful August 24 conversation with Eisner, Katzenberg called Spielberg. The director and his wife, actress Kate Capshaw, were visiting another film director, Robert Zemeckis (*Forrest Gump*), and his wife at their vacation home in Jamaica. During this phone discussion between Katzenberg and Spielberg, Zemeckis piped up in the background, suggesting that the two men "do something together," such as start their own studio. The comment was intended, more or less, as a joke.

A successful studio hadn't been established in Hollywood since 20th Century Fox, the last of the majors, in 1935. In 1969, Barbra Streisand, Sidney Poitier, and Paul Newman had created the short-lived First Artists Production Company. In the 1980s, Francis Ford Coppola hadn't been able to sustain his Zoetrope studio, while Orion had debuted in 1978 and filed for bankruptcy fourteen years later. Two other upstarts, Savoy and TriStar (a part of Columbia), had never developed a strong identity. If opening a new studio would have cost millions upon millions in the sixties or seventies, the numbers now were in the multiple billions.

The day after Spielberg and Zemeckis spoke to Katzenberg from Jamaica, they sent him a gift basket filled with T-shirts from their films. "Get over that Mickey Mouse stuff!" the enclosed note read.

Despite the recent failures of start-up studios, Katzenberg was intrigued with building a new one. He had not only visionary ambition but another agenda as well. He wanted to compete head-to-head with Disney in his specialty, the field of animation, and to beat them. He also wanted acknowledgment as the real engine behind the revitalization of Disney's film studio. If he could get a quarter of a billion dollars out of his former employer, he could not only use this to launch his own studio, but that was a big enough bite to sting Disney itself. He did not have a "no-raid" clause in his walking papers from Disney, which meant that its employees were fair game if he wanted to hire them away.

When Spielberg returned to L.A. from Jamaica, Katzenberg seriously approached him about the plan. The two men were already partners in a local restaurant called DIVE!, so why not try something bigger? Spielberg was initially hesitant, and before taking on such a mammoth project, he needed clearance from two people: Sid Sheinberg, his longtime MCA mentor and boss at that studio, and his wife, Kate, who was worried about the director not having enough time left over for her and their five children. When Sheinberg asked why Spielberg would even consider undertaking something so demanding and risky, he replied that he was an adult now, the idea of owning his own business appealed to him, and he no longer needed to be supported by father figures like Sheinberg or the late Steve Ross.

Without even telling his family members, Spielberg began holding secret meetings with Katzenberg.

Katzenberg was known as a superior corporate manager and Spielberg, of course, was the most commercially successful filmmaker in Hollywood. The late 1993 release of the World War II drama *Schindler's List* had won him Best Picture and Best Director Oscars and established his reputation as the director of a historically important motion picture. Katzenberg and Spielberg had contacts, clout, and money, but they needed someone with even more resources than they had, someone with expertise as a start-up entrepreneur, someone bold and with exceptional business instincts, someone gifted at signing talent, someone whose contract would run out with MCA the following year, when he stepped down as the head of a record label and would be looking for something to do. They called Geffen to feel him out.

At first he thought they were kidding. Remembering his rocky stint at Warner Bros. in the mid-seventies, Geffen had told *Vanity Fair* in 1991, "Today, if you said to me, 'Hey, would you run a movie studio?' I would kill myself. I can't think of a more horrible job." And yet, things looked a little different now. Geffen also relished the idea of competing with Michael Eisner, and two of the people he respected most were asking for his involvement. Hadn't his original hero in the business, Louis B. Mayer, run a studio? Wasn't that the ultimate challenge in entertainment?

At the moment, Geffen wasn't looking for a high-risk, megabillion-dollar investment, but he'd never been one to turn away from new possibilities and explorations. He was at least willing to discuss the subject, and in September he and the other two men spoke among themselves about how to arrange financing and commence such an unwieldy enterprise. None of them was yet committed to the project, but they were gradually finding more reasons to go forward. For years, Katzenberg and Geffen had sniped at the high cost of movie productions, directing most of their criticism at Ovitz and his samurai minions over at CAA. In 1992, at a conference of film executives in New York, Katzenberg had even dared to suggest that the leverage now held by talent agents in Hollywood was a crucial factor in the ever-climbing price of producing motion pictures. He didn't name any names, but he didn't have to; everyone knew who he was talking about.

The year before, at a meeting of the Motion Picture Association of America, one studio executive had told an audience that the biggest problem in their industry was Michael Ovitz. And in a 1992 *L.A. Times Magazine* story about the agent, another studio chief called Ovitz's negotiating tactics "gangsterish," while a Disney executive said, "CAA still has the eighties mentality. With them, it's just kill, kill, kill, and Ovitz has done nothing to rein his agents in."

As the cost of film production had gone higher and higher, and as studios had been faced with paying more and more to stars and their agents, a sense of paranoia had begun to pervade the industry. One man controlled the bulk of the talent and was known to become livid not only at the prospect of losing a client but also at the prospect of losing an agent to a competitor. Virtually everyone in town was afraid of Ovitz, and equally afraid to speak this underlying truth. Quietly, a backlash was building against the king, but it would take a few more years for it to erupt.

Money wasn't the only issue. Ovitz had also helped broker the sale of two studios, Columbia/TriStar and MCA, to the Japanese, and neither of those marriages was going well. Under the leadership of Jon Peters and Peter Guber, Columbia/TriStar had floundered and in 1994 would take a $2.7 billion write off and a $150 million operating loss on the property. Geffen now worked under the MCA umbrella, and neither he nor many other Hollywood insiders cared for the way the Matsushita giant was treating Wasserman and Sheinberg. Lately, to the embarrassment of the Japanese, the outspoken Sheinberg had begun grousing publicly about this. The MCA heads, along with Geffen, were upset when Matsushita refused their proposal to buy a 25 percent stake of General Electric and then rejected their idea of purchasing Virgin Records for $1 billion. Wasserman had also tried to interest the electronics conglomerate in acquiring cable or broadcasting properties, but each time the answer was no. The two Americans were clearly no longer in charge of MCA's destiny, or perhaps even their own.

Katzenberg, Spielberg (an Ovitz client), and Geffen were not at all enamored of the current state of affairs in their industry. They imagined a time when the town would not have an agent as its overlord. They looked back to an era before the average cost of making and promoting a single film, according to the Motion Picture Association of America, was now almost $60 million, a 148 percent increase over the past decade. They envisioned a studio that would offer its talent a profit participation plan in its films, something that currently wasn't being done anywhere. They wanted to cut down on bureaucracy, lower costs, and create more freedom for filmmakers. Spielberg, in particular, had long-standing loyalties to Wasserman, Sheinberg, and MCA, and he did not enjoy seeing the older men answering to people who had no roots in show business and lived on the other side of the globe. If the three younger men were to start their own studio, they naturally wanted success for themselves, but they also wanted to make a statement about the necessity for change. To put it in Geffen terminology, all of them would have qualified as nerds, who were looking for revenge.

In effect, they wanted to create something that had never been created before. At an early meeting of the trio, Katzenberg showed up with a detailed business plan for their new venture. Geffen glanced at it and threw it away. The time had come, he said, to improvise.

On Wednesday, September 28, 1994, Spielberg, Katzenberg, and Geffen were invited to the White House to have dinner with President Clinton and Russian president Boris Yeltsin. Following the meal, Spielberg and Katzenberg returned to their suites at the Hay-Adams Hotel. Bill and Hillary Clinton asked Geffen if he wanted to sleep over in the Lincoln bedroom, an offer the first couple frequently made to people who'd been exceptionally generous in helping them win the Oval Office. Geffen said yes, then retired to his room. At one-thirty A.M., the phone rang near his bed. When he answered it, his two friends over at the Hay-Adams told him that they'd been talking about their proposed studio. Spielberg and Katzenberg had conclusively decided, after dining with the world's two most prominent leaders, that they wanted to go ahead with their plans. Right now. The trappings of power had emboldened them.

Katzenberg told Geffen to get dressed and come over to their hotel so they could talk some more. When Geffen asked how to get there, the former Disney executive told him to call a cab. Geffen replied that you can't call a cab to the White House, and then added that he couldn't walk over because he didn't know the way and didn't want to stumble around in the hallways of the White House in the middle of the night looking for someone to give him the directions to get there. Katzenberg conceded that he had a point. Geffen said he would see them early in the morning and went back to bed. Five hours later, he jumped into a White House car and rode over to the Hay-Adams to join them for breakfast in Spielberg's suite. The three men looked at one another, took a collective deep breath, and said, "Let's do it."

Twelve days later, on Monday, October 10, the trio went to Lew Wasserman's home to tell him of their scheme. This was a wise move, since it was never a good idea, as others were about to discover, to leave the godfather out of the loop. The men gathered in Wasserman's living room, where the eighty-one-year-old patriarch told them stories about the past and showed them a colorful drawing of Mickey Mouse, given to him by Walt Disney himself. He displayed other artifacts from his life in show business, while the younger men sat in front of him, awed at what they were seeing and where their own careers had taken them.

This was the inner sanctum of Hollywood, as close to the throne as one could get, and they mostly listened in silence until Wasserman asked them to talk about their plans. After hearing them out, he said that he believed in all of them and would assist them in any way he could. Then all of them made a pact to support one another in the future, a pact whose importance would only be revealed later on. Leaving Wasserman's, the men went over to Katzenberg's and signed their equity agreements for the new business, splitting the company in three equal parts.

The following day the trio called several journalists and told them to be at a press conference at ten sharp the next morning at the luxurious Peninsula Hotel in Beverly Hills. They hinted that "something big" was about to happen but said nothing more and refused to return any reporters' calls about what was coming. To the new partners' dismay and anger, the following morning's *Wall Street*

Journal, L.A. Times, and *New York Times,* as well as the trade papers, all carried stories saying that Spielberg, Katzenberg, and Geffen were about to launch a startling new venture. The trio were agitated that their news had been leaked, and speculation ran high that the culprit worked right across the street from the Peninsula, over on the third floor of Creative Artists Agency. Ovitz, went this scuttlebutt, was paying Geffen back for his reputed leak to the *Wall Street Journal* during the agent's negotiations with Matsushita and MCA four years earlier. On the other hand, some people contended that Ovitz knew nothing about the new studio and that the pronouncement took him completely by surprise.

For the press conference, Spielberg and Geffen arrived dressed casually, but Katzenberg showed up in a tie. The men tried to appear calm, but nerves were shaking. At four A.M. that morning, Geffen had arisen and vomited. To control his stomach, he'd begun sipping ginger ale; he would later confess that he hadn't felt this much anxiety in twenty years. The three together had an estimated net worth of $2 billion, and each of them had thrown $33 million and change into this unnamed project, giving them $100 million to get started. For the forty-six-year-old Spielberg and the fifty-one-year-old Geffen, $33 million was a significant but not a deadly serious amount. For Katzenberg, forty-three, it meant taking out a second mortgage on some personal property.

Smoked salmon and berries were served at the press conference. Ovitz and Ron Meyer had walked over from CAA to take in the scene, and they stood by quietly, along with a number of other Hollywood heavyweights. Everyone seemed a bit amazed as the trio announced their new venture, couching their plans in language that suggested they were no longer pleased with corporate Hollywood, and wanted to build something more personal and intimate. There were doubters in the crowd who felt that the men didn't really intend to open a studio; instead, along with Wasserman and Sheinberg, they were stealthily planning to buy back a controlling interest in MCA from Matsushita and rescue the two older men from their Japanese superiors. Others believed that Spielberg and Geffen were merely sending a signal across the Pacific, a message saying that these two huge human assets were threatening to walk away from MCA if Matsushita didn't start deferring to the Americans' wishes and judgment.

Many people simply could not imagine that anyone, including

these three Hollywood megasuccesses, would actually attempt something of this scope in 1994. At the press conference it was revealed that their company had no name (although Tom Hanks had recently suggested "DIVE! The Studio"), no budget, no business plan, no staff, no deals, and no office. For the time being, they would work out of Spielberg's abode complex, known as Amblin, on the back lot of Universal. They were looking for $2 billion in investment capital, just to launch themselves. To bring their concept to fruition would take roughly seven years and $7 to $8 billion. After the media began to grasp the magnitude of their plans, they started coming up with names of their own for the new studio: "Egos R Us," "The Pep Boys," and "Money, Money, and More Money."

At the Peninsula Hotel, Katzenberg temporarily christened himself and his partners the "Dream Team," a term first used to describe America's Olympic basketball squad, and more recently applied to O. J. Simpson's defense attorneys in his unfolding double homicide case in L.A. Katzenberg's team would have five different divisions—film, TV, music, animation, and interactive media—so essentially the trio would be taking on the entire world of entertainment.

During the press conference, Geffen said that he'd always run his companies by himself, but this was a "once-in-a-lifetime opportunity to work with partners." Shunning all modesty, he also stated that Geffen Records was "a superb model" for starting the new music division at their fledgling entity. Spielberg glanced over at his wife, Kate Capshaw, and said that over the years he'd vowed with an "almost religious fervor" that he would never invest his own money in show business, but now he wanted to "create a company that will outlive us all....I want to create a playground that filmmakers can play in." Katzenberg attempted to bury the past by saying that his conflict with Eisner and Disney was "behind us" and that he was pointing toward the future. (More than a year would pass before he officially announced his $250 million lawsuit against his former employer.)

The press conference was full of bonhomie and laughter. Now that he was in business with Spielberg, Geffen joked with reporters, he wanted to direct *The Lost World,* the upcoming sequel to *Jurassic Park,* which had generated $900 million for MCA/Universal. The director then turned to Geffen and said he would be more than happy to let him do the film if he—Spielberg—could become a billionaire. Katzenberg told the gathering that he deeply wanted his children in both of his partners' wills.

"There's an opportunity," Katzenberg said, turning serious for a moment, "for us to have a revolution."

One film executive, standing off to the side and watching the proceedings, shrugged at this last remark. Then he mumbled a question that others in Hollywood would soon be pondering. Throughout this morning's media event, it had struck him that the grandiose new studio was still mostly an idea, a dream more than a reality.

"Where's the beef?" he said.

CHAPTER 32

By November of 1994, the situation between the Americans who ran MCA and their Japanese bosses at Matsushita had become intolerable. The month before, Wasserman and Sheinberg had traveled to Osaka to meet with the Matsushita president, Yoichi Morishita, and discuss their ideas about buying CBS for $5 billion. Morishita not only vetoed the purchase but let the esteemed American duo wait for more than an hour in an anteroom before a company official even came out to talk to them. After returning to L.A., Sheinberg wrote a furious letter to the distant corporation, demanding an apology to Wasserman. He also gave Matsushita an ultimatum: let the Americans run MCA their own way or they would resign.

Uncertain what to do with his Hollywood property and his two unruly employees, Morishita contacted New York investment banker Herbert Allen. The banker flew to Japan and advised the Matsushita brass that MCA could be sold for $7 to $8 billion. Then he went home and set in motion the groundwork for the sale. In December, Allen returned to Osaka, and this time he took along Michael Ovitz.

Initially, the Japanese did not want to include Ovitz, because he was Steven Spielberg's agent. Spielberg was very close to Sheinberg, and the heads of Matsushita did not want the volatile Sheinberg to know what was unfolding across the Pacific. If MCA's number two man learned that Ovitz was engaged in clandestine negotiations to sell the conglomerate out from under Lew Wasserman, the fallout could be harsh.

Four years earlier, when Ovitz was brokering the sale of MCA to Matsushita, he'd gone out of his way to keep the two Americans informed of his movements. But now he could not betray the secrets of the men who ran the electronics giant in Osaka. After Allen persuaded the Matsushita leaders that Ovitz could be trusted, the agent quietly flew to Japan with the banker. This was the natural culmination of Ovitz's career as a force behind innumerable Hollywood power plays. And it was fitting that it was taking place in Japan, where the sword has long been the trademark of the samurai warrior, and those who live by the sword often perish the same way.

On January 12, 1995, in their first major announcement since the previous October, Spielberg, Katzenberg, and Geffen told the media that they'd just entered into a $100 million TV production venture with ABC. The deal would guarantee the men a share of future advertising dollars—an unprecedented arrangement for a network to make with a studio. The trio said they expected to have television shows on in the fall. The next day, they officially named their venture: DreamWorks SKG. Geffen, just like Louis B. Mayer nearly seven decades before him, now represented the third letter in the newest and most ambitious studio in Hollywood history.

DreamWorks soon hired away two Disney executives, Helene Hohn and Michael Montgomery, and Paramount's chief financial officer, Ronald Nelson. Then Microsoft cofounder Paul Allen invested $500 million in the young business, while Microsoft's other founder, Bill Gates, announced a $30 million coventure with the studio. Geffen began pursuing One World Media, a Korean firm that would eventually invest $300 million in DreamWorks. The trio were well on their way to leveraging their original $100 million in seed money into $1.9 billion.

In January of the new year, Wasserman and Sheinberg returned to Japan, where the Matsushita brass told them that Ovitz would soon be arriving to assess the Americans' value to MCA. The agent's cover was gone. Wasserman and Sheinberg instantly grasped what they were being told: Ovitz had gone behind their backs and was shoving them out of their jobs. He was, they felt certain, finally making his long-anticipated play for the MCA helm. He had secretly arranged things so that he would become the next Lew Wasserman and godfather to the industry.

Wasserman was steamed. If in the past he'd given Ovitz the benefit of the doubt, because he needed to do business with CAA, the aging man now gave in to his conviction that the agent was just an arriviste with an unlimited supply of ambition.

Ovitz flew to Osaka, gave his opinions about Wasserman and Sheinberg to the Matsushita chiefs, and told them that the Montreal-based Seagram's beverage empire might be interested in purchasing MCA. Then he boarded a plane for home. The following day an earthquake leveled whole sections of Osaka, killing more than five thousand people. To veteran Ovitz observers, this was the supreme symbol of his excellent timing in all things human and nonhuman. He'd not only made an end run around two of Hollywood's biggest players but had also avoided a natural catastrophe. The man simply could do no wrong.

In early March, Edgar Bronfman Jr., the chairman of Seagram's, flew to Kyoto to meet with the heads of Matsushita. He traveled in his Gulfstream IV. (This $26 million aircraft was now so commonplace among the jet set that when the limited edition Gulfstream V became available in 1996, for just $10 million more, Bronfman, Geffen, and Spielberg all jumped on the waiting list.) In Kyoto, Bronfman met twice with the Matsushita president before flying home to put together a formal offer. By late March, rumors of the deal were leaking out and media pundits could not refrain from comparing Matsushita's unloading of MCA to the Japanese surrender on the deck of the *Missouri* at the close of World War II.

On April 9, the deal was consummated over a conference table in Los Angeles. Matsushita sold 80 percent of MCA for $5.7 billion but retained the other 20 percent. This arrangement allowed the electronics behemoth to recoup its losses and save at least some face. The hottest buzz in L.A. was that the long arm of Ovitz was about to take over MCA and was even reaching for an equity position in the House of Seagram.

▪ ▪ ▪

As representatives for Bronfman and Ovitz began preliminary negotiations, the DreamWorks founders continued expanding their business. In May, Silicon Graphics made a $50 million deal to create state-of-the-art animation for the new studio. Katzenberg hired away from Disney Hans Zimmer, the composer for *The Lion King,* and Stephen Schwartz, the lyricist for *Pocahontas.* The studio announced that its first animated film, *Prince of Egypt,* based on the life of Moses, would be released in 1998. The Hasbro company developed a line of DreamWorks toys, and Sega, in conjunction with SKG, planned to open a chain of video programming outlets, known as GameWorks.

In April of 1995, Geffen officially left his old record label to become the head of SKG Music. His first major move was buying singer George Michael out of his contract with Sony, for a reported $30 million. While pitching DreamWorks as a welcome home for Hollywood's corporate refugees, Geffen was able to lure executives Mo Ostin and Lenny Waronker away from Warner Records.

DreamWorks now had start-up capital and talented employees but still lacked a physical plant. The new studio heads wanted to locate on 1,087 acres of land at Playa Vista, near Los Angeles International Airport and close to where Howard Hughes had built his famous *Spruce Goose* plane. Spielberg envisioned a "campus" where hundreds or even thousands of people would be employed turning out not just motion pictures and CDs but the very latest technological advances in entertainment media. Everything would be state-of-the-art and everyone working here would have escaped the old Hollywood grind. It was an inspired, utopian vision that was quickly invaded by reality. The 1,087 acres held some of the last wetlands in L.A., and environmentalists were soon protesting the development.

The most intriguing issue for DreamWorks during its first year concerned who would distribute the studio's movies. The founding trio had for years made films for three old-line entertainment giants: Spielberg for MCA/Universal, Katzenberg for Disney, and Geffen for Warner Bros. Because of the Eisner-Katzenberg rift, Disney was not an alternative. Warner still handled Geffen's films, but for the past five years Geffen had been an MCA employee and had grown increasingly closer to its top management.

With Seagram's purchase of MCA, that management was

stepping down. Wasserman would become chairman emeritus, while Sheinberg would open his own production company, called the Bubble Factory. Spielberg, Katzenberg, and Geffen, along with other well-informed Hollywood players, knew that Ovitz was the logical candidate to take over MCA. He could make more money as a corporate chief, but there were other, murkier reasons for him to leave his agency.

In recent months, a rebellion had been building inside CAA, a revolt that was astonishly similar to something that had happened in the agency business twenty years earlier. Just as Ovitz and his four original partners had wanted to leave William Morris in 1974 because they were impatient and hungry, five young men at Creative Artists—the Young Turks, the media had dubbed them—were now asking their boss for power, more independence, and an equity stake in CAA. In order to mollify them, Ovitz had been tossing some of his most prominent clients their way, such as David Letterman, Dustin Hoffman, Tom Hanks, Robert Redford, Brad Pitt, and Woody Harrelson, but he was unwilling to give them a piece of the business. The Turks, according to scuttlebutt, were about to take a stand against Ovitz or bolt with some of CAA's biggest clients and start their own agency.

The king of Hollywood was being encircled by enemies, both real and potential, outside of CAA and within its elegant marble walls.

"Given the ugliness of some of the criticism and gossip that surrounds our industry," says a film executive in L.A., "Ovitz had to feel, in the spring of 1995, that if he slipped just a notch or two, it would be hard to recover and get back on top. All your allies can easily turn into jackals, especially in Hollywood. There's a certain delight in tearing apart someone who's been so successful for so long, a certain revenge factor."

CHAPTER 33

Geffen had a gift for knowing who was vulnerable and when to strike. In mid-1990, he'd quietly moved Bruce Springsteen and Michael Jackson away from Walter Yetnikoff, helping to bring down the most powerful man in the music business. Now he was a player in the turmoil spinning around the most potent individual in the movie industry. In the spring of 1995, Geffen and Katzenberg knew they were holding an extremely valuable card—the distribution rights to their future films—in Ovitz's negotiations with MCA's new owner, Edgar Bronfman Jr. These two longtime Ovitz enemies may have even been holding a key to the man's fate in Hollywood. The third DreamWorks partner, Steven Spielberg, was in a more delicate position. As a CAA client, he had a certain loyalty to Ovitz, yet his deeper loyalty ran toward his two mentors, Wasserman and Sheinberg, and the film director had not been pleased when Ovitz sold MCA out from under them.

Over the Memorial Day weekend, the DreamWorks founders were closely following the negotiations between Ovitz's people and Bronfman's in New York. They were also following the lead of Lew Wasserman, who'd let it be known that if Ovitz assumed the MCA helm, he would quit as chairman emeritus. Spielberg, Katzenberg, and Geffen had earlier decided to sign a ten-year film distribution deal with MCA but had not yet signed the papers. Now they were reconsidering their options. If they threatened to take their business elsewhere, this might affect Bronfman's plan to hire Ovitz. It might even persuade him to dump the agent.

Geffen was still close to the heads of Warner Bros., Bob Daly and Terry Semel, and had already begun speaking with them about distribution rights. Daly and Semel were only too happy to join forces with men as accomplished as S, K, and G. Warner Bros. was also prepared to give them better terms than they had at MCA.

By June 1, Ron Olson, the L.A. lawyer representing Ovitz in the negotiations, had flown to New York to conduct formal meetings with Bronfman attorney Kenneth Edgar. With the talks reaching a critical stage, the DreamWorks trio played their hand, informing Bronfman's people of their decision: get rid of Ovitz or we're going with Warner Bros.

Four days later, Ovitz gathered his troops before him at CAA and made a brief speech. He would not be going to MCA but would stay put and run his agency, just as before. Things would go on as they always had, and there was nothing for his employees to worry about. No one close to the failed negotiations in Manhattan openly discussed why the deal had collapsed, but Bronfman had clearly not wanted to lose the most commercially successful filmmaker in Hollywood history, or the man who'd helped turn Disney around, or the first billionaire in the entertainment business. And Ovitz had just as clearly overreached himself. The smallest amount of money he reportedly asked for was $250 million, plus a piece of the Seagram's empire. Someone finally told him no.

A week after the talks between Seagram's and Ovitz fell apart, DreamWorks signed the distribution deal with MCA, and Wasserman stayed on as chairman emeritus.

Just as talk of these events was settling down in Hollywood, Geffen launched another gossip grenade. Earlier in 1995, he'd been contacted by Robert Sam Anson, the journalist who'd written the colorful 1982 profile of him in *Esquire*. Anson called to say that he was writing a book about the Disney company and wanted to know if the billionaire cared to evaluate Michael Eisner. Geffen complied, and his remarks soon showed up not in a book but in the July 1995 issue of *L.A. Magazine*. He was enraged with Anson, publicly declaring that the reporter had betrayed him by not stating up front that his comments would be used in the magazine. At the same time, Geffen did not say that Anson had misquoted him or that he wanted to retract anything he'd said in the article. He hadn't forgiven Eisner for firing Katzenberg, and Anson had merely given him the chance to vent.

In *L.A. Magazine,* Geffen called the head of Disney a "liar. And anyone who has ever dealt with him, genuinely dealt with him, knows he is a liar." Then he said that Eisner was "a little bit woo-woo" and had "character flaws" and "something very damaged in his background."

When Anson raised the sticky notion that Katzenberg hadn't become the president of Disney because he was too close to some prominent Hollywood gays, Geffen said, "When they want to say the worst about you, they call you a fag."

"I'm not afraid of Michael Eisner," he added. "That's why he's so angry with me. Because in this town, where people are all about business and making money, I am the only one willing to say the truth.... Michael is a very, very ungenerous guy who suffers when anyone else shares the credit."

By the story's end, it seemed certain that Geffen had torched his Disney bridges, but Hollywood is stranger than that.

On July 10, Ovitz got rocked again when Ron Meyer, his closest ally at CAA, announced that he was taking the very MCA job that had earlier eluded the most powerful man in Hollywood. Unbeknownst to Ovitz, Edgar Bronfman had invited Meyer to New York, and during dinner they'd quickly reached an agreement that had Meyer leaving the agency business in Beverly Hills and moving over to MCA headquarters in the San Fernando Valley. His compensation would be approximately a third of what Ovitz had been asking. As Meyer was leaving the restaurant that evening, he called his wife, the model Kelly Chapman, and then phoned Ovitz. The head of CAA had spent the past decade stunning people with his secret negotiations and deals. Now it was his turn to be shocked.

Then he got stunned once more.

On the afternoon of July 28, Eisner called Ovitz and asked him to come over to his house in Bel-Air. The agent was alarmed, assuming that something had again gone wrong with Eisner's health. The two men had known one another for twenty years and had vacationed together with their children and wives. They were close in the peculiar way that industry associates are close in Hollywood, where genuine intimacy often runs a distant second to business friendship.

Arriving at Eisner's estate, Ovitz was relieved to learn that the man had not had a relapse of bad health. Eisner told him that Disney was about to buy ABC/Cap Cities, Inc., for $19 billion—once more surprising the agent with information that had escaped him. Then Eisner gave him a much bigger surprise, asking Ovitz if he wanted to become the number two man at the largest media corporation on the planet. You don't have to respond today, Eisner told him, just think about it.

On the last day of July, Eisner announced the Disney purchase at a press conference in New York. It was the second largest takeover in American business history, and the new conglomerate would now include Walt Disney Pictures, Touchstone Pictures, ABC Productions, eleven TV stations, 228 TV affiliates, twenty-one radio stations, and the cable networks ESPN, Lifetime, A&E, and the Disney Channel, plus newspapers in thirteen states. The vast had just gotten vaster.

One of the tens of thousands of people who would be employed by this megacompany had just publicly said some very nasty things about his new boss. Because of the production deal that DreamWorks had recently made with ABC, Geffen was now, in the roundabout way that Hollywood specializes in, working for Michael Eisner. So was Jeffrey Katzenberg, who was in the process of suing Disney for $250 million.

Eisner needed an answer from Ovitz. If the agent took the Disney job, his compensation package could eventually approach half a billion dollars. That was an astounding amount of money, of course, but it was Batya Geffen who had once told her son that the devil always arrives with the biggest check.

Ovitz said yes.

CHAPTER 34

Geffen's power and influence were steadily spreading, along with his name. First, there was the David Geffen Foundation, which by the mid-1990s had dispersed $35 million. Then there was DreamWorks SKG. In August of 1995, Geffen's foundation gave $4 million to two AIDS organizations in New York: $2.5 million to Gay Men's Health Crisis and $1.5 million to God's Love We Deliver. The $1.5 million was to be used to renovate a structure for homebound AIDS patients and would be known as the David Geffen Building. The foundation also gave $5 million to the Westwood Playhouse on the UCLA campus. It was now called the Geffen Playhouse, ensuring that the university he'd once lied about attending would carry his name in perpetuity.

The late comedian Danny Thomas had founded the St. Jude's Children's Research Hospital in Memphis, and his daughter, Marlo, oversaw fund-raising for the institution. In March of 1996, at the Beverly Hilton Hotel in Los Angeles, Marlo put on a black-tie affair for St. Jude's, featuring performances by Roseanne Barr and Tony Bennett. The audience for this $20,000-a-table event held Bob Hope, Sid Caesar, and David Geffen. During the showing of an emotionally charged film about the hospital, Geffen leaned over to Marlo and asked his former paramour how much money she'd raised this evening.

"One-point-one million dollars," she said.

"Now you've got another million," he replied.

She took the money but did not rename St. Jude's.

One branch of L.A.'s Museum of Contemporary Art, known for years as the "Temporary Contemporary," was comprised of two large warehouses in the city's Little Tokyo district. Initially, the warehouses were meant to be a stopover for works of art until a permanent home could be found, but the funky location was so popular that the trustees decided to keep the museum there. In May of 1996, Geffen gave $5 million to the "Temporary," and in exchange for this gift, the museum was rechristened the Geffen Contemporary.

Disgruntled art patrons immediately began grousing in the *Los Angeles Times* and elsewhere about attaching Geffen's moniker to these warehouses. The consensus was that if the trustees were going to alter the name, they should never have sold out so cheap, but squeezed the benefactor for another $20 or $25 million.

After this last change was announced, one Hollywood pundit asked, "Why don't we just get it over with and rename L.A. after the man?"

In addition to giving money away, Geffen was also generating huge amounts for his friends in the White House. In 1993, he'd persuaded oilman Marvin Davis to hold a Hollywood fund-raiser for President Clinton that brought in $2 million. The next year, Geffen oversaw a similar event at Steven Spielberg's, which raised $2.1 million. Geffen's foundation funded *The War Room,* the mostly flattering documentary about James Carville and George Stephanopoulos, the two strategists who masterminded Clinton's 1992 election.

In June of 1995, Kansas senator and presidential hopeful Bob Dole had made a point of attacking Hollywood in a major speech, calling its entertainment products "nightmares of depravity." If the industry had not been stocked with Republicans before Dole's comments—individuals in Hollywood gave ten times as much money to Democrats as to their opponents—the GOP would now find it even harder to recruit new members from show business. Dole had done nothing but make Geffen and his wealthy colleagues that much more committed to defeating the Kansan, once he officially became the 1996 Republican presidential candidate.

In February of 1996, Geffen held a dinner for the president at his Malibu home, attended by Katzenberg, Sheinberg, Wasserman, producer Steve Tisch, and White House chief of staff Leon Panetta. The following month Geffen hosted another presidential dinner, featuring duck and caviar, for a guest list that included Steve Jobs of the Apple Corporation, Edgar Bronfman Jr., beer magnate August Busch IV, and Warren Buffett's wife, Susie. Each person at the table pledged $50,000 to $100,000 to the cause. The Geffen Foundation was also supporting Democrats other than Clinton, giving money to Senator Ted Kennedy of Massachusetts, Senator Joseph Lieberman of Connecticut, and Senator Bob Kerrey of Nebraska.

Over the past five years, the DreamWorks founders alone had given $1.5 million to Democrats. Geffen was the top donor in Hollywood, at $575,000, followed by Wasserman, at $507,000, then Spielberg, at $503,000, and Katzenberg, at $408,000. Democratic candidates from across the country now made pilgrimages to an office on the twenty-seventh floor of a tower near Universal Studios, where they asked Andy Spahn, the head of DreamWorks SKG's corporate affairs, for money. In political circles, Spahn had been dubbed "Geffen's gatekeeper."

In March of 1996, during an informal campaign visit to California, President Clinton spoke at Pepperdine University, just up the road from Geffen's Malibu residence. His address concluded, the chief executive and his accompanying Secret Service agents drove down to Geffen's home, where the president, Steven Spielberg, and the host stayed up late watching videos, while the feds lurked around the beach house with their walkie-talkies. The baby boom generation had truly come into power, and not everyone was comfortable with that.

"President Clinton and David Geffen watching movies on the beach—how perfect," says author George Trow. "They're naturals together. Here are two people not entirely secure in their adulthood."

By the time Clinton began running for reelection, Geffen had clearly replaced Lew Wasserman as *the* Democratic fund-raiser in L.A. He'd also become a regular at 1600 Pennsylvania Avenue. Since 1992, Geffen had been invited to sixteen separate functions at the White House and, like other large Clinton contributors, he had spent the night in the Lincoln Bedroom. The Democrats contended that these sleepovers, while looking tacky to the public, were really nothing but slumber parties. The Republicans howled that the president was peddling the Lincoln Bedroom to the highest bidder—and that everything in the White House was for sale.

Money ruled, but some people felt that Geffen should be using his extreme wealth to wield even greater political influence.

"He could do a lot more," says Michelangelo Signorile. "Geffen has become enamored of having access to power in Washington. He's in Bill Clinton's pocket now, and Clinton has disappointed the gay community. Geffen should push him harder on issues like gays in the military and more funds for AIDS research and safe-sex education. With David's money backing Clinton, the president will continue to suck up to him. He needs Geffen more than Geffen needs him."

Two months before the 1996 general election, Geffen, supermarket tycoon Ron Burkle, and the Hollywood Women's Political Committee hosted a gala fund-raising affair for the president and first lady at Green Acres, formerly the Bel-Air estate of the silent film star Harold Lloyd. It was the highlight of the political season, drawing a thousand people and raising $4.5 million for Clinton's reelection campaign. Tom Hanks was the master of ceremonies, poet Maya Angelou gave a reading, and the Eagles, Chicago, and the Neville Brothers all performed their music. $2,500 bought you a ticket to the concert, $5,000 moved you up to a cocktail reception with the president, and for $12,500 you got to break bread with the first family. The celebrity list included Sharon Stone, Shirley MacLaine, Rob Reiner, Richard Dreyfuss, and Barbra Streisand, who sang a revised rendition of "The Way We Were." The new lyrics took some humorous shots at the advanced age of seventy-three-year-old Senator Dole.

In November, the president was handily reelected to a second term, but the most significant political event of 1996 may have come that spring. In several early Republican primaries, Pat Buchanan had made a strong showing and looked as if he might be a serious candidate for the GOP nomination. But his own party then turned its back on him, and the man who'd declared cultural war on certain parts of American society in Houston in 1992, was relegated, at least for the moment, to history's dustbin. Even mainstream Republicans were uncomfortable with his bitterly divisive and openly anti-homosexual message.

Buchanan's defeat was a signal victory for gay Americans, but not the only one in 1996. The U.S. Supreme Court overturned Colorado's Amendment Two, making possible the passage of gay rights legislation in the state. After the introduction of new combinations of drugs, AIDS deaths in New York City were cut in half. The Centers for Disease Control and Prevention in Washington, D.C., produced statistics showing an 11 percent drop in AIDS deaths nationwide in the first half of 1996, compared to the previous year—the first decline since the epidemic began.

In the fall of 1996, TV viewers eagerly debated whether comedian Ellen DeGeneres, the star of the sitcom *Ellen,* would come out on the show as a lesbian (she did so in late April of 1997). Prime-time television now featured twenty-two openly gay characters, a development that would have been unimaginable half a decade earlier. In late December of 1996, capping a remarkable twelve months, *Time* named AIDS researcher Dr. David Ho as its Man of the Year.

All these events were, in one form or another, beneficial to Geffen, who was now being touted as Hollywood's most forceful behind-the-scenes player. His press coverage reflected this.

He was featured on the cover of the January 1997 issue of the gay magazine *genre*. His left hand was stuffed into his pocket, and he wore an untucked flannel shirt—a distinctly casual pose. The cover story was entitled "men we love," and although several names were listed under this banner, the only one in bright orange was DAVID GEFFEN. The article on him was as fawning as those from two decades earlier had been deprecating and snide.

In the magazine, Geffen acknowledged that he'd become a role model for younger gay men and that he took this responsibility seriously.

"Find the courage to be yourself," he told the *genre* audience. "Because you can't fully succeed at anything unless you're who you are. If you try to be something else, you're likely to fail."

He also acknowledged that he'd been in a "very intimate" but not exclusive relationship with a man for the past five years. The old bisexual question surrounding him had essentially faded, but he did make a point of saying that "women are better in relationships and men are better with sex."

For decades, people had contended that Geffen was not the sort of person who would ever find any peace or happiness, but he held a different view.

"My friends," he told *genre,* "know that I'm quite happy, but there is no such thing as *simply* happy. From time to time I'm unhappy, from time to time I'm depressed, from time to time I feel anxious, but overall I would say I'm a happy person. That's not to say that you couldn't see me a week from Thursday and I might be unhappy. I think that comes with a normal life."

Even an old Geffen nemesis had softened. One warm October afternoon, Michelangelo Signorile entered a coffee shop on Manhattan's lower Fifth Avenue and sat down at a small table. He had a short frame and a muscular build. With his strong yet delicate features, close-cropped hair, and warm blue eyes, the thirty-five-year-old resembled someone else, but it took a second glance to determine who. The Brooklyn native looked unmistakably like a younger, stockier version of David Geffen.

Signorile's manner was very calm, and he spoke quietly. He did not conjure up a "terrorist" or other, less pleasant terms people had used to describe him. In *Queer in America,* he'd written that at the start of every revolution, someone has to step forward and behave outrageously, to throw the Molotov cocktails that ignite political change. In the process, feelings get smashed, emotional damage is done, and one may later have second thoughts, but that can be sorted out in the future.

Near the end of his book, he'd made peace with some of his targets, calling both Liz Smith and Geffen "heroes" for the work they'd done on behalf of those with AIDS. And when he talked this afternoon, he had the relaxed tone of a man who'd drained himself of considerable venom.

"I took on Geffen," he said, "in a particularly brutal way. In our media-obsessed culture, you have to yell to get someone's attention, so I yelled loudly. I felt I had nothing to lose. People were dying, and celebrities were making millions of dollars, avoiding all of this. I might as well go out kicking and screaming, because this would be the end of my career. I kept attacking Geffen, and eventually he began to respond. Of course, he was furious with me, and hated me, and still does to this day. That's okay with me, as long as he came out in public and then gave money to AIDS causes. He's changed dramatically and given $4 million to Gay Men's Health Crisis.

"I know that David has called me a terrorist, and people used to tell me how enraged he was with me. My name would come up and he would go off the deep end. I'm told that during 1991 and 1992, when things were really hot, he went into deep therapy over all this. It must have been very painful.

"He once said that I did what I did because my nose was pressed up against the glass of a glamorous party, but I could never get into that party myself. I think he's got it backwards. For years his nose was pressed up against my glass because I'd come out and been honest about myself and he hadn't. I think my behavior really got to him. It's one thing to have one nut yelling at you, but when other gay people began protesting his appearances and asking him to do more, that's something else. We were saying to him, 'You're a billionaire and very powerful. You socialize with us—you sleep with us—and you owe something back to us.'"

Signorile's career, like NBC's Pete Williams's, was not destroyed after he openly confronted his sexuality and became the pioneer of outing. On the contrary, he is now writing his third book and regularly lectures about gay issues on the college circuit. The theme of his talks still centers around opening the closet doors of the powerful.

"The strange thing was that even when we were fighting, David and I were only a few degrees apart," Signorile said. "The gay community is relatively close—I know people Geffen has dated—and we all struggle with the same things. We struggle with love and with being lonely and with being in relationships. Men in general deal with the impulsive sexual part of relationships fairly well, but the other parts are harder. In straight relationships, women deal with the emotional parts better, but when you have two men and neither of them has been taught how to nurture something, it can be difficult.

"Also, gay men were brought up to hate homosexuality and to hate ourselves. David said in *Vanity Fair* that he wanted to be six feet tall and have blond hair and blue eyes—to look like the straight, very masculine man. I think he's started to shift and work through some of that. What I did hurt him, but it was also pushing him into dealing with these things."

Did Signorile have any regrets?

"No. I've never regretted taking on any of these people. Every journalist feels for his subjects, but I felt I had to be as forceful as I was, given the times we were in. Today, gay men are coming out in cities and in small towns and even in suburbs. We don't have to live in big-city ghettos any more. This is a huge change. We've seen a new wave go out across the country, and it's happening everywhere. The last few years have been extraordinary. When I watch C-Span on television and see the Congress debating gays in the military, I think, 'My God, my tax money is finally being put to use.' If we lose this issue now, I know we'll win it in twenty years. That's progress."

CHAPTER 35

Despite Geffen's increasing clout in Hollywood, DreamWorks was running far behind its original schedule. By mid-1996, fewer albums had been released than planned, and *Older,* George Michael's first LP for SKG Music, had sold softly and been critically panned. SKG's initial TV show, *Champs,* had been canceled, and its second, *High Incident,* was not a hit. *Spin City,* starring Michael J. Fox, was growing in popularity, but *Ink,* a much-ballyhooed adult comedy starring Ted Danson and Mary Steenburgen, debuted as a high-budget disaster. Its first four pilots (at $1 million per pilot) were scrapped, before new writers were hired to start from scratch.

On the movie side, the new studio had only one feature nearing the end of production—*Peacemaker,* starring George Clooney—while the original business plan had called for three live-action films to be released by late 1996. The interactive department was faring better, with four CD-ROMs ready for the 1996 Christmas season and other potentially lucrative projects underway. When detractors raised their voices against DreamWorks, Geffen reminded them that his last record label had lost money for twenty-four straight quarters before he'd turned it around and sold it to MCA for $545 million. His public optimism notwithstanding, Hollywood was filled with rumors of Geffen's dismay over the difficulty of launching something as unwieldy as DreamWorks SKG.

"The buzz in town," says L.A. author and film historian Alain Gansburg, "is that just because they've called DreamWorks a studio, it isn't really a studio yet. Their first TV shows tarnished their reputation and hurt their credibility with the networks. They haven't produced any features, and certainly not the kind of blockbuster pictures that Spielberg has been associated with in the past. Geffen and Spielberg were never buddy-buddy, and I think Geffen expected Spielberg to come up with a 'franchise' movie by now, something huge. He just hasn't done that.

"DreamWorks has to be a new reality for these men. Katzenberg was a corporate animal who ran an established studio like Disney, not a start-up business. Geffen made his money in music, not films. At Universal, Spielberg was used to having people bring him a glass of water wearing knee pads. Those days are over, and they're on their own now. There's been some tension over these issues, not to mention all those land problems."

The problematic real estate was the Ballona Wetlands in Playa Vista, the site the partners had selected for their campus. A group called the Citizens United to Save All of Ballona protested this decision by taking out a two-page ad in *Daily Variety.* Addressed to the DreamWorks founders, it read, "Although you have hired well-respected environmental consultants to work on this project, placing a development this massive on and around a wetlands ecosystem is not environmentally sound—no matter how many recycling programs it has."

The 1996 Environmental Media Association's awards show in Beverly Hills had been planned as a celebration of Hollywood's ecological awareness. Instead, a gate-crashing activist named Valerie

Sklarevsky, clad in a black jumpsuit and a ballerina skirt, slipped into the party, leaped onto the stage, and began shouting, "Please stop DreamWorks! They're putting a nightmare in the Ballona Wetlands!" She was carted away by security guards, but not before embarrassing the fledgling studio and its creators.

Even if the DreamWorks partners wanted to build their studio elsewhere, 1,087 acres of open, affordable land were nearly impossible to find in Los Angeles. And there were other difficulties. DreamWorks had initially joined forces with the Maguire Thomas development firm, which then became entangled in financial and political troubles. Members of L.A.'s city council asked developer Robert Maguire to remove himself from the project, and if he didn't comply with this request, the studio might lose the $70 million in incentives that the local government had offered DreamWorks to build at Playa Vista.

"At least a year behind schedule," the *L.A. Times* said of DreamWorks in December of 1996, "the $8-billion, 1,000-acre project remains very much a question mark—and costing DreamWorks invaluable time in its race to create Hollywood's cutting-edge entertainment company....

"The longer Playa Vista is delayed, the greater the potential price of grandiosity of vision. Instead of showing the way for the rest of Hollywood, the venture could end up as a kind of Jurassic anachronism, badly outmaneuvered by the quicker-witted mammalian life swarming around it."

Compared to Michael Ovitz, Geffen and his partners were having a glorious year. Since Ovitz had become the president of Disney in the autumn of 1995, nothing had gone well for him. By the following July, the *New Yorker* was anonymously quoting a source close to Michael Eisner saying that the Disney CEO had made a mistake in hiring the former agent. "Big Mike" and "Little Mike," as they were now called, were constantly surrounded by rumors of discord. Some people contended that Eisner wouldn't give Ovitz anything substantial to do, for fear of losing power at the company, while others claimed that Ovitz had simply refused to learn the nuts and bolts of running a multibillion-dollar enterprise.

In the late summer of 1996, the former agent had gone around town trying to make up with some of the people he'd angered in the past, so that Disney would now have a smoother time conducting its business in Hollywood. He met with Don Ohlmeyer, the president of NBC West Coast, who several months earlier had called Ovitz the "Antichrist" in *Time* magazine. He met with Jeff Berg, the head of the ICM agency. This face-to-face confrontation began with hostility but ended productively. The same thing could not be said about Ovitz's meeting with Geffen in the DreamWorks private dining room at Amblin Entertainment. The two men tried to have a civil discussion, but it quickly became heated. Accusations and hurt feelings flew around the table, and when it was apparent that nothing could be accomplished by further conversation, Ovitz left.

In September, in order to quell the mounting gossip, Eisner and Ovitz appeared on the *Larry King Live* show. The host peppered the men to reveal what was really going on between them, and the Disney duo vigorously denied any hint of friction. The words spoken were secondary to Ovitz's body language—his twisting in the chair, his tightening of the lips and clenching of teeth. The man who'd once squeezed all of Hollywood was now being squeezed by his boss in front of millions of people; clearly, this didn't feel very good. When Ovitz tried to muster some enthusiasm for the animal safari exhibit at a Disney theme park, it was embarrassingly obvious that he was out of his element, or downright indifferent to the whole thing.

In October, *Vanity Fair* rated the most powerful people in "The New Establishment." Geffen was number ten; Ovitz had fallen to twenty-fifth. Two months later, the magazine ran an article on the problems between Eisner and Ovitz at Disney, entitled "The Mouse Trap." When asked to comment on this situation, Geffen told *Vanity Fair*:

"He's not Michael Ovitz anymore. He's a guy who has a job working for Michael Eisner. And if you think everyone's not aware of it, you're very wrong."

Then Geffen was asked about Don Ohlmeyer's calling the ex-agent the Antichrist.

"Apparently," he replied, "Don Ohlmeyer thinks more highly of Mike Ovitz than I do."

On December 12, 1996, two days before his fiftieth birthday, Ovitz left Disney, after only fourteen months on the job. His severance package was reportedly $90 million, causing media commentators from coast to coast, not to mention Disney shareholders, to wail in anger and disgust. Ovitz had publicly and strikingly failed, but he made off with 7.5 percent of his company's 1996 net income. Disney stockholders were so outraged that they began clamoring for the corporation to alter its executive pay packages, a suggestion that Eisner staunchly resisted.

The wheel had turned in Los Angeles, and someone new was perched atop it. Hollywood had a new Rajah.

"Ovitz shaped the eighties in L.A., but that time has passed," says Marc Strassman, the president of Transmedia Communications in Los Angeles. "Now we have a more informal style, one that is far more suited to a man like Geffen. It's ironic that Ovitz had this very conscious, long-term strategy for acquiring power through fear and intimidation. That worked—for a while—but then the general lost his horse. Geffen was less visible in the eighties and didn't seem to have any great need for accumulating power or any overall plan. Yet he's emerged as the new force.

"Anyone who can master the style of a period is going to be favored by it. This is a time of enormous change, and the one who is the most flexible and can grow the most quickly will triumph. It's also a time of diversity and crossover. Geffen embodies those things in almost every aspect of his life. He combines the looser sixties style with the nineties style, which has a more political agenda attached to it. He has good interpersonal skills, with both women and men. We saw that in the intimate relationships he built in the music business, with Joni Mitchell, Jackson Browne, and other performers. He can make people feel good about themselves, so they want to be around him.

"In the nineties, the key thing is being able to manage increasingly complex systems of technology, finance, and business. How do you manage complexity in a relatively simple way? How do you create new products around this idea? If you can do this, markets will open up and advertising will follow. There's an enormous amount of information out there, and you need to know how to manage not just this information but other people and yourself. Geffen is adept at all these things. He does them better, for example, than the president of the United States. With these skills coming more into favor, Geffen is riding the wave as well as anyone."

CHAPTER 36

Not everyone was pleased by Geffen's ascension. In Fred Goodman's recent book about the rock-'n'-roll industry, *The Mansion on the Hill,* the former *Rolling Stone* editor documented his largely negative feelings about Geffen's rise through the ranks of the music business. It did not escape Goodman's attention that in 1996, more than thirty years after Bob Dylan had become a world-renowned singing prophet, and more than twenty years since Neil Young and Bruce Springsteen had become celebrated rock figures, none of these men was talked about as much nowadays as the slight figure with the curly hair who'd gone to work in the William Morris mailroom in 1964. The brief David Geffen vogue that George Trow had written about disparagingly in the 1970s was evolving, in the 1990s, into the David Geffen decade. Fred Goodman, and many others, took a dim view of this development.

"If the acquisition of wealth and influence is rock's ultimate meaning," he wrote, "then the most meaningful figure it has produced is the billionaire mogul David Geffen. Indeed, it's more than ironic that Geffen's appreciation of the dollars-and-cents value of music has placed him in a position to exert a greater influence and power over society and politics than the artists—it may be the measure of a profound failure by the musicians and their fans. Geffen is a visionary businessman and a generous philanthropist, but I never sat around the shack behind the kitchen when I was sixteen trying to divine the secret language of business, and I don't know anyone else who did. I wasn't looking for the mansion on the hill [a remarkably accurate description of Geffen's unoccupied estate on Angelo Drive], and I didn't think rock 'n' roll was, either."

Goodman's essential point was difficult to challenge. In a culture that had commercialized every possible thing in the past few decades, including a bedroom in the White House, rock music had also been engulfed in this trend. Driven by Geffen and other talented executives, rock had become another huge and successful business rather than anything resembling a serious cultural or political revolt.

Radio was the lifeblood of that business, and whole genres of brilliant American music—bluegrass, the blues, jazz, show tunes—had been marginalized to an hour or so on the weekends, while at any moment one could hear this month's rock chartbusters pounding out another formulaic song.

Indeed, anyone strolling along Sunset Strip in the mid-nineties could have sensed these changes. Three decades earlier, the Whisky-a-Go-Go, housed in a former Bank of America building, had opened on the Strip and soon became the latest hipster hangout in L.A. Go-go girls spun records and shimmied in glass bubbles high above the floor. Sexual liberation was new and titillating. The music was provocatively fresh. The Whisky's house act was Johnny Rivers, and two thousand people showed up some evenings to hear Otis Redding, Led Zeppelin, the Doors, the Who, or Jimi Hendrix. In the mid-sixties, when a *New York Times* reporter first wandered into the club, he declared that the Whisky would be nothing more than a fad because "girls are admitted in slacks and ties are not required on men." The reporter faded; the Whisky lived on.

The disco craze of the seventies did not kill the venue, and in the eighties, it was revitalized by such punk bands as Fear and Black Flag. During the nineties, it featured headliners like Van Halen and Smashing Pumpkins, who wanted the chance to play in a more intimate setting.

By the spring of 1997, the air on the Strip felt flat, and no name bands were appearing at the Whisky or On the Rox, the new version of the club Geffen and his partners had created more than twenty years earlier. One small, ragged palm tree stood in front of the old Roxy, and the building's off-white-and-brown façade was in need of refurbishing. A big neon *R* rose above the club, like an archeological relic from the great age of rock 'n' roll, a reminder of the magical nights that had once unfolded on this fast stretch of pavement.

The Strip seemed quieter now, perhaps waiting for a bold new sound or perhaps ready to fade into American cultural history. Bill Graham, one of Geffen's partners in the Roxy, was dead, and Geffen himself had long since left his record label, headquartered just across the street on Sunset Boulevard. Otis Redding, Jim Morrison, Keith Moon of the Who, Jon Bonham of Led Zeppelin, and Jimi Hendrix had all played the Strip in its prime, and all of them were gone, too. Some people may have believed that David Geffen killed rock-'n'-roll; if he did, he had plenty of help.

Beneath the irony that Fred Goodman wrote about in his book was another stranger irony. The original impulse behind rock music was freedom—from convention, from sexual repression, from bigotry, and from the potential drudgery of the adult world. But most of all, it was freedom from the emotions and psychological prisons that limit, bind, and hurt people once they've become adults themselves. Rock was an implicit attack on business as usual, and the very best of the music carried one to the edge of transcendence, where one could feel, at least for the duration of a song, what it was like to live without pain and suffering and unnecessary boundaries. Something in the basic rock beat—the heavy four-four-time signature—broke through the walls and gave listeners a surge of hope.

Yet very few rock stars ever achieved such heights of liberation for any length of time.

John Lennon, who devoted as much time and energy as any rocker to penetrating his own soul, was shot to death at age forty. In 1995, Jerry Garcia's heart gave out after too much heroin. In 1997, Laura Nyro died of cancer. Mick Jagger liked to advertise the Rolling Stones as the "world's greatest rock-'n'-roll band," but for years they'd really been the world's greatest rock-'n'-roll business. Bob Dylan was indecipherable. During the past two decades, he'd done a number of self-conscious interviews with reporters, which some people had charitably described as containing little more than gibberish.

David Crosby had been in and out of drug rehab. Like many rockers, he'd sought the short cut to transcendence and paid the price. Freddie Mercury, the lead singer of Queen, had died of AIDS. Joni Mitchell was groping with her emotional past, by searching for and eventually finding the daughter she'd given up for adoption many years earlier. Neil Young was still angry and creative. And after a quarter century of writing and performing, gender-bending David Bowie, perhaps more than anyone else, had continued to forge an exciting, unpredictable career in music.

The story in business and politics was essentially the same. In recent years, Walter Yetnikoff and Irving Azoff had both tumbled, and Michael Ovitz had been deposed. President Clinton, who was constantly touted as the most powerful man on earth, had been caught in so many inconsistencies and inner contradictions that at times he seemed barely able to govern himself, let alone the United States of America. He'd never quite learned the value of speaking the truth.

The fundamental challenge for people of Geffen's age was to integrate into their psyches, in a healthy way, the experiences, new ideas, and enormous changes of the past several decades—the music, the drugs, the politics, the sexual alternatives, the financial demands, the therapies and spiritual adventures. This was a huge, complicated task, and there were casualties everywhere, but some people had kept muddling toward their own freedom.

Geffen lived with a parrot in a house by the ocean. He was surrounded by works of art and stunning views of the Pacific. He communicated with the world through a ten-button telephone and managed the ever-greater complexity of global business while sitting on his deck and suntanning. He moved out into the world and then retreated to spend some time alone. He ate healthy foods and exercised each day. He spoke his mind without fear, both privately and publicly, and was willing to accept the consequences of his actions. He not only had clear access to his feelings, which was rare enough, but he confronted and expressed them directly.

When he wanted sex, he found it, and not only with men. Occasionally, he went to bed with a woman just to keep himself from being too strictly defined by anyone, including David Geffen. When he wanted emotional involvement, he took that from others and gave back what he had to give. The rock world had succumbed to middle age, but Geffen, clad in his ever-present blue jeans and tennis shoes, still conjured up a jaunty teenager.

While Bob Dylan was chanting nonsense in *Rolling Stone,* Geffen had learned to speak openly and without irony about the value of accepting, and loving, the most challenging parts of himself. That kind of power, freedom, and simplicity was hard to find, not just in Hollywood but anywhere in American life. Grace remained elusive—Geffen couldn't shake his bitter Brooklyn tongue—and when he fought, he fought viciously, but as an adult he'd avoided many of the things that kids had wanted to escape when they got their first taste of rock-'n'-roll.

In early 1997, *Us* magazine sent noted gay author Edmund White to interview Geffen for an article about sex and clout in Hollywood. To White, Geffen was impenetrable. The writer kept looking for an opening, a clue to this confounding man, and when he couldn't find one, he grew exasperated. Finally, he asked Geffen who took care of him when he needed to be taken care of.

Geffen didn't seem to understand the question.

Whom did he lean on for support, for example, when he had to go to the dentist?

It was a perfectly natural inquiry among people who expect others to manage their fears or needs for them. It was a perfectly acceptable question for those who unconsciously want others to protect them from conflict or painful things. But it was not so natural or acceptable for someone who'd devoted time to distancing himself from that kind of dependency and self-victimization.

Geffen replied that he didn't lean on anyone when he had to go to the dentist.

"I take care of me," he replied flatly, and that was the end of the story.

Surfers can momentarily ride the ocean, and birds can float upon the waves, but to stay above the water requires a peculiar sailor with a distinct gift. It has something to do with being in a constant state of change and flux, like the ocean itself, and then catching its drift. And something else to do with embracing the water's turbulence. As you go sailing by, people will glance your way, but if they're not really looking, they'll only see your wake.

ACKNOWLEDGMENTS AND SOURCES

After a year or so of studying David Geffen, I came to believe that he was a more unusual creature than one might have guessed from reading about him in magazines. Most people who wrote about Geffen focused on his great wealth, and they were struck by his refusal to give up his beach house and live in more grandiosity and splendor. His money was irrefutably a large part of his story, but without some other things—some ability to deal with his own interior and commitment to his own independence—he would be a far less interesting man. He might also be a less successful man. Many people feel that Geffen has simply been lucky, but luck does not explain his thirty-plus years of triumphs in the field of entertainment. Jim Ellison, my editor at Carol Publishing, pushed me to try to understand more about the mysteries behind Geffen's good fortune, and I'm glad that he did.

In 1995, while writing another book for Carol Publishing Group, about Michael Ovitz, I interviewed hundreds of people in Los Angeles and absorbed the prevailing emotional atmosphere in the movie business. It was controlled by Ovitz and can only be described as paranoid. Film executives and others were palpably afraid of the man, and Ovitz's air of secrecy, mystery, and boundless power had led many to believe that he could not be toppled. Two years later, everything has changed, and the Ovitz saga is now just a piece of the larger tale of David Geffen's continuing success, an outcome that few Hollywood insiders could have predicted.

All of the people I interviewed in 1995 were helpful in giving me the full context for this book about David Geffen. They included motion picture executives, screenwriters, producers, network employees, agents, actors, mailroom trainees, entertainment lawyers, secretaries, and many others in L.A. In 1996, I broadened my interview process to include ex-Brooklynites, former William Morris agents and clients, musicians, rock managers, fans, critics, erstwhile Time Warner employees, est students, media experts, politicians, gay activists, New Age commentators, and Hollywood historians.

As time went on, I was struck again and again by how many places and people Geffen had touched in his career. He represents significant trends in our national life from the 1960s to the present, and his progression through the years reveals something about the evolution and maturation of our entire culture. There may be only a handful of Americans left who have not seen a movie or Broadway play that he produced or heard a record that one of his labels brought to the marketplace. He has touched and helped shape our collective sensibility.

As part of my research, I also read widely in the field of entertainment. My periodical sources included the *Wall Street Journal,* the *New York Times Magazine, genre,* the *Advocate,* the *New Yorker, Time, Newsweek, Business Week, Spy,* the *L.A. Times Magazine, Buzz, L.A. Magazine, POZ,* the *National Perspectives Quarterly, Wired, Vanity Fair, BAM* magazine, *Daily Variety,* the *Hollywood Reporter, Esquire, New York* magazine, *ComputerLink,* the *L.A. Times,* the *New York Times, Advertising Age, L.A. Weekly, Premiere, Entertainment Weekly, Out, OutWeek, GQ, Playboy,* and *Rolling Stone.*

On the book side, I read or reread Frank Rose's *The Agency,* Bill Carter's *The Late Shift,* Sun Tzu's *The Art of War,* Fredric Dannen's *Hit Men,* Fred Goodman's *The Mansion on the Hill,* my own *Power to Burn: Michael Ovitz and the New Business of Show Business,* Neal Gabler's *An Empire of Their Own: How the Jews Invented Hollywood,* Julia Phillips's *You'll Never Eat Lunch in This Town Again,* David McClintick's *Indecent Exposure: A True Story of Hollywood and Wall Street,* George W. S. Trow's *Within the Context of No Context,* Michelangelo Signorile's *Queer in America: Sex, the Media, and the Closets of Power,* Connie Bruck's *Master of the Game: How Steve Ross Rode the Light Fantastic From Undertaker to Creator of the Largest Media Conglomerate in the World,* Steven Gaines and Sharon Churcher's *Obsession: The Life and Times of Calvin Klein,* Anthony Scaduto's *Bob Dylan: An Intimate Biography,* and Budd Schulberg's *What Makes Sammy Run?*

My wife, Joyce, and my agent, Reid Boates, were very helpful with this project. So was Gillian Speeth, who located the photos reprinted here. Finally, the *Penguin Encyclopedia of Popular Music,* edited by Donald Clarke, was extremely useful for reminding me of bands or songs I'd nearly forgotten. I was prompted to go listen to some old albums again, like *Retrospective* by Buffalo Springfield, and that's always a pleasure.

INDEX